Microsoft® SQL Server® 2008

HIGH AVAILABILITY WITH CLUSTERING & DATABASE MIRRORING

Michael Otey

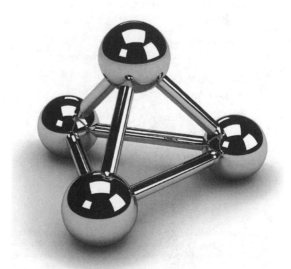

New York Chicago San Francisco Lisbon
London Madrid Mexico City Milan
New Delhi San Juan Seoul Singapore
Sydney Toronto

The McGraw·Hill Companies

Cataloging-in-Publication Data is on file with the Library of Congress

Microsoft® SQL Server® 2008 High Availability with Clustering & Database Mirroring

1234567890   DOC DOC   019

ISBN   978-0-07-149813-5
MHID   0-07-149813-3

Sponsoring Editor Wendy Rinaldi	**Indexer** Karin Arrigoni
Editorial Supervisor Janet Walden	**Production Supervisor** George Anderson
Project Manager Vipra Fauzdar, Glyph International	**Composition** Glyph International
Acquisitions Coordinator Joya Anthony	**Illustration** Glyph International
Technical Editor Dan Jones	**Art Director, Cover** Jeff Weeks
Copy Editors Jan Jue and Bob Campbell	**Cover Designer** Jeff Weeks
Proofreader Debbie Liehs	

To Sherry. Thank you for being there for me.
You are the best, and you will always be my star.

About the Author

Michael Otey is technical director for *SQL Server Magazine* and *Windows IT Pro* and is a founding editor for both magazines He is also president and founder of TECA, Inc., a software development and consulting firm that specializes in systems integration. Michael is also author of *SQL Server 2008 New Features*, as well as numerous other SQL Server books. Michael works extensively with Windows Server, virtualization, and Microsoft development technologies. Previously, Michael managed the IT for a division of a Fortune 500 manufacturing company.

About the Technical Editor

Dan Jones has been with Microsoft's SQL Server business unit since 2004 and is currently the Group Program Manager of the SQL Server Manageability Team. In SQL Server 2008, Dan's team delivered Policy-Based Management, SQL Server Agent, PowerShell, SQLCMD, Management Studio, and Database Mail. Prior to joining Microsoft, Dan worked for several small and Fortune 50 companies in software development and enterprise IT. Dan regularly presents at top industry conferences, including Microsoft TechEd, SQLPASS, and VSLive!

Contents at a Glance

Contents

Acknowledgments

I would like to thank all of the people at McGraw-Hill who helped make this book possible. You are great to work with and I really appreciate all your efforts. I would like to convey a special thanks to Dan Jones for his most excellent and detailed technical edits. He significantly helped to improve the quality of this book.

Introduction

This book is intended as a guide for DBA and IT professionals tasked with implementing high availability technologies using SQL Server. The first chapter of this book discusses the organizational and technical factors that go into creating a highly available database environment and provides an overview of all the SQL Server high availability features.

The body of this book is split into three main sections that focus on the main technologies that can be used to address both planned and unplanned downtime. The first part of this book focuses on Windows failover clustering. Windows failover clustering primarily addresses the issues of unplanned downtime and is Microsoft's premier high availability technology. This section starts with Chapter 2, where you will get an overview of the Windows failover clustering architecture. Chapter 3 shows how to set up a two-node Windows failover cluster. Chapter 4 shows you how to install SQL Server on both of the cluster nodes. This section concludes with Chapter 5, where you will learn the essential techniques for managing the Windows failover cluster.

Part II covers database mirroring. While Windows failover clustering is a server-level technology, database mirroring is a database/application-level solution for availability. Database mirroring can address both planned and unplanned downtime. Chapter 6 provides an overview of the database mirroring architecture. Chapter 7 steps you through setting up database mirroring in a high availability configuration. Chapter 8 guides you through the database mirroring management tasks.

Part III takes a different tack on availability and shows how you can use virtualization to address the issues of planned downtime and disaster recovery. In this section you will learn how live migration can reduce the planned downtime associated with system maintenance and system updates. Chapter 9 provides you with an understanding of virtualization and shows how virtualization addresses the issues of availability. This chapter also gives you an introduction to Microsoft's live migration technology. Chapter 10 shows how you can implement a Windows failover cluster that supports virtualization and live migration. Chapter 11 steps you through setting up SQL Server on a highly available virtual machine. Finally, this section concludes by showing you the fundamental techniques for managing a SQL Server in the virtual environment.

Chapter 1

Planning for High Availability

In This Chapter

▶ **Defining High Availability**
▶ **Factors Influencing Availability**

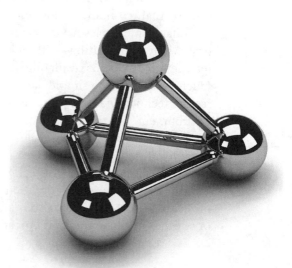

Although the database administrator (DBA) has a lot of important responsibilities, none is more important than making sure that the database resources are available to the end users. Sure, performance and a plethora of cool features are nice, but if the database isn't available to the end users, then what value does it really have? Which call from the IT manager evokes the faster response from the DBA? A call telling him that a particular query is running slow or a call telling him that the database is down and the company can't take any orders until it is up again?

Different methods of measuring availability have been used by different vendors to highlight the robustness of their offerings. For example, how often have you seen availability referred to as "server uptime"? However, server uptime is only a part of the true availability picture. True measures of availability cannot be made at the server level. Real availability can only be measured from the end user perspective. After all, if the server is available but the applications that the users or the customers require are not available, then the bottom line is that the application and support database are essentially not available. If end users and customers cannot access the database and application resources that they depend upon to conduct business, then the organization will be adversely impacted. Essentially, the database and servers that support those applications need to be available during the times that the end users require those applications, and the infrastructure that supports end-user connection must be available as well.

Clearly, downtime can be costly both in terms of a loss of direct revenue for online sites as well as in terms of customer and even employee satisfaction. Depending on the organization and the application, the direct costs for service outages can be extremely high. Gartner estimates the average cost of downtime for a large business to be about $42,000 per hour. However, for businesses that rely on their Internet presence for income, the costs can be much higher. A study by Forrester Research showed that a one-hour outage for the online brokerage firm eTrade cost $8 million. The same study showed that ten hours of downtime at Dell cost $83 million.

Today's enterprises have greater requirements for availability than at any time in the past. Many organizations with online ecommerce sites and other global organizations require full 24×7×365 availability. Achieving these high levels of availability requires much more than the simple data protection provided by traditional backup and restore technologies or by an onsite backup server. Creating a high availability environment for your organization can be a challenging undertaking. There are multiple levels of availability, plus each level has different costs. Typically, the higher the level of availability that is required, the higher the cost to implement the solutions. Although selecting the right technology certainly plays a large role in achieving high availability in the organization, achieving high availability is more than just a question of technology. Availability also is affected by several other factors including your organization's personnel and operational processes.

In the next section of this chapter, you'll get a basic understanding of how availability is measured, and then you'll learn about the most significant human and organizational factors that influence availability. Finally, you'll learn about the different high availability technologies that Microsoft has provided with SQL Server 2008, as well as see which types of availability scenarios each technology addresses.

Defining High Availability

Availability is traditionally measured according the percentage of time that the system is available to its end users. Therefore, 100 percent availability means that the system is available all of the time and there is no downtime. However, achieving 100 percent availability is virtually impossible. Too many technical and human factors are involved for that to be a realistic possibility. Even so, by utilizing technology and creating a suitable operating environment, very high levels of availability are achievable. The highest practical measure of availability is typically expressed as "five nines" or 99.999 percent. The percentage of availability can be calculated using the following formula:

Percentage of availability = ((total elapsed time – sum of downtime)/total elapsed time)

The percentage of system availability equals the total elapsed time minus the sum of the system downtime. This result is then divided by the total elapsed time.

Let's take a little deeper look at what this means in a practical sense. A year has a total of 8,760 hours (24 hours per day × 365 days per year = 8,760 hours). Therefore, an availability of 8,760 hours over a year would be 100 percent uptime as you can see in the following equation:

100 = ((8,760 – 0)/8,760) × 100

A much more common scenario is for a system to have a regular period of downtime every month. For many organizations this might be as little as eight hours of downtime in every month, or essentially two hours per week. This downtime might be the result of planned system maintenance such as system backup procedures. Two hours of downtime per week or eight hours per month results in 98.9 percent availability, as the following formula illustrates:

98.9 = ((8,760 – (8 × 12)/8,760)) × 100

Many organizations don't achieve that level of availability. However, when expressed as a measure of nine, 98.9 percent isn't even two nines, as the base level of availability is lower than 99 percent. While one nine may not seem like a high level of availability, for many organizations one day of downtime per month would be perfectly adequate.

Number of Nines	Percentage Availability	Downtime per Year	Downtime per Month	Downtime per Week
Two nines	99.0%	3.65 days	7.30 hrs	1.68 hrs
Three nines	99.9%	8.76 hrs	43.8 mins	10.1 mins
Four nines	99.99%	52.6 mins	4.38 mins	1.01 mins
Five nines	99.999%	5.26 mins	26.28 secs	6.06 secs

Table 1-1   *Number of Nines and Downtime*

However, many businesses are running critical lines of business and e-commerce applications where one nine of availability is not enough. These organizations require three nines or even five nines of availability. So how much actual downtime is associated with these levels of availability? Table 1-1 gives you an idea of the amount of downtime that is permitted with each increasing level of "nines."

Table 1-1 shows how each increasing nine level of availability requires significant decreases in downtime. While reaching two nines of availability can be accomplished with a total of 1.68 hours per *week* of downtime, five nines of availability is only slightly more than five minutes of downtime per *year*.

Five minutes of downtime per year is an impressive and difficult number to achieve. Another important factor to remember is that the costs and operational disciplines increase substantially with each successive level of availability. Achieving these higher levels of availability cannot be accomplished using technology only. Creating a highly available environment requires a combination of several factors.

Factors Influencing Availability

The ability to achieve high availability for information systems is not just about technology. Technology does not operate in a vacuum. The most important factors influencing availability include people, processes, and matching the right availability technology to the current business problem. Operational systems are managed by people. People implement operational procedures. Let's look in more detail at some of the factors that go into creating a highly available environment.

Personnel Factors

The single largest cause of downtime for all organizations is not hardware or software failure. Although it does fail, hardware is typically quite reliable and failures are rare. Instead, the single largest cause of downtime is human error. System administrators typically perform numerous administrative tasks daily, and it only takes one poor choice and a couple of seconds for an administrative or operations error to cause a system failure or to corrupt a database, but it could take hours or even days to recover from that error. Human error is unavoidable in even the best of circumstances; however, the resulting downtime usually is avoidable—with preparation. If you are planning to create a highly available environment for your organization, planning for the ability to recover from human errors must be a priority for your organization.

You can proactively take steps to minimize downtime and to recover from these errors. Human error stems from two main sources: administrative errors and end user errors. End user errors can cause any number of data corruption issues such as mistakenly deleting critical data or incorrectly updating a database with the wrong information. These types of errors often require the database to be rolled back to a point in time before the corruption. Administrative errors can be more serious. Administrative errors such as incorrectly changing a database schema or submitting incorrect T-SQL update batches can cause the applications to fail and even require complete database restores. Several steps can help reduce both the number of human errors as well as the time required to recover from those errors. The first step in reducing the human error factor starts with hiring the best and most qualified personnel for your administrative and operational duties. The next step is the establishment of a regular training routine for your administrative personnel to ensure they are up to date with the operational best practices and the technologies in use. Additionally, one of the most important steps to curtail potential downtime due to user error is restricting all users' access to just the data and services that are required for them to perform their jobs.

Application developer errors can also have a major impact on application availability. For example, coding errors that delete rows from the wrong table or a coding error that results in corrupt data being written to the database can require application updates and even the need to roll back and restore the database. To reduce the possibility of such errors, it's important to increase awareness of management about the complexities and responsibilities that are associated with continuous information availability. This translates to establishing or maintaining training budgets, as well as ensuring proper development and practices like code walkthrough where peer developers review each other's code changes and adequate quality assurance (QA) processes.

Operational Factors

Another area that can profoundly affect your ability to create a highly available environment is your organization's internal processes. Establishing efficient and standardized operational procedures can eliminate unnecessary downtime as well as enable more rapid recovery in the event of a system failure. The creation of documented operating procedures is one of the most important steps to ensuring high availability.

The organization should possess written procedures for performing routine operational tasks as well as for performing the steps required to recover from various types of predictable and probable system failures. The establishment of standard problem-resolution procedures can help operational staff to identify common problem scenarios and give them the ability to more quickly diagnose and resolve a variety of situations. These documented operational procedures are usually referred to as *run books*. Lack of documentation leads to haphazard recovery from service outages. Inadequate or missing documentation increases the likelihood of omitting required steps or procedures. It can also increase the overall time required to troubleshoot a problem or to recover from a system or service failure. Additionally, the lack of documentation for routine operational procedures increases the possibility of operator error. This is especially true where there is a change in personnel due to either illness or other factors like changes in personnel.

The establishment of standard change management procedures can also be an important factor in systems availability. Change management procedures enable an organization to keep track of the application and database schema changes that occur over the lifetime of an application. In addition to providing a standard mechanism for tracking source code and database schema changes, the establishment of change management procedures also enables an organization to roll back to prior know-good configurations in the event that an application or database change results in an error. The absence of change management procedures can lead to gross recovery errors, where database schema and application updates can be lost or overridden by subsequent changes that failed to incorporate more recent updates. Similarly, the establishment of a standardized QA process will result in higher application quality and fewer code failures. Standardized QA processes ensure that code is tested in a safe QA setting before it is deployed in a production environment.

Two other important processes that have a direct bearing on availability are the creation of standardized hardware and software configurations. Whenever possible it's advantageous to create a standardized environment for both the hardware and software configurations your data centers on. On the hardware side, uniform hardware components make it easier to effect system repairs and/or replacements in the event of hardware failure. In the same way, consistent software configurations make routine operations easier and reduce the possibility of operator error. For example, ideally, all servers should be running with the same operating system and service pack level. Likewise, all database servers should use the same version of SQL Server with the same service pack level and client data access components. Further, systems should utilize standard naming convention and setup practices. For instance, all servers should use a standard naming scheme and have standardized drive letters, mapped directories, and share names. Likewise, all database servers should use standard database- and object-naming conventions. The lack of standard hardware and software configurations increases the possible points of error, leading to lengthier troubleshooting times and the increased probability of administrative and recovery errors.

One final factor that can help in establishing a high availability environment is making sure your administration and helpdesk personnel have up-to-date knowledge. One way to do that is to make sure that your organization has regular training for its technical employees. Establishing a regular training schedule for all IT personnel helps to ensure that your staff has up-to-date technical skills as well as making it more likely that your organization will adopt the most effective technologies and tools. Outdated or incorrect technological knowledge can result in reduced availability by increasing the time to solve problems as well as increasing the possibility of incorrect troubleshooting or uninformed choices for the systems management and database development issues of future projects.

Technical Factors

Technical solutions for high availability address the two types of possible downtime: unplanned downtime and planned downtime.

- ▶ **Unplanned downtime**   Unplanned downtime is any unexpected period where the organization's services are not available to the end user. Unplanned downtime can be caused by hardware failure such as a server going down or the failure of network infrastructure devices. Application or service failure can be another cause of unplanned downtime. Disasters or other site-level catastrophes can cause unplanned downtime. In some cases operational error can also cause unplanned outages.

- ▶ **Planned downtime**   Planned downtime is any period where the organization expects and has planned for system or application unavailability. Scheduled hardware upgrades and database maintenance are common causes for planned downtime.

Taking advantage of today's high availability technologies can reduce or eliminate downtime associated with planned maintenance.

SQL Server's High Availability Technologies

SQL Server 2008 has a number of high availability technologies: *Windows failover clustering* provides protections against server failure; *database mirroring* and *log shipping* provide protection against site and database failure; *peer-to-peer replication* can provide protection against site and system failure; *database snapshots* provide protection against database corruption; and *fast recovery* reduces the time required to recover a database from a backup. To give you an idea of the big picture of SQL Server availability, the next section of this book will give you an overview of each of these different technologies and how they contribute to availability. Then the remainder of the book will provide more detail about how to use the primary availability technologies of failover clustering, database mirroring, and Hyper-V live migration.

> **NOTE**
>
> *It's important to remember that these technologies are not mutually exclusive. They can be combined for different levels of protection. For instance, you can combine failover clustering with database mirroring for both the server-level protection afforded by failover clustering and the database-level protection provided by database mirroring.*

Windows Failover Clustering   Windows failover clustering provides server-level protection from both unplanned and planned downtime. With Windows failover clustering, multiple servers join together to form a *cluster*. The cluster allows other servers, called *nodes,* to take over the services provided by another cluster node in the event of a failure on one of the servers in the cluster. All of the nodes in a cluster are in a state of constant communication. If one of the nodes in a cluster becomes unavailable, another node will automatically assume its duties and begin providing users with the same services that were provided by the node that failed. You can see an overview of Windows failover clustering in Figure 1-1.

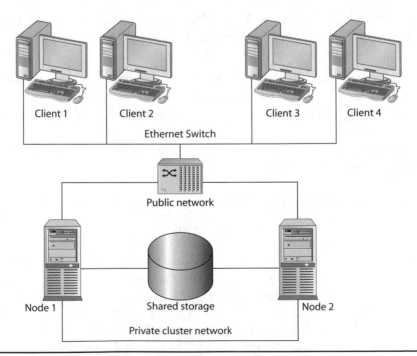

Figure 1-1   *Windows failover clustering*

The failover process is very fast, but it does require a short interval to complete. The time required depends on the speed of the servers involved in the failover and the type of resources that are protected by the cluster. In the case of SQL Server, the databases on the protected server must be recovered in order to ensure transactional consistency. The length of this recovery period depends on the level of database activity on the failed server. Clients that were connected to the failed node will be disconnected. However, when they attempt to reconnect, they will be redirected to the cluster node that assumes the failed node's duties. More detailed information about Windows failover clustering can be found in Chapter 2.

Database Mirroring   Database mirroring provides database-level protection from unplanned downtime. With database mirroring, all the changes in a protected database called the *principal database* are sent to a backup database called the *mirrored database*. If the principal database fails, the mirrored database located on a different SQL Server instance will be almost-instantly available. Database mirroring can be set up with a single database, or it can be set up for multiple databases on the same server.

While Windows failover clustering provides server-level protection, database mirroring provides database protection. The main difference to recognize is that all of the assets on the server are protected by Windows failover clustering—including the database service itself, database logins, and system database. This is not the case with database mirroring. Database mirroring just protects user databases. You can see an overview of database mirroring in Figure 1-2.

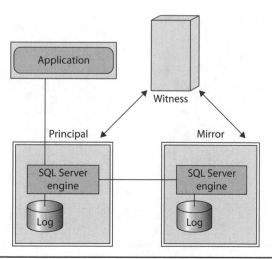

Figure 1-2   *Database mirroring*

Database mirroring is initialized by making a backup of the principal database and restoring it to the mirror server. When database mirroring is active, the transaction log is monitored for changes to the principal database. Those changes are then copied out of the transaction log of the principal server and sent over the network to the mirror server. The *witness* serves as a monitor. It detects if the principal database is not available and tells the mirror database to become the principal in the event that the original principal cannot be contacted. The switch from principal to mirror server is very fast and can be automated so it happens without user intervention. Transparent client redirection can automatically connect network client systems to the new principal server after a database mirroring failover. More detailed information about database mirroring can be found in Chapter 6.

Log Shipping Log shipping is a high-availability and disaster-recovery solution that can be used to protect against unplanned downtime. Originally introduced with SQL Server 2000, log shipping was designed as an inexpensive protection against server failure. Like database mirroring, log shipping works by first restoring a full backup of the primary database to a backup server. Then transaction log backups are periodically sent from the primary server's database and applied to the database on the backup server. Unlike database mirroring, which is limited to using a single mirror server, log shipping can send the captured transaction logs to multiple destinations. While database mirroring forwards log data to a mirror server as it occurs, log shipping sends transaction logs back, allowing you to choose the time when the transaction log will be captured and sent. All recovery for log shipping is manual. There is no automatic failover. You can see an overview of log shipping in Figure 1-3.

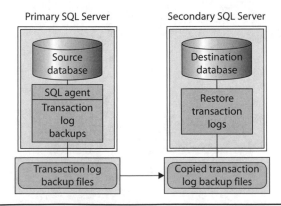

Figure 1-3 *Log shipping*

Peer-to-Peer Replication   Peer-to-peer transactional replication is another data replication technology that can be used to protect against unplanned downtime. All nodes in a peer-to-peer transaction replication topology are peers. Peer-to-peer transactional replication is designed for bidirectional replication and high availability scenarios. The database schema of the replicated databases must be identical between each of the nodes. Database inserts, updates, and deletes can be made to any of the peer nodes, and each node publishes the updates to the other peer nodes. Replicated data is uniquely identified to prevent it from being replicated more than once. You can see an overview of SQL Server's peer-to-peer transactional replication in Figure 1-4.

One advantage to using replication is that the peer servers are continually available. They can be readily used by applications or used as distributed reporting servers. Peer-to-peer replication does not offer any automatic failover. The process for promoting a peer server to assume the role of a primary server is manual and not automatic. In addition, to return the primary server to its original role after a server failure requires you to restore the database from a backup.

Database Snapshots   Database snapshots are a tool that can enable your organization to recover more quickly from unplanned downtime. Database snapshots allow you to quickly restore a database to a previous point in time. Database snapshots create copies (or "snapshots") of a database without the overhead of performing a physical copy of the entire database. The database snapshot makes a copy of the original database schema. As changes are made to the database, the changed pages are copied into the snapshot. For all of the unchanged data, the database snapshot shares the pages of the base database. You can see an overview of SQL Server 2008's Database Snapshot capability in Figure 1-5.

To recover from a data corruption problem, you can use the database snapshot to restore the database from its earlier saved state. You restore the database by copying to it the original pages saved in the snapshot, returning the database to its state when the database snapshot was created.

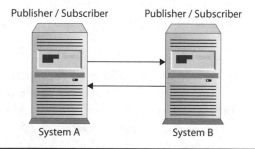

Figure 1-4   *Peer-to-peer transactional replication*

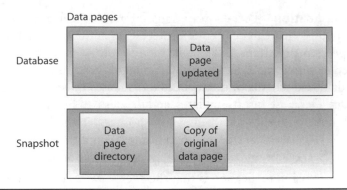

Figure 1-5   *Using Database Snapshot to make point-in-time copies of a database*

Backup and Restore   A sound backup and recovery plan is an essential component to high availability. SQL Server database backups can be performed to disk, tape, or to other media. Without a doubt, disk-based backups are the fastest mechanism for backing up and restoring data. However, to protect against drive failure, backups should always be directed to a separate drive and preferably to a separate system from your database server.

SQL Server supports three types of database backup: full, differential, and transaction log backups, as follows:

▶ **Full backup**   A *full* database backup is a complete copy of the database. Full backups provide a known point from which to begin the database restore process.

▶ **Differential backup**   A *differential* backup copies only the database pages modified after the last full database backup. Frequent differential backups minimize the number of transaction log backups that need to be applied to bring your database up to the last current transaction.

▶ **Transaction log backup**   The *transaction log* backup copies the changes that have occurred since the last full or differential backup. You can make multiple transaction log backups per day depending on the activity level of your system. Transaction log backups may be applied after the last full or differential backup has been restored.

SQL Server's backup and restore process allows an entire database to be recovered to any given point in time. For example, if an application error occurred at 03:00 that resulted in a corrupted database, you could restore the database and then use SQL Server's transaction log backup to recover the database to 02:59, which would be just before the point that the data corruption occurred. Restoring a database is often a lengthy operation, and depending on the type of failure, a small loss of data can occur.

Selecting a High Availability Technology   Selecting the appropriate high availability technologies requires matching your organization's availability needs and budget to the capabilities and requirements of the different high availability technologies. The different technologies provided by SQL Server 2008 are designed to give different levels of availability and data protection. They each have different costs as well as hardware and technological skill level requirements. Table 1-2 summarizes some of the key availability technology to best fit your organization's requirements.

| Feature | Very Low Latency | | Medium Latency | | High Latency | |
	Failover Clustering	Database Mirroring	Peer-to-Peer Transactional Replication	Log Shipping	Database Snapshots	Backup/ Restore
Data loss	No data loss	No data loss	Some data loss possible	Some data loss possible	Some data loss	Some data loss
Automatic failover	Yes	Yes	No	No	No	No
Transparent to client	Yes	Yes	No	No	No	No
Downtime	20 sec + database recovery time	< 10 seconds	Minutes—time to perform manual failover	Minutes— time to perform manual failover + database recovery time	Minutes— time to restore database from snapshot	Minutes to hours—time to restore database from backup media
Standby data access	No	Mirror accessible via database snapshot	Yes	Intermittently accessible	No	No
Protection level	All system and user databases (SQL Server instance level)	User database	Table	User database	User database	User database
Complexity	High	Medium	Medium	Medium	Low	Low

Table 1-2   *Summary of SQL Server 2008's High Availability Options*

Part I

Implementing Windows Failover Clustering

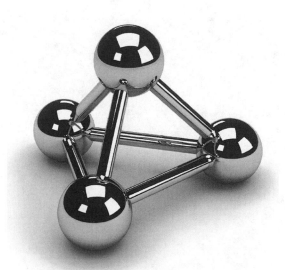

Chapter 2

Windows Failover Clustering Architecture

In This Chapter

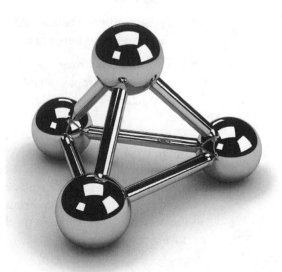

Windows failover clustering is designed to protect your critical business applications like SQL Server from unplanned downtime. In this chapter, you'll get an overview of Windows Server 2008 Failover Clustering. Here you'll learn about the architecture and components that comprise a Windows failover cluster, some of the new features in Windows Server 2008 Failover Clustering, and SQL Server 2008's support for failover clustering.

Overview

Windows failover clustering is Microsoft's primary technology for providing high availability at the server level. Windows failover clustering essentially involves utilizing multiple servers in a group or cluster. If one of the servers in the cluster has a system failure, then one of the other servers in the cluster can take over the workload of a failed server. Each physical server in the cluster is called a *node,* and the nodes work together to form the cluster. All of the nodes in a failover cluster constantly communicate. If one of the nodes in a cluster becomes unavailable and loses communication with the other nodes in the cluster, another node will automatically assume its duties and begin providing users with the same services as the failed node. This process is called *failover.* When the failed node is repaired, services can be restored to the node. This process is referred to as a *failback.*

Windows failover clustering provides the following features:

▶ **Automatic failover**   When a node fails, the cluster automatically switches the services to a backup node.

▶ **Rapid failover**   In many cases the failover process can complete in less than 30 seconds.

▶ **Transparent to clients**   After a failover, clients can immediately reconnect to the cluster with no network changes.

▶ **Transactional integrity**   There is no data loss. For SQL Server, all committed transactions are saved and reapplied to the database after the failover process completes.

The failover process does have some downtime associated with it, but it is a totally automated process. When a failover occurs, the Windows failover cluster will restart the failed services or applications on one of the remaining nodes. The period required to complete the failover depends in part on the hardware used and in part on the nature of the service or application. From a hardware standpoint the clustered services or application must be restarted on the backup node. Then the application or service must perform its own startup tasks. For a database application like SQL Server, the length of time for the failover depends largely on the level of database activity that was occurring at the time of failover. SQL Server records database activity in its transaction log. After a failover all committed transactions in the transaction log that have not been saved must be applied to the database, and all the uncommitted transactions must be rolled back to ensure database integrity. If the database is not very active, the time required for this will be brief. If the database is an enterprise-scale database with a very high activity level, then the time to apply the transaction log entries will be longer.

Clients that were connected to a node that fails will be temporarily disconnected. When they attempt to reconnect, the clients will be automatically and transparently redirected to access the cluster services running on the backup node.

Windows Failover Cluster Configurations

Windows failover clusters have a minimum of 2 nodes and a maximum of 16 nodes depending on the edition of Windows Server that you are running. More information about the multiple node support found in Windows Server 2008 and SQL Server 2008 is presented later in this chapter. In addition, failover clusters can be set up in a couple of basic ways: *active-active* clustering, where all of the nodes are performing work, or *active-passive* clustering, where one or more of the nodes are dormant until an active node fails.

Two-Node Clusters

Most Windows failover clusters in small and medium organizations are implemented using two-node configurations. In a two-node configuration, both nodes can be active or one can be passive. If both nodes are active, the key point is to ensure that the nodes have adequate system resources to run both their primary workload as well as the workload from the failed node.

In Figure 2-1 you can see an example two-node cluster. Both nodes have a private network that connects them together. This private network is used for the cluster's heartbeat. In addition, they have a public network connection that network clients use to connect to the cluster.

Each cluster node requires the following hardware:

▶ A hard disk for the Windows Server operating system. This is typical local Direct Access Storage (DAS). This disk is not shared and is not connected to the controller used by the shared storage. Instead, this disk uses its own controller and can be mirrored for improved availability.

▶ A NIC (network interface card) or Fibre Channel adapter that connects to the cluster's shared disk storage.

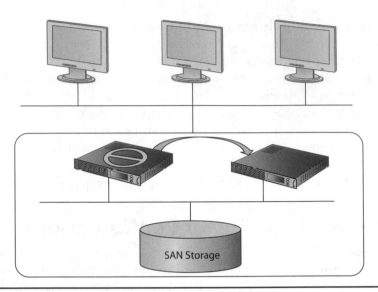

Figure 2-1 *A two-node Windows failover cluster*

▶ Two network interface cards (NICs). One NIC is used to connect the cluster node to the external network. The second NIC is used for the private cluster network, which the cluster nodes use to notify the other cluster nodes of their availability.

In addition, SAN storage is used for the cluster's quorum drive and application storage. Because the nodes in a cluster use a shared storage subsystem, they typically need to be in relative proximity to one another. This distance that the nodes can be apart depends on the connection that the nodes use for the storage subsystem. Failover clusters using iSCSI (Internet Small Computer Systems Interface) storage can be geographically dispersed. More information about cluster components and multisite clusters is presented later in this chapter.

Networked clients connect to the cluster using the cluster's virtual IP address. The cluster then connects these clients to their desired clustered resources. If the first node fails, the clustered services and applications running on the first node will be restarted on the second node.

Multinode Clusters

While two-node clusters are more common in SMB (small and medium business) and departmental installation, larger business and enterprise-level organizations tend to take advantage of multinode clusters. As you would expect, multinode clusters provide great levels of protection and more flexibility in their deployment options. For example, with a 16-node cluster you can set up 12 of the 16 nodes to be available and providing different services, while the 4 nodes act as a passive node that can assume the services of any of the 12 active nodes.

The combination of SQL Server 2008 and Windows Server 2008 multinode clustering provides a very flexible and cost-effective clustering scenario to enable highly available applications. For example, with an eight-node cluster you can have seven of the eight nodes set up to actively provide different services, while the eighth node is a passive node that is ready to assume the services of any of the seven active nodes in the event of a server failure. Figure 2-2 illustrates an example eight-node cluster where seven nodes are active and one node is in standby, waiting to step in if any of the seven active nodes fails.

Multisite Clusters

Geographically dispersed clusters (aka multisite clusters or geoclusters) address the issue of site-level protection by separating the cluster nodes geographically. Multisite clusters have nodes residing in different geographic locations. Typically, these nodes provide clients with local access to data that is spread over a wide geographic range. Multisite clusters don't have a true shared disk. Instead, they rely on SAN replication to keep storage in sync between sites. Because the nodes are at a different site, you need to use a quorum model that can accommodate the distance differences between the sites. More information about the different types of Windows Server 2008 failover cluster quorum types is presented in the next section of this chapter. You can see an overview of a multisite cluster in Figure 2-3.

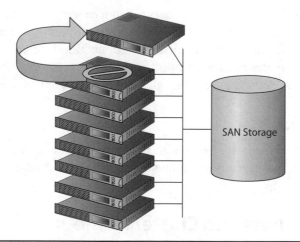

Figure 2-2 *An eight-node Windows failover cluster*

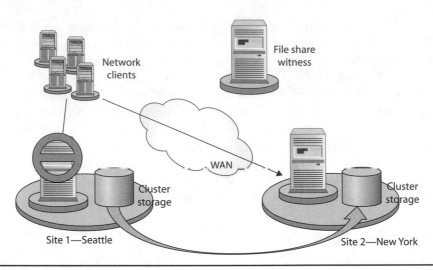

Figure 2-3   *A multisite Windows failover cluster*

Windows Failover Cluster Components

Apart from the nodes themselves two other important cluster components are the cluster quorum and the cluster resources. In this section you'll learn about the different components that are used by a Windows failover cluster.

Cluster Nodes

Each server that participates in the cluster is called a *cluster node*. These nodes need to be networked together. Cluster nodes remain in constant communication with each other to determine each node's availability. This connection is referred to as the *cluster heartbeat*. All cluster nodes need to be running the same version of the Windows Server operating system. For example, they must all run Windows Server 2008.

Cluster Service

The Cluster service is the core component that controls the operation of the failover cluster. The Cluster service runs on all cluster nodes and is managed by the Failover Cluster Manager.

Virtual IP Address and Cluster Name

The virtual IP address and cluster name are unique to the cluster, and they are different from the values that are used by any of the cluster nodes. The virtual IP address and cluster name are the information that networked clients use to connect to the cluster. The virtual IP address and cluster name remain consistent no matter which cluster node is running the clustered services or applications. This allows network clients to transparently reconnect to the clustered service or application after a failover.

Cluster Quorum

The cluster quorum essentially defines the number and type of elements that must be online for the cluster to be available. The purpose of the cluster quorum is to determine which nodes will participate in the cluster in the event that hardware failures or network outages make it impossible for some of the cluster nodes to communicate with other cluster nodes.

Elements that make up a quorum can vary depending on the type of quorum that you elect to use. Cluster quorum elements can be cluster nodes, a disk witness, or a file share witness. A disk or file share witness is a shared cluster disk resource or a file share that is available on the cluster that the administrator has especially designated to serve as a part of the quorum. The *disk witness* quorum is a Windows disk that resides on shared storage and contains a copy of the cluster configuration. The *file share witness* is a file share that resides on a networked server that is accessible by all cluster nodes. The file share quorum does not maintain a copy of the cluster configuration.

Windows failover clusters support multiple types of quorum to address the different sorts of cluster arrangements and differing numbers of nodes. Windows Server 2008 supports the following types of quorums.

Quorum Types

▶ **Node majority**   Each node in the cluster can vote. The cluster will only function if more than half of the nodes are available. This is recommended for clusters with an odd number of nodes.

▶ **Node and disk majority**   Each node in the cluster plus the designated disk witness can vote. The cluster will only function if more than half of the nodes are available. This mode is recommended for clusters with an even number of nodes. It is not recommended for multisite clusters.

▶ **Node and file share majority**   Each node in the cluster plus the designated file share witness can vote when they are in communication. The cluster will only function when more than half of the nodes are available. This mode is recommended for multisite clusters, for clusters with an even number of nodes, and for clusters with no shared storage.

▶ **No majority disk only**   The cluster is available as long as one node is available and that node can communicate with a designated disk storage. Other nodes can join the cluster only if they can communicate with the designated disk. This mode is recommended for clusters with an even number of nodes where there is no shared storage.

The Create Cluster Wizard will typically pick the best quorum type for the cluster that you create. You can see the Create Cluster Wizard in Chapter 3.

Services and Applications

Cluster services and applications essentially define the unit of failover. In earlier versions of failover clustering, these were defined as resource groups. At any point in time the service or application is owned by one cluster node. If that cluster node fails, another cluster node will become the owner of the resource, which essentially means the service or application will be started on that node. You can configure the preferred nodes that a service or application will failover to. Resources can also have a LooksAlive check, which is a basic health check for the applications. By default, SQL Server uses a LooksAlive test every five seconds.

Shared Storage

Clusters require shared storage and cannot be built using just direct access storage. The cluster's shared storage can either be an iSCSI SAN (storage area network) or a Fibre Channel SAN. For SQL Server a shared disk resource contains all of the system and user databases, logs, FILESTREAM files, and integrated full-text search files. In the event of a failover, the disks are mounted on the backup node, and the SQL Server service is restarted on that node.

Additional Resources

You can find more detailed information about Windows Server 2008 Failover Clustering at http://www.microsoft.com/Windowsserver2008/en/us/failover-clustering-main.aspx.

New Failover Clustering Features in Windows Server 2008

Windows failover clustering was significantly revamped with the release of Windows Server 2008, and additional improvements have been made with Windows Server 2008 R2. The new improvements simplify cluster setup and management as well as enhance their flexibility and security.

Cluster Validation

One of the biggest changes in failover clustering in Windows Server 2008 was the removal of the requirement that the hardware used in the cluster must be listed in the Microsoft Hardware Compatibility List (HCL) in order for the cluster to be supported. To participate in the HCL, OEM vendors had to submit specific hardware configurations for testing. While this ensured the systems worked with failover clustering, it also tended to limit the number of systems available for failover clustering and contributed toward making these systems expensive.

This process was eliminated with Windows Server 2008 and replaced by the new Cluster Validation Wizard. A Windows Server 2008 failover cluster will be supported if it passes the cluster validation tests. The cluster validation tests are a suite of system and configuration tests that determine the suitability for all of the nodes to successfully participate in the cluster. The Cluster Validation Wizard performs the following tests:

- ▶ **System configuration tests**   This set of tests determines if each of the servers meets the hardware and operating system requirements for the failover cluster.

- ▶ **Network tests**   This set of tests determines if the network configuration meets the failover cluster requirements. For example, this will check whether the cluster nodes can communicate with each other.

- ▶ **Storage tests**   This set of tests determines if the storage meets the failover cluster requirements. For example, the tests will determine if there are available drives for shared storage and if there is a suitable quorum disk available.

Running the Cluster Validation Wizard is shown in Chapter 3.

Simplified Cluster Setup and Management

Other important improvements in Windows Server 2008 Failover Clustering are the changes to the failover cluster setup and management process. The new Create Cluster Wizard makes it easier to create clusters, and the new Failover Cluster Manager streamlines the management experience. You can see both the Create Cluster Wizard and the Failover Cluster Manager in Chapter 3.

Support for Cluster Shared Volumes

Support for Cluster Shared Volumes (CSV) was released with Windows Server 2008 R2. With previous versions of Windows Server, each node owned its own LUN (Logical Unit Number) storage. Nodes were not able to share LUNs. This made storage management difficult because it required multiple LUNs. CSV answered this problem by allowing multiple nodes to share and access the same LUNs. This was a virtual improvement to support live migration. You can find more information about virtualization, live migration, and CSV in Chapter 9. You can see an example of configuring failover clustering to use CSVs in Chapter 10.

Support for GUID Partition Table Disks

Recent advances in storage technologies have resulted in very large capacity storage. Windows Server 2008's support for GUID (Globally Unique Identifier) Partition Tables (GPT) enables Windows Server clusters to utilize partitions that are larger than 2TB. In addition, GPT disks provide built-in redundancy for the storage of their partition information.

Support for IPv6

Another important improvement to Windows Server failover clustering is full support for IPv6 (Internet Protocol version 6). IPv6 can be used for both node-to-node communications as well as network client-to-node networking.

Support for Multiple Subnets

Windows Server 2008 Failover Clustering also now allows cluster nodes to be placed on different subnets. This is an important improvement for supporting geographically dispersed clusters.

   For more information about all of the new features in Windows Server 2008 Failover Clustering, you can refer to: http://technet.microsoft.com/en-us/library/cc770625(WS.10).aspx.

SQL Server 2008 Failover Clustering Support

Taking advantage of the enhanced clustering support found in Windows Server 2008, SQL Server 2008 can now be implemented on up to 16 node clusters in Windows Server 2008 Datacenter Edition and Windows Server 2008 Enterprise Edition. SQL Server 2008 Standard Edition supports a maximum of two nodes. In addition, SQL Server 2008 supports eight-node clustering on Windows Server 2003 Enterprise Edition and on Windows 2000 Datacenter Server. A maximum of two-node clustering is supported in Windows 2000 Advanced Server. A summary of Windows Server and SQL Server 2008 failover clustering maximum node support is shown in Table 2-1.

Windows Server Edition	SQL Server 2008 Enterprise Edition	SQL Server 2008 Standard Edition	SQL Server 2008 Web Edition	SQL Server 2008 Workgroup Edition	SQL Server 2008 Express Edition
Windows Server 2008 Datacenter Edition	16	2	0	0	0
Windows Server 2008 Enterprise Edition	16	2	0	0	0
Windows Server 2008 Standard Edition	0	0	0	0	0
Windows Server 2008 Web Edition	0	0	0	0	0
Windows Server 2003 Datacenter Edition	8	8	0	0	0
Windows Server 2003 Enterprise Edition	8	8	0	0	0
Windows Server 2003 Standard Edition	0	0	0	0	0

Table 2-1   *Windows Server and SQL Server 2008 Failover Cluster Nodes*

Some of the clustering-specific improvements in SQL Server 2008 include support for an unattended cluster setup. In addition, all of the different services within SQL Server 2008 are fully cluster-aware including the following:

▶ Relation database engine

▶ Analysis Services

▶ Integration Services

▶ Reporting Services

▶ SQL Server Agent

▶ Full-Text Search

▶ Service Broker

Summary

In this chapter you learned about the different types of Windows failover clusters including two-node clusters, *n*-node clusters, and multisite clusters. Next, you got an overview of the failover cluster architecture and received an introduction to the different components that compose a failover cluster. Then you got an overview of some of the most important new features in Windows Server 2008's Failover Clustering. In the last part of the chapter, you learned about SQL Server 2008's support for failover clustering.

In the next chapter, you'll see how to put all this into practice by building a two-node failover cluster with Windows Server 2008.

Chapter 3

Configuring Failover Clustering

In This Chapter

- ▶ **Configuring Windows Server 2008 Shared Storage**
- ▶ **Adding the Failover Clustering Feature**
- ▶ **Configuring Failover Clustering**

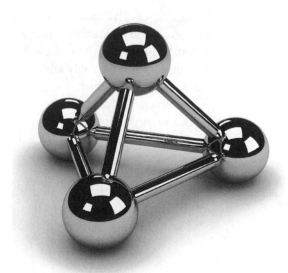

I n the previous chapter, you got a basic understanding of the important concepts, requirements, and capabilities of Windows failover clustering. In this chapter, you'll see how to put that knowledge to good use and learn how to configure Windows Server 2008 Failover Clustering. Here you'll see how to add the Failover Clustering feature to a Windows Server 2008 system. Then you'll see how to configure a two-node cluster.

Configuring Windows Server 2008 Shared Storage

As you learned in Chapter 2, one of the vital prerequisites for setting up a Windows Server 2008 failover cluster is shared storage. Shared storage can be accessed by all of the nodes in the failover cluster, and it is provided either by a Fibre Channel SAN (storage area network) or an iSCSI (Internet Small Computer Systems Interface) SAN. In this section, you'll see how to connect Windows Server 2008 to an iSCSI SAN.

The iSCSI Network Connections

The first step to getting your iSCSI SAN connected is planning the network configuration. At a minimum you need two network connections in each of the Windows Server 2008 systems that will function as cluster nodes. First, you need a connection to your organization's public LAN. This connection is used by the network clients to connect to services that will be available on the cluster. Next, you need a second network connection that connects each Windows Server 2008 system to your SAN. This connection should be on a completely separate physical network from the network that you use for client connectivity. In addition, the SAN network should be configured to use a different IP subnet than the client network. Also, for some configurations, Microsoft recommends the use of a third network connection for node-to-node connectivity that is separate from both the client network and the SAN network. This example will use two network connections. You can see an overview of the network connectivity and devices to implement failover clustering for this two-node cluster shown in Figure 3-1.

The network connections on the client network can run at whatever speed is in use at your organization. Most corporate networks today run at either 100MB or 1GB. The network connection for the iSCSI SAN should be running at a minimum of 1GB. If the network is any slower, it has the potential to become a bottleneck for your organization.

After you've completed all of the required network connections for both servers that will be nodes on the cluster, the next step is to configure the iSCSI connection for each of your Windows Server 2008 nodes.

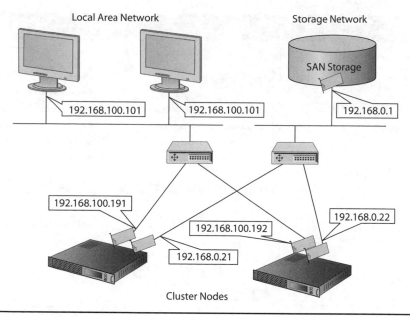

Figure 3-1   *The network configuration overview*

Configuring the Windows Server 2008 iSCSI Initiator

The exact configuration steps of the SAN itself depend highly on each vendor's hardware. The examples in this chapter were built using a LeftHand Networks SAS Starter SAN. The LeftHand Networks Starter SAN is an iSCSI SAN. In this example the SAN is configured to provide four different volumes:

► Quorum—500MB

► SQL Server Data Files—500GB

► SQL Server Log Files—500GB

► MS DTC—200MB

You can see an overview of the SAN configuration for the LeftHand Networks SAN in Figure 3-2.

The LeftHand SAN is highly scalable and has the ability to aggregate multiple SAN nodes together. To accomplish that, it uses a concept of a virtual IP address. The virtual IP address is used by the iSCSI clients to connect to the SAN. This insulates the iSCSI clients from needing to know any configuration information about nodes that are added. Instead, clients that connect using the iSCSI Initiator are configured to use the

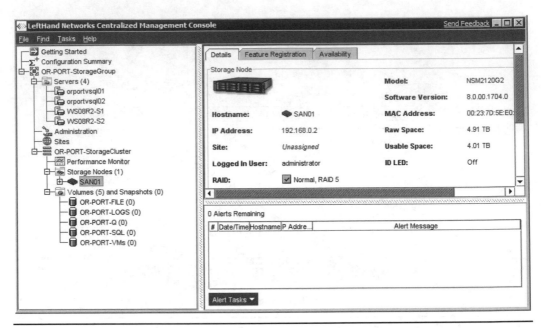

Figure 3-2   *SAN configuration overview*

SAN's virtual IP address. In this example, the SAN nodes use addresses 192.168.0.2 and 192.168.0.3, and the SAN itself is configured to use a virtual IP address of 192.168.0.1.

Next, you need to configure the iSCSI Initiator on each of the Windows Server 2008 systems. To configure the iSCSI Initiator, choose Start | Administrative Tools | iSCSI Initiator. If you've never run the iSCSI Initiator option before, you'll see two prompts. The first prompt will alert you that the iSCSI service is not running. The second will ask you about unblocking the Windows firewall.

For the first prompt, in almost all cases you will want the iSCSI Initiator service to automatically start when you start the computer. You should respond Yes to this prompt. You can always change this option by manually configuring the iSCSI service using Administrative Tools | Services.

The second prompt will ask you if you want to unblock the Microsoft iSCSI service so it can communicate across the Windows firewall. Again, you'll want to answer Yes. You can also control this by manually configuring the Windows firewall and unblocking port 3260. To configure the Windows firewall, open the Control Panel, and then select the Windows Firewall applet.

After you respond to these two prompts, the iSCSI Initiator will be displayed as you can see in Figure 3-3.

iSCSI Initiator Properties   Send Feedback ☒

| Targets | Discovery | Favorite Targets | Volumes and Devices | RADIUS | Configuration |

Target portals

The system will look for Targets on following portals: [Refresh]

Address	Port	Adapter	IP address

To add a target portal, click Discover Portal.   [Discover Portal...]

To remove a target portal, select the address above and   [Remove]
then click Remove.

iSNS servers

The system is registered on the following iSNS servers: [Refresh]

Name

To add an iSNS server, click Add Server.   [Add Server...]

To remove an iSNS server, select the server above and   [Remove]
then click Remove.

More about Discovery and iSNS

                                    [OK]   [Cancel]   [Apply]

Figure 3-3   *Starting the iSCSI Initiator*

NOTE

Before connecting to the SAN, you may need to configure the SAN with the iSCSI Initiator name. The iSCSI Initiator name can be found on the iSCSI Initiator's Configuration tab. The example presented here uses the name "iqn.1991-05.com.microsoft:orportvsql01.contoso.com". The name used in your configuration will be different depending on the system and domain names that are in use.

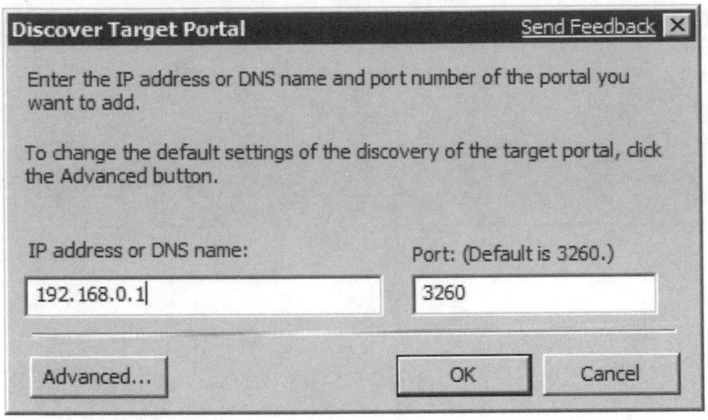

Figure 3-4   *iSCSI Initiator: Discover Target Portal*

To configure the iSCSI Initiator, select the Discovery tab, and then click Discover Portal. This will display the Discover Target Portal dialog box that you can see in Figure 3-4.

Using the Discover Target Portal dialog box, enter the IP address used by the SAN. In this example, you can see that the SAN address is 192.168.0.1 and that it will be using the default port of 3260. After entering the IP address, click OK, and the iSCSI Initiator will discover the storage resources that are available on the SAN. All of the storage resources will be listed on the iSCSI Initiator's Targets tab. At this point you can select each of the discovered targets, and then click the Connect button. This will display the Connect To Target dialog box, like the one in Figure 3-5.

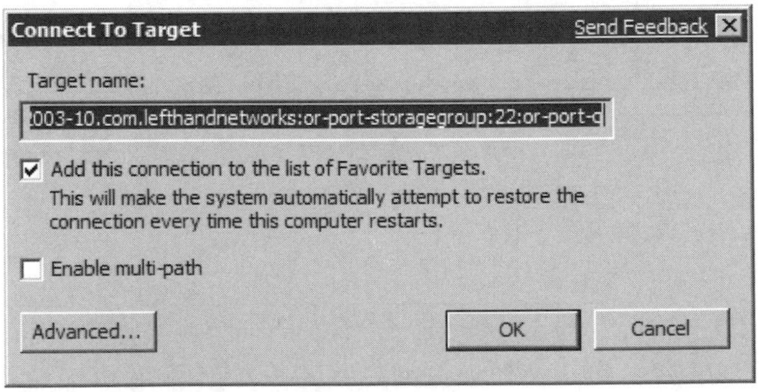

Figure 3-5   *iSCSI Initiator: Connect to Target*

The target name for each of the SAN resources will be listed in the Targets Name field. Be sure that the "Add this connection to the list of Favorite Targets" check box is selected. This will ensure that the Windows Server system will automatically connect to the iSCSI SAN resource when the system is started. After all of the resources have been connected, the iSCSI Initiator properties will appear as shown in Figure 3-6.

All of the connected SAN resources will be displayed in the Targets list box. The Status for each of the targets should show "Connected." At this point the drives can be viewed using Disk Manager exactly as if they were locally attached storage. Clicking OK ends the iSCSI Initiator.

Next, to prepare the drives for use, start Windows Server 2008's Disk Management by selecting Start | Administrative Tools | Server Manager. Then expand the Storage node and click Disk Management to display the drives as shown in Figure 3-7.

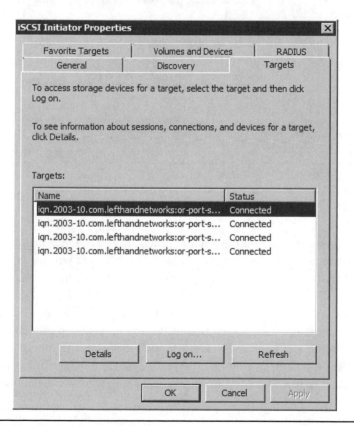

Figure 3-6 *iSCSI Initiator Targets tab with connected storage*

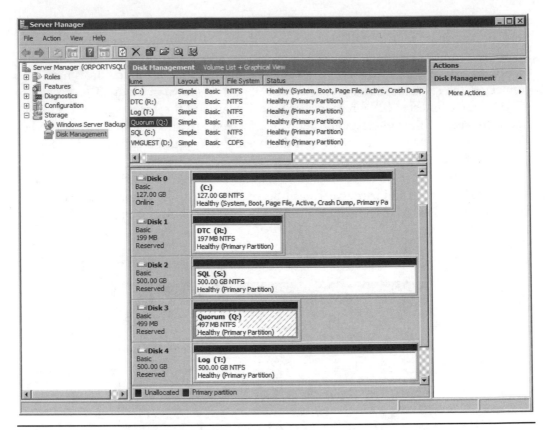

Figure 3-7 *Working with iSCSI SAN storage using Disk Management*

In Figure 3-7 you can see the three iSCSI volumes: Disk 2, Disk 3, and Disk 4. Disk 2 will be used as the failover cluster quorum, while the others will be used for SQL Server or file storage. You can assign drive letters by right-clicking each of the drives and selecting the Online option to bring the drives online. Then you can right-click the drive volume and select Change Drive Letter And Paths. In Figure 3-7 you can see that Disk 3, which will be used as the cluster quorum drive, has been assigned the letter *Q*. It doesn't have to be *Q*, but using *Q* makes it a bit easier to remember that it is being used as the cluster quorum. In this example, I assigned the other iSCSI volumes drive letters *R, S,* and *T*. Before you use the drives, make sure that you have formatted them using the NTFS (New Technology File System). After preparing the drives, be sure to bring them offline so that the Create Cluster Wizard can use them as storage. To bring the drives offline, right-click the disk icon displayed by the name *Disk 2, Disk 3,* and *Disk 4,* and then select Offline from the context menu.

You will need to repeat the iSCSI configuration steps for the other nodes in the cluster.

Adding the Failover Clustering Feature

Windows Server 2008 implements failover clustering as an operating system feature. Windows Server 2008's Server Manager is the tool that enables you to add support for failover clustering. Server Manager is Windows Server 2008's primary system configuration utility. Server Manager enables you to configure Windows Server 2008 by adding roles and features. *Roles* essentially define the type of server that the Windows Server 2008 system will be used for. For example, there are roles for Active Directory Domain Services, DHCP Server, DNS Server, File services, Hyper-V virtualization, and Web Server (IIS). Roles essentially define the overall function of the Windows Server 2008 system. You can install multiple roles on the same server. *Features* define the different optional components that you can add to the server. Installed features apply to all of the roles used on the server. Features include support for the .NET Framework 3.5, BitLock Drive Encryption, Multipath I/O, Network Load Balancing, and Failover Clustering.

You need to use Server Manager to add the Failover Clustering feature to all of the servers that will participate in the cluster. In this example, you'll see how to set up a two-node cluster, so Server Manager must be used to add failover clustering support to both servers. It doesn't make any difference which server is configured first.

Adding the Failover Cluster Feature with Server Manager

To add failover clustering support to Windows Server 2008, first run Server Manager by selecting Start | Administrative Tools | Server Manager. This will start Server Manager and display the Server Summary screen. To add the failover clustering feature, click the Features node in the Server Manager pane shown at left onscreen. This will display the Features Summary window you can see in Figure 3-8.

The Features Summary window shows the currently installed features. To add the Failover Clustering feature, click Add Features at right on the Features Summary screen you can see in Figure 3-8. This will display the Select Features window you can see in Figure 3-9.

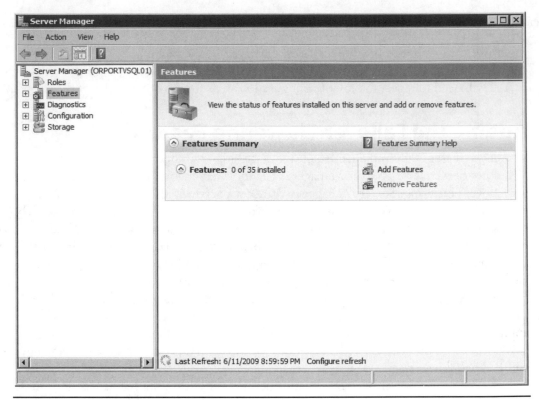

Figure 3-8 *Adding a feature using Server Manager*

Scroll through the list of features in the Select Features window until you see Failover Clustering. To add the Failover Clustering feature, select its check box and then click Next. The Confirm Installation Selections screen, displayed in Figure 3-10, will appear.

The Confirm Installation Selections dialog box confirms that you have elected to install the Failover Clustering feature. To proceed with the installation, click Install. This will take a couple of minutes, as the wizard copies the binary files that provide failover clustering support on the Windows Server system. Windows Server 2008 installs all of the binaries required for all of the roles and features as a part of the initial Windows Server installation. There's no need to find the original installation media.

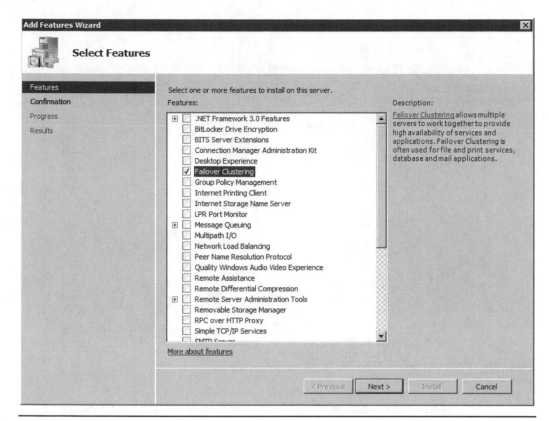

Figure 3-9 *Selecting the Failover Clustering feature*

After the files required for failover clustering have been copied to the system, the Installation Results dialog box shown in Figure 3-11 will be displayed.

The Installation Results screen reports the success or failure of the installation. If the feature installation failed, you will see a red *x* along with the message indicating the feature installation failed. If the installation of the Failover Clustering feature succeeded, you will see a green check mark followed by an "Installation succeeded" message like the one shown in Figure 3-11.

Clicking Close ends the Add Features Wizard, and the Server Manager's Features Summary screen will be displayed as you can see in Figure 3-12.

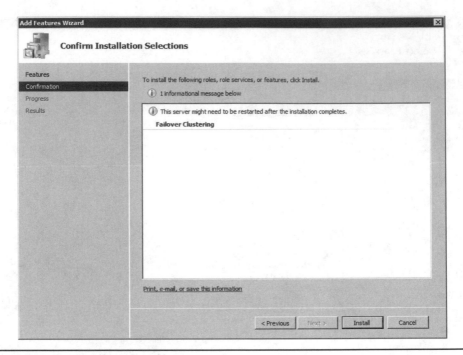

Figure 3-10   *Confirming the feature selection*

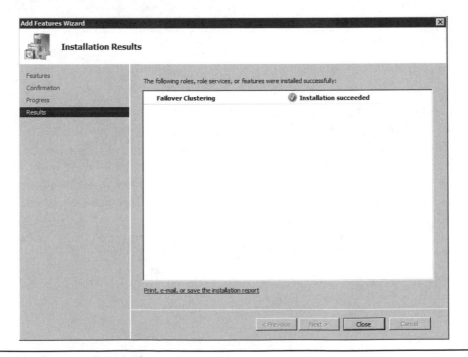

Figure 3-11   *Feature installation results*

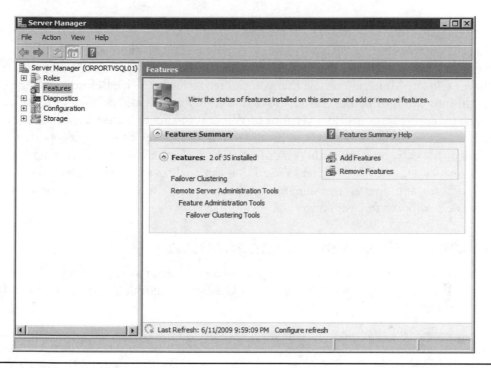

Figure 3-12   *Feature installation results*

Following the successful installation of the Failover Clustering feature, you'll see the feature listing in the Server Manager Features Summary as you can see in Figure 3-12. No reboot was required.

At this point the basic support for failover clustering has been added to the first node in the cluster. These same steps need to be performed for all of the servers that will participate in the failover cluster. This example uses a two-node cluster, so you would need to go to the second node and perform the steps for adding the Failover Clustering feature. The process is exactly the same as described in this section.

Configuring Failover Clustering

After the Failover Clustering feature has been added to all of the nodes in the cluster, the next step is to configure failover clustering on the first cluster node. To configure failover clustering, you need the Failover Clustering Wizard.

Running the Failover Cluster Manager

To start Windows Server 2008's Failover Clustering Wizard, choose Start | All Programs | Administrative Tools | Failover Cluster Manager. This will display the Failover Cluster Manager console that you can see in Figure 3-13. Before jumping straight into configuring the cluster, the first task that you should perform is to validate the cluster configuration. Older versions of Windows Failover Clustering required that you buy hardware that had been specifically tested for failover clustering support. That's no longer the case. Starting with Windows Server 2008, the Failover Clustering feature now provides a Cluster Validation Wizard that can analyze the different hardware, configuration, and operating system requirements in order to verify that the proposed systems can support failover clustering.

Validating the Cluster Configuration

To validate the Windows failover clustering configuration, start the Failover Cluster Management, and then select the Validate A Configuration link shown in Figure 3-13.

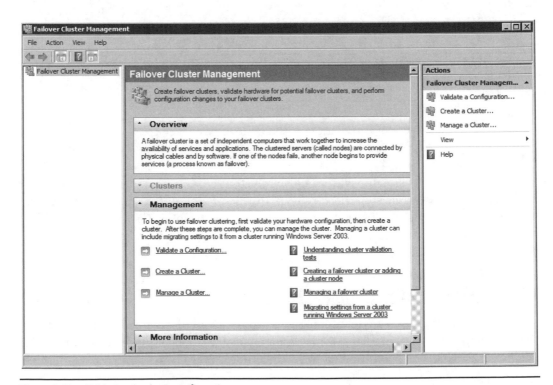

Figure 3-13 *Validating the cluster configuration*

Before running the cluster validation, you must have installed the Failover Clustering feature on all of the cluster nodes that you want to validate.

Clicking on the Validate A Configuration link starts the Validate A Configuration Wizard to verify that all of the components in the cluster will work with Windows Server 2008 Failover Clustering. You can see the initial screen of the Validate A Configuration Wizard displayed in Figure 3-14.

The initial dialog box of the Validate A Configuration Wizard simply warns you that the wizard is about to run a series of tests on your system and that the storage connected to your server will be momentarily unavailable while the tests are run. To start the Validate A Configuration Wizard, click Next. This will display the Select Servers or a Cluster dialog box that you can see in Figure 3-15.

You can use the Validate A Configuration Wizard either to test an existing cluster for errors or configuration problems, or to test new clusters nodes for their compatibility with Windows Server 2008 Failover Clustering. To test an existing cluster, you would

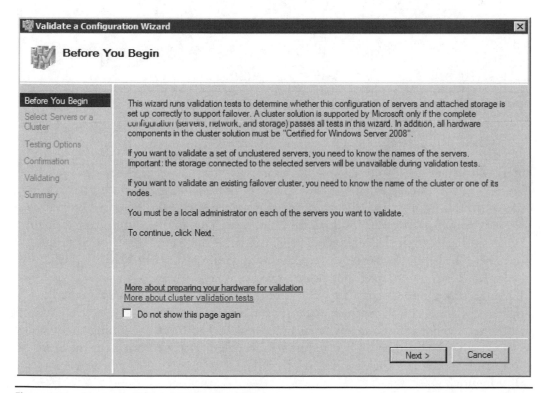

Figure 3-14   *Running the Validate A Configuration Wizard*

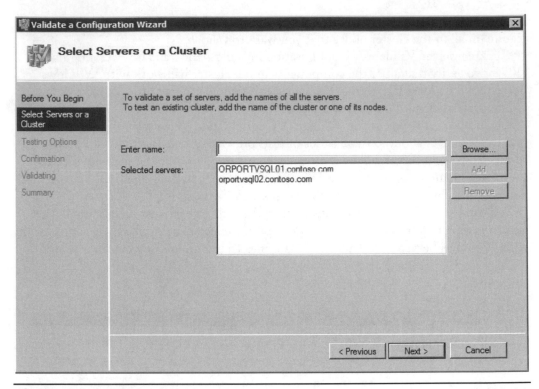

Figure 3-15   *Selecting the servers to validate*

enter the cluster name. To test a new cluster node, you would enter the node name. In Figure 3-15 you can see where the node names of both nodes in the cluster have been entered. In this example the first cluster node is named ORPORTVSQL01 and the second is named ORPORTVSQL02. Both nodes are part of the contoso.com domain. If your cluster has more than two nodes, you can enter the names of the other cluster nodes here. To begin the cluster configuration validation tests, click Next. This will display the Testing Options dialog box that you can see in Figure 3-16.

The Testing Options screen lets you select the validation tests that you want to run. You can choose to run the entire battery of validation tests, or you can selectively run just the tests you choose. If this is a new failover cluster or if you are adding a new node to an existing cluster, then it's best to just go ahead and choose to run all of the tests as shown in Figure 3-16. Clicking Next displays the Confirmation dialog box that you can see in Figure 3-17.

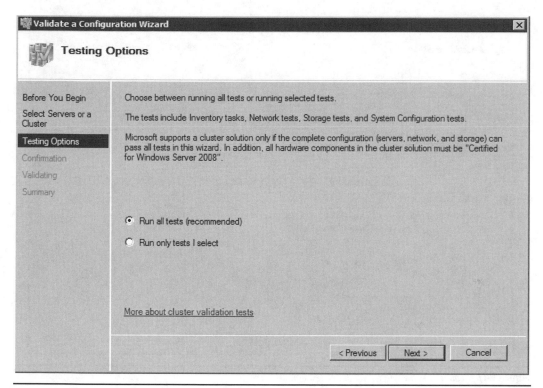

Figure 3-16   *Selecting the validation testing options*

The Confirmation dialog box lets you verify the tests that will be run. It also allows you to confirm the server nodes that the validation tests will be run on. If you've selected to run a set of individual tests, you can use the Previous button to go back and change your test selections. If you opted to run the entire test suite, then you probably won't have any need to change the test selections. Clicking Next fires off the cluster validation tests as shown in Figure 3-18.

As each test is run, the progress is displayed in the Validating list. Running all of the tests takes several minutes. When the tests have finished, you'll see the Summary screen shown in Figure 3-19.

The Summary dialog box shows the results of the set of failover cluster validation tests. The Summary dialog box will show one of three types of results: success, warning, or errors. You can proceed with the cluster configuration if you see a success message.

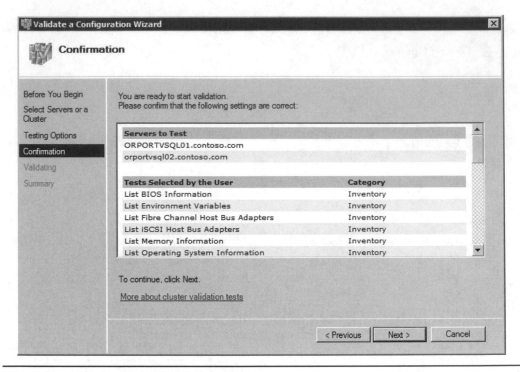

Figure 3-17   *Confirming the selected validation test options*

You can also proceed if you see a warning message. However, in the case of a warning, you'll want to click View Report to see the test results. If you see an error indication on the Summary screen, then you need to find and fix the error before you can proceed with the cluster configuration.

To view any warnings or errors, click View Report. The test results will be displayed in the browser. All the tests that are passed are marked with a green check mark. Any warnings are marked with a yellow triangle. If a given test isn't passed, it's marked with a red *x*. You can find more information about each of the validation tests and its results by clicking the links next to each test. When configuring a two-node cluster, it's common to see a warning about the quorum type. You'll see how to adjust the quorum configuration later in this chapter. You may also see warning messages if your Windows Update levels are not the same. Clicking Finish ends the Validate A Configuration Wizard and returns you to the Failover Cluster Manager.

After the cluster nodes have been validated to support the Windows Server 2008 Failover Clustering feature, you're ready to go ahead and create the cluster on the first node.

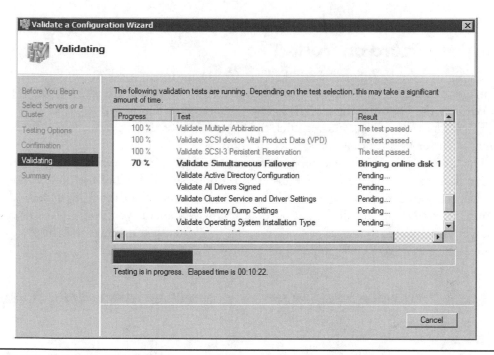

Figure 3-18   *Running the selected validation test options*

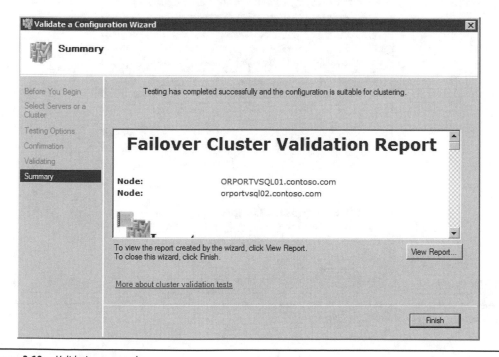

Figure 3-19   *Validation test results summary*

Creating the Cluster Using the Create Cluster Wizard on Node 1

To configure Windows Server 2008 Failover Clustering, open the Failover Cluster Manager by selecting the Start | Administrative Tools | Failover Cluster Manager. This will display the Failover Cluster Manager as illustrated in Figure 3-20.

To create a new failover cluster, click the Create A Cluster link. This will start the Create Cluster Wizard that you can see in Figure 3-21.

The Create Cluster Wizard steps you through the process of creating a new failover cluster. Before running the Create Cluster Wizard, be sure that all of the nodes that you are going to configure have passed the validation tests. In addition, set up a local administrator account on all the cluster nodes. This will enable you to perform system changes and updates to the other cluster nodes. Clicking Next displays the cluster wizard's Select Servers dialog box, which you can see in Figure 3-22.

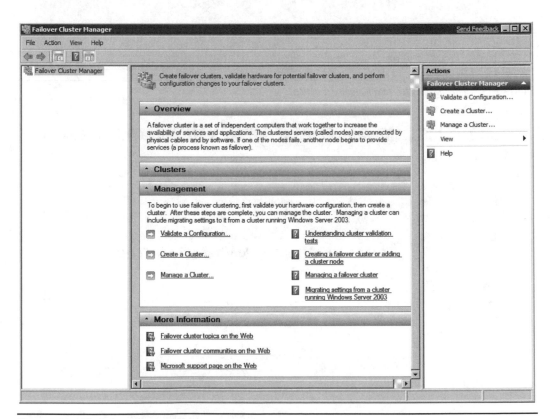

Figure 3-20   *The Failover Cluster Manager*

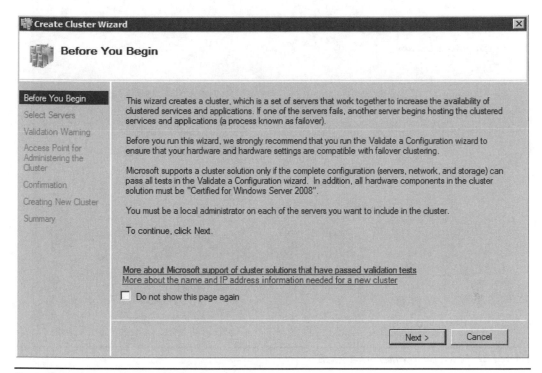

Figure 3-21   *Starting the Create Cluster Wizard*

As its name implies, you use the Select Servers dialog box to choose the servers that will act as nodes in the failover cluster. You can either type the fully qualified server names directly into the Enter Server Name prompt, or if your nodes are registered in the Active Directory, you can click Browse and select the names using the Active Directory Find dialog box. In the example shown in Figure 3-22, you can see that the names of both servers that will make up this two-node cluster have been entered. In this example I added nodes ORPORTVSQL01 and ORPORTVSQL02. Clicking Next displays the Access Point for Administering the Cluster dialog box that you can see in Figure 3-23.

You use the Access Point for Administering the Cluster dialog box to name the cluster and to assign it an IP address. This will be the name and address that network clients use to access the cluster. In the example shown in Figure 3-23, you can see that the cluster will be named ORPORTSQLCL01. You also need to manually assign the cluster's IP address. It cannot be assigned by DHCP. The IP address assigned should be on the same subnet as the networked clients. In this case the IP address of the cluster will be 192.168.100.210. After giving the cluster a name and public IP address, clicking Next displays the Confirmation screen that you can see in Figure 3-24.

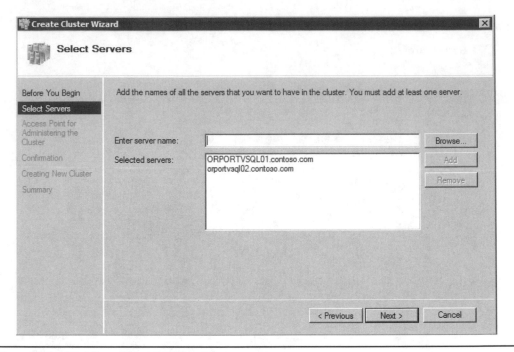

Figure 3-22 *Create Cluster Wizard: Select Servers*

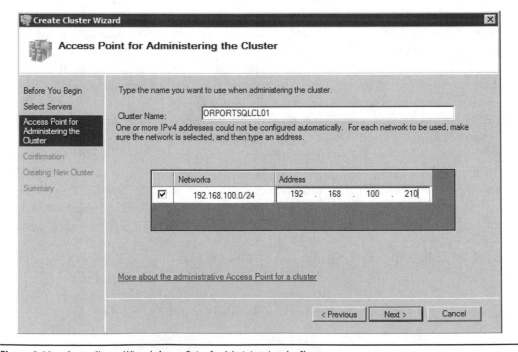

Figure 3-23 *Create Cluster Wizard: Access Point for Administering the Cluster*

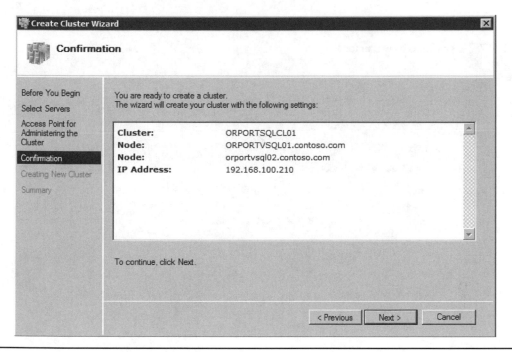

Figure 3-24 *Create Cluster Wizard: Confirmation*

The Confirmation screen presents a summary of the failover cluster configuration options that have been selected to this point. In Figure 3-24 you can see that the public cluster name will be ORPORTSQLCL01, and the IP address of the failover cluster is 192.168.100.210. The two Windows Server 2008 nodes that will compose the cluster are named ORPORTvSQL01 and ORPORTvSQL02. Both nodes are in the contoso .com domain.

If you need to make changes to these values, you can use the Previous button to page back through the previous wizard screens, where you can change any of the values displayed. If all of the values are acceptable, clicking Next will begin the cluster creation process. While the Create Cluster Wizard is creating the cluster, the Creating New Cluster dialog box shown in Figure 3-25 will be displayed.

It takes several minutes for the Create Cluster Wizard to create the cluster. The total amount of time depends on the number of nodes that will make up the cluster and the processing power of the machines involved. After the Create Cluster Wizard has successfully created the cluster, you'll see a Summary screen like the one shown in Figure 3-26.

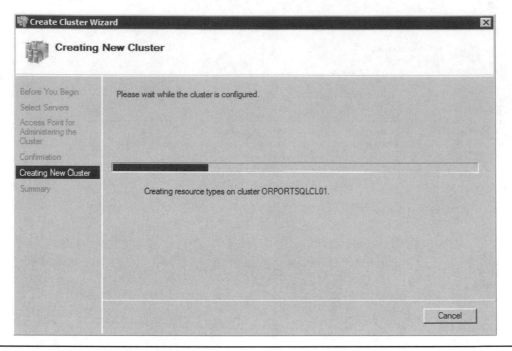

Figure 3-25 *Create Cluster Wizard: Creating New Cluster*

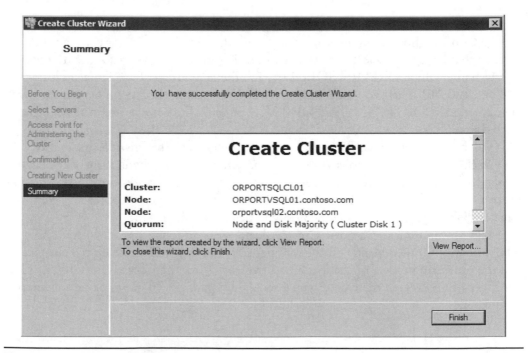

Figure 3-26 *Create Cluster Wizard: Summary*

The Create Cluster Wizard displays the Summary screen after the cluster has been successfully created. At this point you could begin to configure SQL Server to use the cluster. However, while the Create Cluster Wizard does a great job of setting up the required services on all of the cluster nodes, it doesn't always select the correct quorum drive to use. The Create Cluster Wizard often selects the first shared drive available, and that's not always the drive that you want to use as the quorum. For more information about the function of the failover cluster quorum, you can refer back to Chapter 2.

To change the quorum drive, you'll need to start the Failover Cluster Management. To start the Failover Cluster Management, choose Start | Administrative Tools | Failover Cluster Manager. This will start the Failover Cluster Management that you can see in Figure 3-27.

To use the Failover Cluster Management to change the quorum drive that's used by your new failover cluster, right-click the cluster name displayed. This will display the context menu. In Figure 3-27 you can see that I've right-clicked ORPORTSQLCL01. To configure the quorum, select More Actions | Configure Cluster Quorum Settings from the context menu. This will start the Configure Cluster Quorum Wizard that you can see in Figure 3-28.

The Configure Cluster Quorum Wizard enables you to select the type of quorum that will be used by the cluster. As you learned in Chapter 2, different cluster

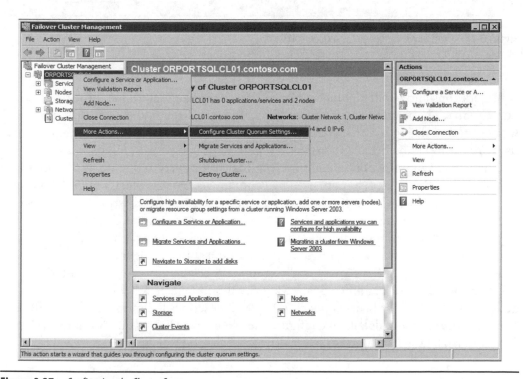

Figure 3-27 *Configuring the Cluster Quorum*

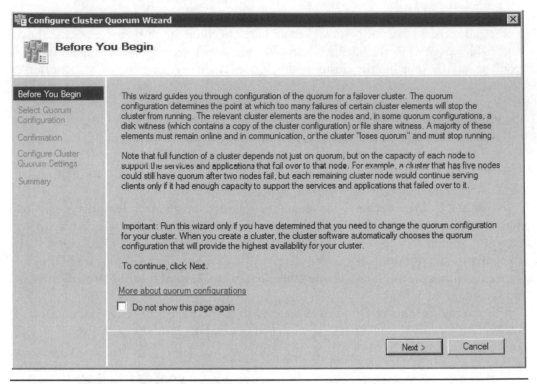

Figure 3-28 *Starting the Configure Cluster Quorum Wizard*

configurations and varying numbers of nodes in the cluster determine the type of quorum that's best suited to the cluster. Clicking Next displays the Select Quorum Configuration dialog box that enables you to configure the type of quorum that will be used. You can see the Select Quorum Configuration dialog box in Figure 3-29.

The Select Quorum Configuration screen that you can see in Figure 3-29 allows you to choose the type of quorum used by your failover cluster. The Configure Cluster Quroum Wizard automatically chooses the type of quorum that best fits the number of nodes that are in the cluster. In Figure 3-29 you can see that the Configure Cluster Quorum Wizard recommends using the Node and Disk Majority cluster for a two-node cluster. This is the best configuration for a typical two-node failover cluster. The other configuration options are typically used for special-purpose implementations. For example, the Node and File Share Majority might be a better choice for geographically dispersed cluster nodes. Chapter 2 describes the purpose of the different quorum types in more detail. To configure the Node and Disk Majority quorum, click Next to display the Configure Storage Witness dialog box shown in Figure 3-30.

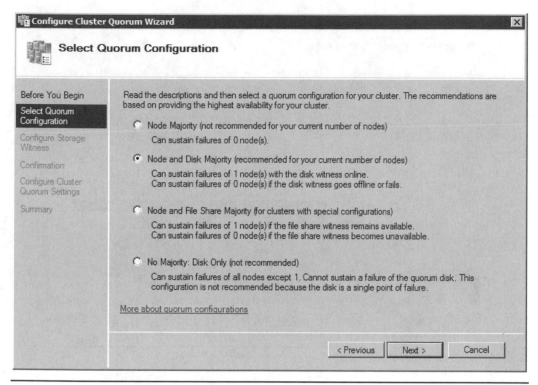

Figure 3-29   *Configure Cluster Quorum Wizard: Select Quorum Configuration*

On the Configure Storage Witness dialog box, select the disk that you want to use as the cluster quorum.

NOTE

If the drives you expect to see aren't listed, be sure all of the drives are visible to all of the cluster nodes. Then make sure all of the drives are offline on all nodes. Next rerun the Cluster Validation Wizard. Then add the missing storage to the cluster by selecting the Storage node in the Failover Cluster Management console and then clicking the Add A Disk task. This will display the Add Disks to a Cluster dialog box, where you should be able to select the disks you want to add to the cluster.

In Figure 3-30 you can see that Cluster Disk 4 has been selected. This was the drive that was previously assigned the letter *Q*. Clicking Next displays the Confirmation window that you can see in Figure 3-31.

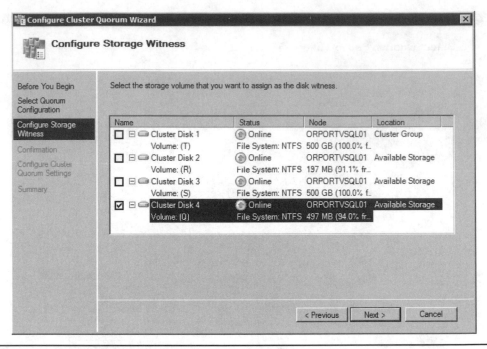

Figure 3-30   *Configure Cluster Quorum Wizard: Configure Storage Witness*

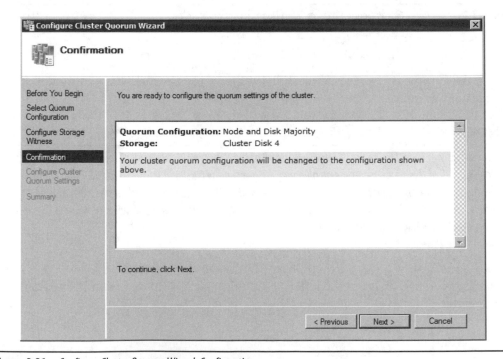

Figure 3-31   *Configure Cluster Quorum Wizard: Confirmation*

The Confirmation dialog box lets you review the new quorum settings. If you want to change these settings, clicking Previous allows you to page back through the previous configuration screens. To accept the new quorum configuration, click Next. This will display the Summary dialog box that you can see in Figure 3-32.

The Summary screen is displayed after the cluster quorum has been configured.

At this point the Windows Server 2008 Failover Cluster has been set up on both nodes, and you're ready to proceed with the SQL Server 2008 installation.

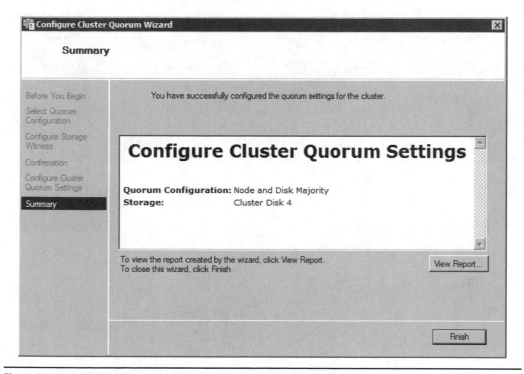

Figure 3-32   *Configure Cluster Quorum Wizard: Summary*

Chapter 4

Configuring SQL Server Failover Clustering

In This Chapter

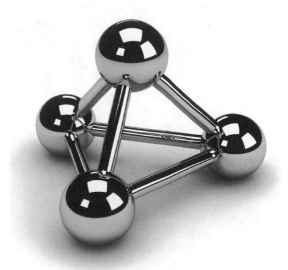

I n the last chapter, you saw how to create a two-node failover cluster by using Windows Server 2008. In this chapter, you'll see how to use that Windows Server 2008 failover cluster to provide high availability to SQL Server 2008. In the first part of this chapter, you'll see how to install the Microsoft Distributed Transaction Coordinator to the cluster. In the second part of this chapter, you'll see how to install SQL Server 2008 on the first cluster node. Then in the third part of this chapter, you'll see how to install SQL Server 2008 on the second cluster node.

Installing Microsoft Distributed Transaction Coordinator on the Cluster

The Microsoft Distributed Transaction Coordinator (MS DTC) is required for most SQL Server failover cluster installations. If you are installing only the relational database engine or just Analysis Services, then MS DTC is not required. MS DTC is required if you are installing the workstation components, SQL Server Integration Services, or if you intend to use distributed transactions. You can install MS DTC either before or after you install SQL Server 2008 on the cluster, but as it is a requirement, it's simpler to install it before you begin the SQL Server installation.

MS DTC must be installed as a separate cluster resource from SQL Server 2008. It must also have its own shared storage that's separate from the shared storage used by SQL Server. To install MS DTC to the cluster, go to the first cluster node, and then start Failover Cluster Management by choosing Start | Administrative Tools | Failover Cluster Management. This will display the Failover Cluster Management window shown in Figure 4-1.

To install MS DTC to the cluster, expand one of the cluster nodes, and right-click Services And Applications. This will display the context menu that you can see in Figure 4-1. Then select "Configure a Service or Application." This will launch the High Availability Wizard that you can see in Figure 4-2.

The Before You Begin dialog box warns you that you are about to begin the process of setting up a clustered service or application. This essentially means that the service or application that you configure will be highly available; that is, if it fails on the primary node, it will be restarted on one of the remaining cluster nodes.

NOTE

You cannot use the High Availability Wizard to install SQL Server on the cluster. You must use SQL Server 2008's Installation Center to create a SQL Server 2008 clustered installation.

Clicking Next begins the cluster installation for MS DTC and displays the Select Service or Application dialog box that you can see in Figure 4-3.

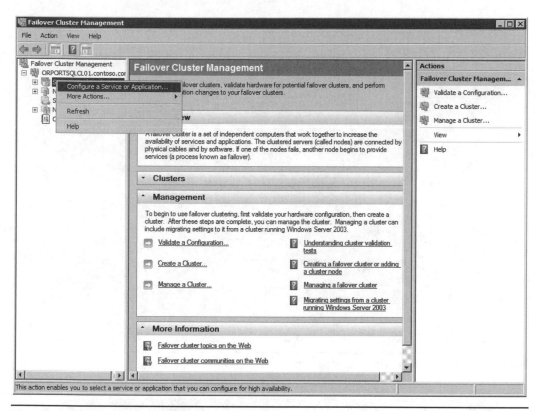

Figure 4-1   *Installing MS DTC from Failover Cluster Management*

To install MS DTC on the failover cluster, scroll through the "Select the service or application that you want to configure for high availability" list until you see the Distributed Transaction Coordinator (DTC). Select the Distributed Transaction Coordinator (DTC) and then click Next. This will display the Client Access Point dialog box that you can see in Figure 4-4.

In the Name prompt enter the name for the clustered service. In Figure 4-4 you can see that I use the name of ORPORTSQLCL0Dtc for the clustered service name. Next, enter an IP address that will be used. This IP address can't be used by the existing cluster configuration. For this example, you can see that I used the address of 192.168.100.213. After you've named a service and assigned it an IP address, clicking Next displays the Select Storage dialog box that you can see in Figure 4-5.

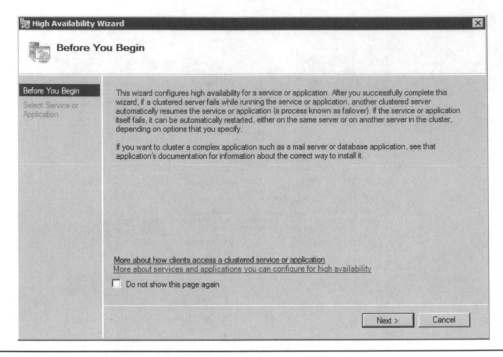

Figure 4-2   *High Availability Wizard: Before You Begin*

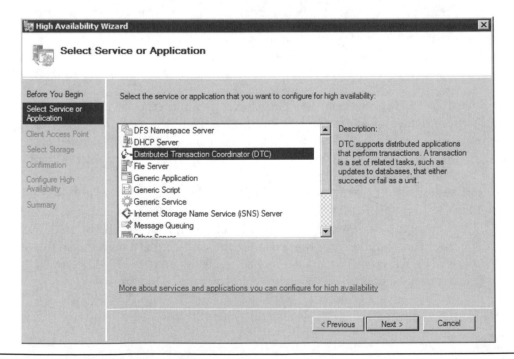

Figure 4-3   *High Availability Wizard: Select Service or Application*

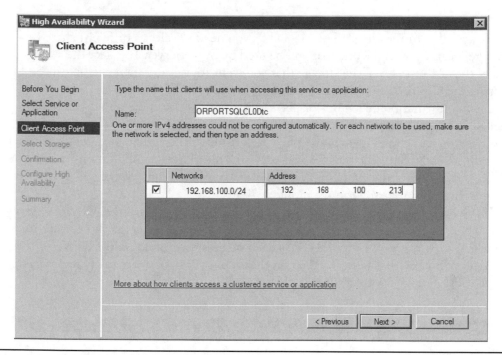

Figure 4-4   *High Availability Wizard: Client Access Point*

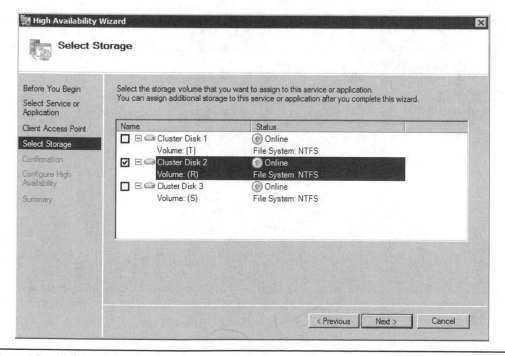

Figure 4-5   *High Availability Wizard: Select Storage*

The High Availability Wizard's Select Storage dialog box displays the shared storage that's available to the cluster. For MS DTC, you need to select a different shared storage location than the one that will be used by SQL Server. To select the storage, select the box in front of the storage that you want to use, and then click Next to display the Confirmation dialog box that you can see in Figure 4-6.

The Confirmation dialog box displays a summary of the choices that you have made using the High Availability Wizard. If you want to change any of the configuration options, you can click Previous and page back through the earlier configuration screen. Clicking Next accepts the settings and performs the cluster configuration for the MS DTC service. After the configuration has been completed, the wizard will display the Summary screen that you can see in Figure 4-7.

If the High Availability Wizard was able to successfully install the MS DTC service to the cluster, the Summary screen will display a success message, as you can see in Figure 4-7. At this point MS DTC has been successfully set up on the cluster.

After MS DTC has been installed on the failover cluster, you're ready to proceed and install SQL Server 2008 on the first cluster node.

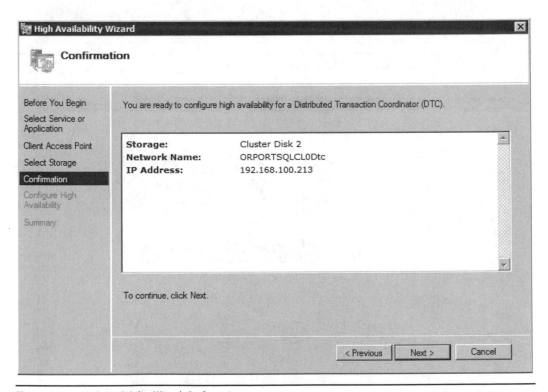

Figure 4-6   *High Availability Wizard: Confirmation*

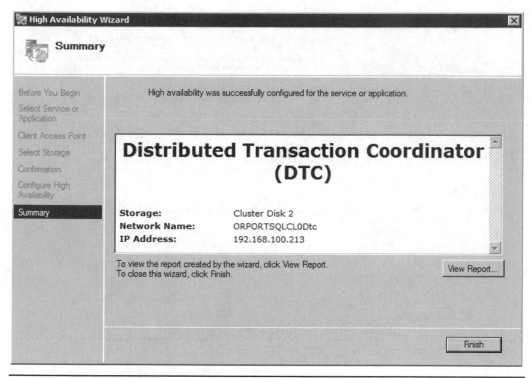

Figure 4-7   *High Availability Wizard: Summary*

Installing Server 2008 on the First Cluster Node

To install SQL Server 2008 on the failover cluster, you need to use SQL Server 2008's Installation Center. The Installation Center is started by running setup.exe from the SQL Server 2008 installation media. After the Installation Center has started, you select Installation from the action links presented on the left side of the screen. This will display the SQL Server Installation Center's Installation options, which you can see in Figure 4-8.

To install SQL Server 2008 on the first cluster node, select "New SQL Server failover cluster installation" from the list of installation options displayed by the SQL Server Installation Center. This will start the SQL Server 2008 setup process. The Setup Support Rules dialog box that you can see in Figure 4-9 appears.

NOTE

If this is first time you've run the SQL Server 2008 installation, you may be prompted to apply an update to Windows Installer and the .NET Framework. This update will require that you reboot the system.

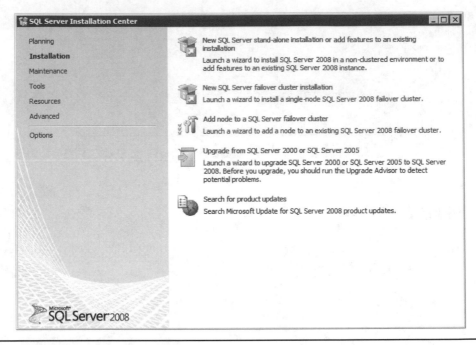

Figure 4-8   *SQL Server Installation Center: Installation*

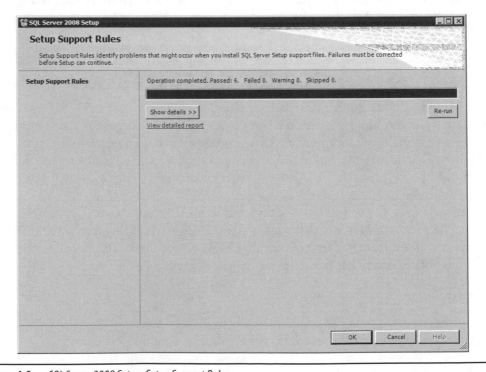

Figure 4-9   *SQL Server 2008 Setup: Setup Support Rules*

The Setup Support Rules dialog box checks your system for problems that might prevent the successful installation of SQL Server 2008. The Setup Support Rules portion of the SQL Server 2008 installation performs tests for six different system requirements including tests for the minimum operating system level, tests to determine if you have administrative privileges, and tests to check if the WMI service is running. Clicking OK displays the Setup Support Files dialog box illustrated in Figure 4-10.

The Setup Support Files dialog box installs the components that are required by the SQL Server 2008 setup program. Clicking Install copies the required setup files to the system and displays the SQL Server 2008 Setup Support Rules dialog box you can see in Figure 4-11.

The Setup Support Rules dialog box performs a second set of tests to determine if there will be any problems running the setup program. A green check mark indicates the condition is OK and that the installation can proceed. A Red *x* indicates a problem needs to be corrected before the setup can proceed. Clicking the link under the Status column will provide more information about any error conditions that weren't met. If all of the conditions are passed, green check marks are next to all the items, as you can see in Figure 4-11.

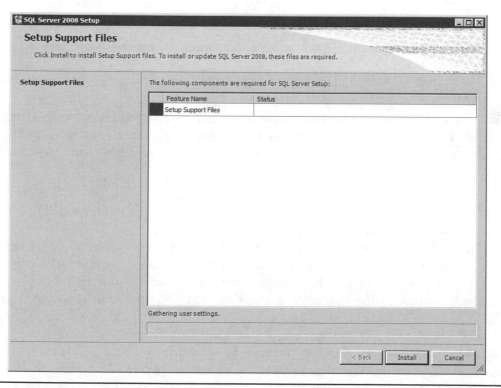

Figure 4-10 *SQL Server 2008 Setup: Setup Support Files*

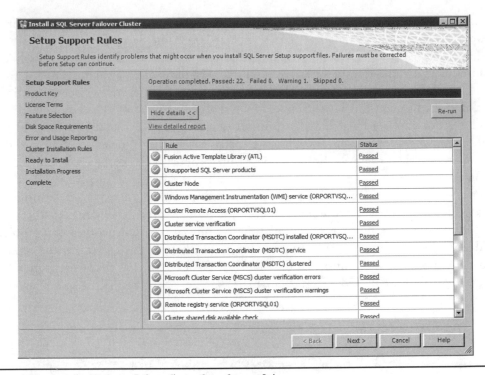

Figure 4-11   *Install a SQL Server Failover Cluster: Setup Support Rules*

> **NOTE**
>
> *If you receive an error regarding the network binding, you can verify and change the binding order by opening Network Connections, pressing ALT to display the menu, and then selecting Advanced | Advanced Settings. This error is typically caused by disabled or ghosted network adapters. You can find more information about this issue at http://support.microsoft.com/kb/955963.*

Clicking Next continues the installation process and prompts you for the SQL Server 2008 Product Key dialog box you see in Figure 4-12.

The Product Key screen in the SQL Server 2008 setup process prompts you to enter your product key information. If you're installing one of the evaluation versions of SQL Server 2008, you would select the "Specify a free edition" radio button and click Next. Otherwise, if you are installing a licensed version of SQL Server 2008, you would select the "Enter the product key" radio button, and then type in the product installation key and click Next. This will display the End User License Agreement (EULA) in the License Terms dialog box that you can see in Figure 4-13.

The installation process will not proceed until you accept the SQL Server 2008 license agreement. You accept the license agreement by selecting the "I accept the license terms" check box.

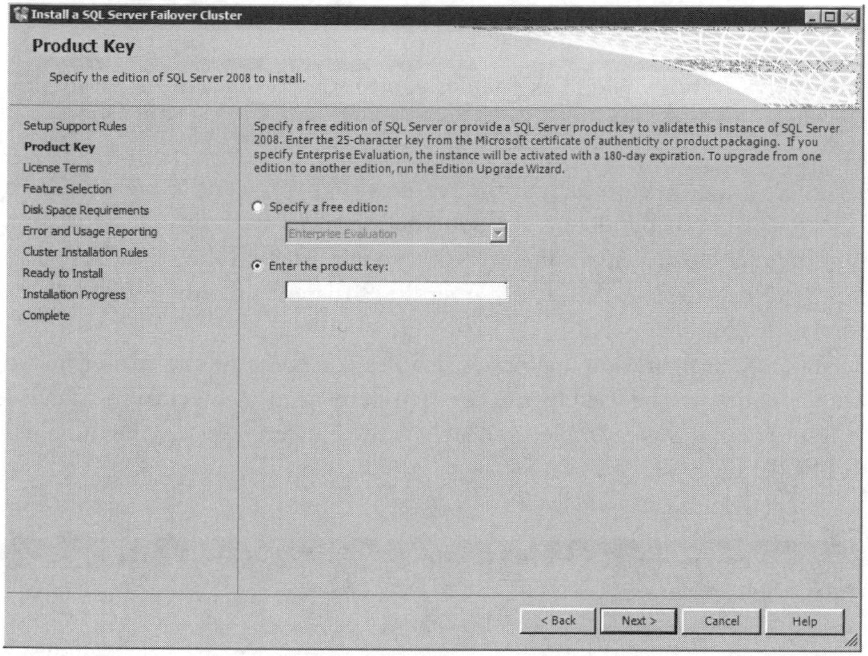

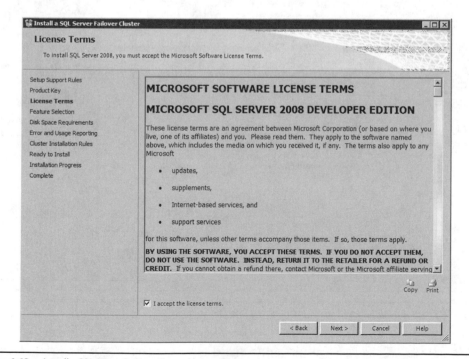

Figure 4-12   *Install a SQL Server Failover Cluster: Product Key*

Figure 4-13   *Install a SQL Server Failover Cluster License Terms*

Clicking Next will display the SQL Server 2008 Feature Selection dialog box that's shown in Figure 4-14.

The Feature Selection dialog box enables you to select which SQL Server 2008 components you want to install. Table 4-1 describes the available SQL Server 2008 features.

Place a check mark next to each of the features that you want to be installed on the failover cluster. Analysis Services and Reporting Services are fully supported in a high availability failover cluster environment. After you've selected the features that you want, clicking Next displays the SQL Server 2008 Instance Configuration screen like the one shown in Figure 4-15.

The Instance Configuration dialog box enables you to name the cluster instance. This instance name will be used by the client systems that connect to the clustered database resources. In this example, you can see the clustered instance will be named ORPORTSQLHA.

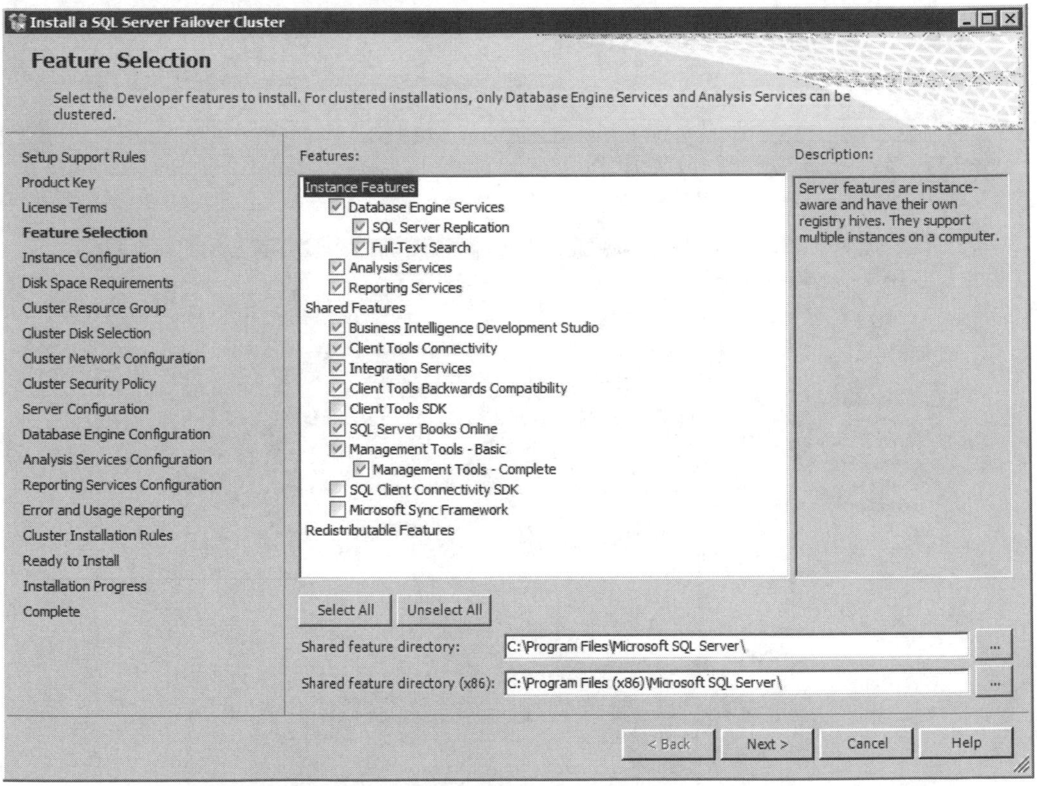

Figure 4-14 *Install a SQL Server Failover Cluster: Feature Selection*

Feature	Description
Database Engine Services	Installs the core relation database engine
SQL Server Replication	Installs support for replicating database objects
Full-Text Search	Installs the Full-Text search engine, which allows linguistic-aware searching for text words and phrases in columns
Analysis Services	Installs the online analytical processing (OLAP) subsystem
Reporting Services	Installs the reporting subsystem
Business Intelligence Development Studio	Installs the IDE (Integrated Development Environment) for developing BI objects like cubes, Integration Services packages, and Reporting Services reports
Client Tools Connectivity	Installs the middleware that enables network clients to connect to SQL Server
Integration Services	Installs the data transfer and transformation subsystem
Client Tools Backwards Compatibility	Installs the components required to run existing DTS packages that were created with SQL Server 2000
Client Tools SDK	Installs the software development samples and tools
SQL Server Books Online	Installs the online product documentation
Management Tools—Basic	Installs SQL Server Management Studio, SQLCMD, and the SQL Server PowerShell provider
Management Tools—Complete	Installs SQL Server Management Studio support for Analysis Services, Integration Services, and Reporting Services as well as SQL Profiler and the Database Tuning Advisor
SQL Client Connectivity SDK	Installs software development samples and tools
Microsoft Sync Framework	Installs the components to support synchronization with offline applications and mobile devices

Table 4-1   *SQL Server 2008 Installable Features*

You have the option to either set up the default instance or set up a named instance. If you've already set up a default SQL Server instance, the setup program will detect that instance and offer you only the option to set up a named instance. ISPs and web hosting providers are the types of business that usually make the most use of named instances. However, they can be used by other organizations as well. A named instance is essentially another copy of SQL Server installed on the same server. The Enterprise Edition supports up to 50 named instances on a given system. The Standard Edition supports a maximum of 16 instances. If you create a named instance, each name must be 16 characters or less. Instance names are not case sensitive, but the first character of the name must be a letter. They cannot have any embedded spaces and must not

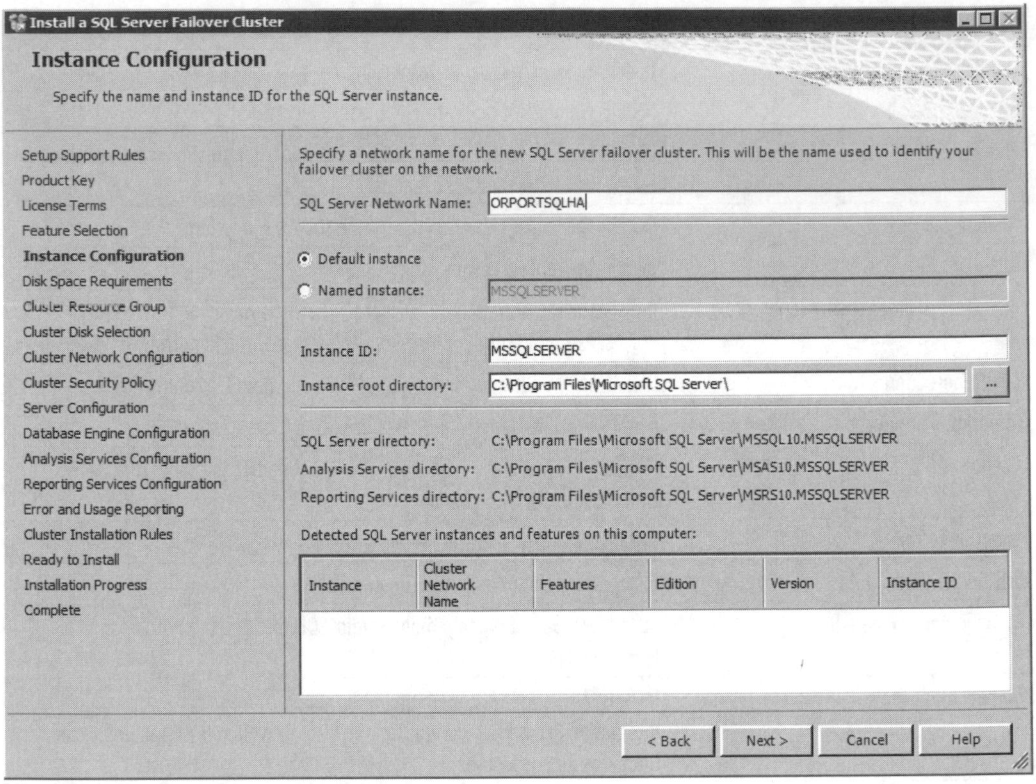

Figure 4-15   *Install a SQL Server Failover Cluster: Instance Configuration*

contain the backslash (\), comma (,), colon (:), single quote ('), dash (-), ampersand (&), number sign (#), or *at* sign (@). Instance names also cannot contain the reserved words "Default" or "MSSQLServer."

NOTE

If you create a named instance, the SQL Server service name will be named as follows: MSSQL$InstanceName (where InstanceName *is replaced with the* instance name *that you create).*

For a typical two-node failover cluster, select the default instance name of MSSQLSERVER.

The Instance Configuration dialog box also allows you to specify the directory that you want to use to install the SQL Server instance. The default installation directory is C:\Program Files\Microsoft SQL Server\. Clicking Next displays the Disk Space Requirements dialog box shown in Figure 4-16.

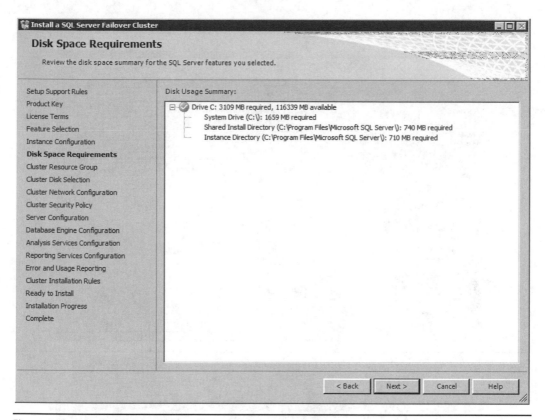

Figure 4-16   *Install a SQL Server Failover Cluster: Disk Space Requirements*

The Disk Space Requirements dialog box displays the installation directories that you previously selected as well as the required and available storage space for each drive. If you need to change the selections, you can use the Back button to page back to the Features Selection and Instance Configuration dialog boxes to change the target directories. If the selected disk storage configuration is acceptable, then clicking Next displays the Cluster Resource Group dialog box that's shown in Figure 4-17.

The Cluster Resource Group screen allows you to specify the SQL Server cluster resource group name. This is the name of the SQL Server resources that are used by Windows failover clustering. By default the Install a SQL Server Failover Cluster Wizard uses the resource group name of SQL Server (MSSQLSERVER)—the same name as the SQL Server instance name. You can also specify a different name by typing in the new name. In Figure 4-17 you can see that the example cluster will use the default value. Clicking Next displays the Cluster Disk Selection dialog box that you can see in Figure 4-18.

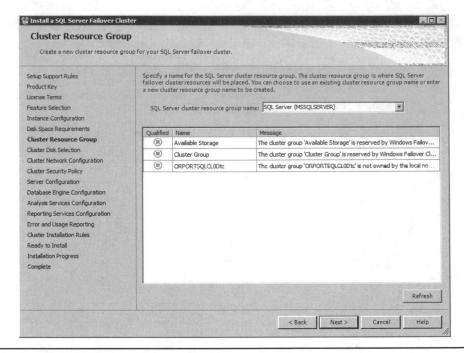

Figure 4-17   *Install a SQL Server Failover Cluster: Cluster Resource Group*

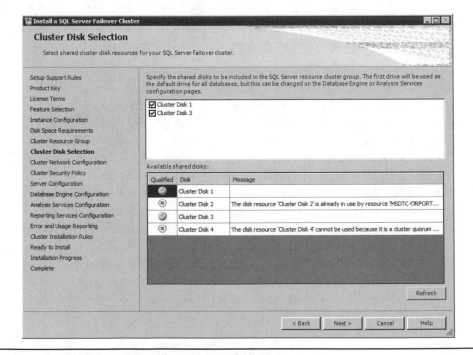

Figure 4-18   *Install a SQL Server Failover Cluster: Cluster Disk Selection*

The Cluster Disk Selection dialog box allows you to select the available storage that will be used by the cluster resource group. All of the cluster storage is shown in the list in the bottom portion of the window. Note that two of the disks are not available because they have already been used by other cluster services. Cluster Disk 2 was used by the MS DTC service, and Cluster Disk 4 has been used as the cluster quorum. The available storage will be shown in the list box in the upper portion of the screen. As you might expect, the storage must be visible to cluster before it can be included in the SQL Server resource group. However, you can also add storage to the resource group after the cluster has been configured.

Initially the check boxes in the upper list box will be empty. To include the storage, select the box in front of each of the cluster disks that will be used by SQL Server. In Figure 4-18 you can see that both of the available cluster disks will be included in the SQL Server cluster resource group. Click Next to display the Cluster Network Configuration dialog box that you can see in Figure 4-19.

The Cluster Network Configuration screen allows you to assign an IP address that will be used by the cluster. If both IPv4 and IPv6 are used, they will both be listed here. In this example IPv6 is not used, so it isn't listed. By default, the cluster address on this

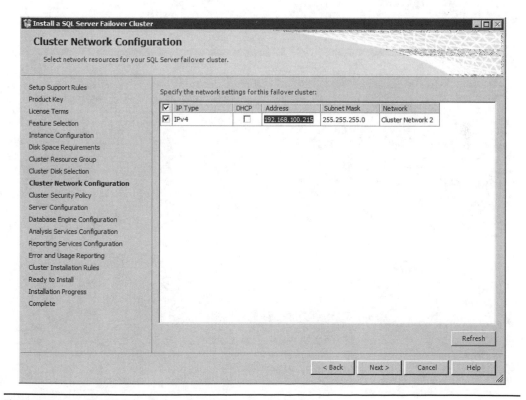

Figure 4-19 *Install a SQL Server Failover Cluster: Cluster Network Configuration*

dialog box is assigned by DHCP. However, it is usually a better practice to manually assign the IP address of your infrastructure servers. In Figure 4-19 you can see that I've manually assigned the cluster an IP address of 192.169.100.215 and used the corresponding subnet mask of 255.255.255.0. Note that the cluster address is different for the IP address of any of the cluster nodes or other services. It must be unique on your subnet. This is the address clients will use when they connect to the SQL Server cluster resources. Clicking Next displays the Cluster Security Policy dialog box that is shown in Figure 4-20.

The Cluster Security Policy dialog box allows you to select the security context that the clustered SQL Server services will use. You can choose to use either the service security IDs (SIDs), or you can specify a domain group. A service SID is a security ID that the system can assign to each service. Service SIDs provide services a way to access specific objects without having to either run in a high-privilege account or weaken the security protection of the object. For more information about using service SIDs with

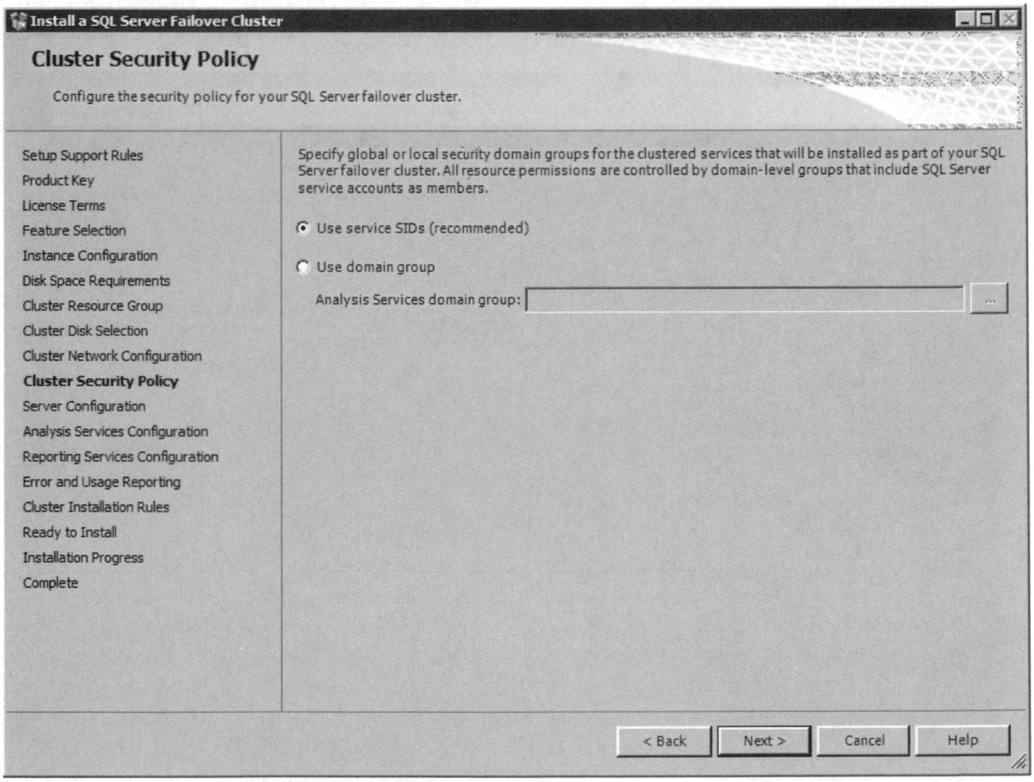

Figure 4-20   *Install a SQL Server Failover Cluster: Cluster Security Policy*

SQL Server, you can refer to http://msdn.microsoft.com/en-us/library/ms143504
.aspx#Service_SID. In Figure 4-20 you can see that the example cluster uses the default
Use service SIDs. Clicking Next will display the Server Configuration window like the
one shown in Figure 4-21.

You use the Server Configuration dialog box to specify the accounts that each of the
SQL Server services will run under. For security the SQL Server service should run
under a domain account, and it doesn't need and shouldn't have Windows administrator
privileges. Microsoft recommends that you run each of the services using a separate
account, ideally, but that isn't required, and it buys you very little in the way of additional
security.

In Figure 4-21 you can see that all of the SQL Server services are being started using
the SQLServiceUser account, which is a domain account in the CONTOSO domain.
If you elect to use a domain account rather than one of the built-in accounts like the
Local Service account, then you will need to supply the account's password as well.

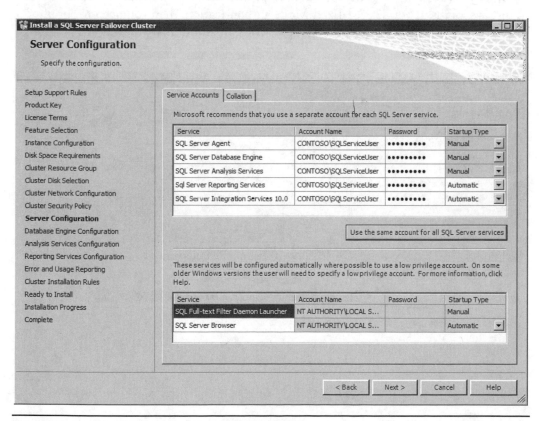

Figure 4-21   *Install a SQL Server Failover Cluster: Server Configuration*

NOTE

Don't be alarmed that the Startup type is manual. That is standard for cluster-aware services and it can't be changed.

After the startup accounts for the SQL Server services have been entered, you can click Next to display the Database Engine Configuration dialog box, as shown in Figure 4-22.

The Database Engine Configuration dialog box is essentially the same as the stand-alone SQL Server 2008 installation process. The Account Provisioning tab enables you to select the type of SQL Server authentication you want to use. The Data Directories tab lets you select the directories that SQL Server will use. The FILESTREAM tab allows you to enable FILESTREAM support for SQL Server.

In Figure 4-22 you can see that I selected Mixed Mode authentication, which essentially means that SQL Server can have its own set of logins that are separate from Windows logins. If you select Mixed Mode authentication, then you need to supply SQL Server's built-in sa account with a password. In addition, if you want to add the

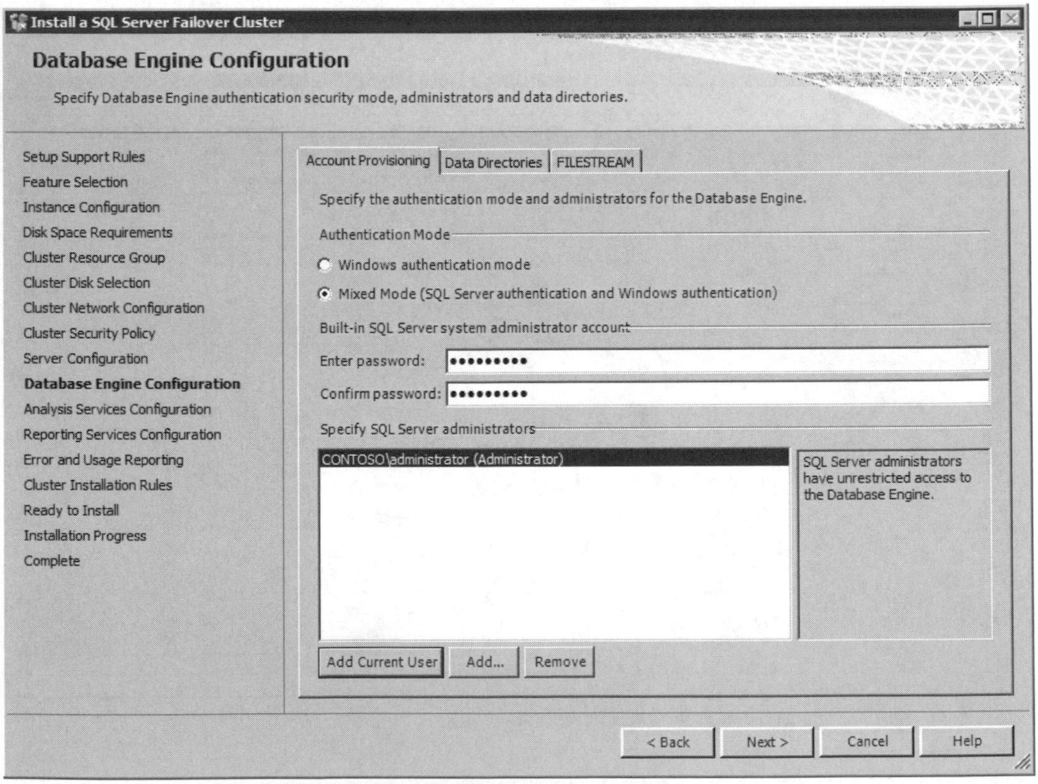

Figure 4-22 *Install a SQL Server Failover Cluster: Database Engine Configuration*

current login to the SQL Server administrators group, then you will need to click the Add Current User button. This will add an entry for the current login account to the list box at the bottom of the screen and will provision this account as SYSADM within the SQL Server relational database engine.

In this example, I also wanted to enable FILESTREAM support by clicking the FILESTREAM tab. This will display the FILESTREAM configuration options dialog box that you can see in Figure 4-23.

SQL Server 2008's new FileStream data type is supported on clustered SQL Server systems just as it is on stand-alone installations. To enable FileStream support during the setup process, click the FILESTREAM tab; then select the "Enable FILESTREAM for Transact-SQL access" check box. In addition, if you want to allow networked clients to access the FileStream data, then you need to check the "Enable FILESTREAM for file I/O streaming access" check box. This will also create a Windows file share. By default the file share will be named MSSQLSERVER, but you can rename it if you choose.

When you've completed configuring the SQL Server database engine, click Next to display the Analysis Services Configuration screen that is shown in Figure 4-24.

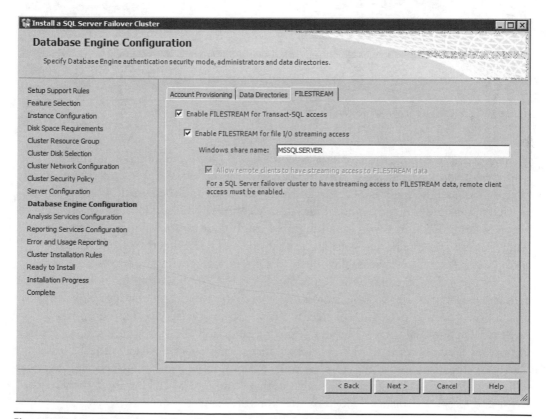

Figure 4-23   *Install a SQL Server Failover Cluster: Database Engine Configuration*

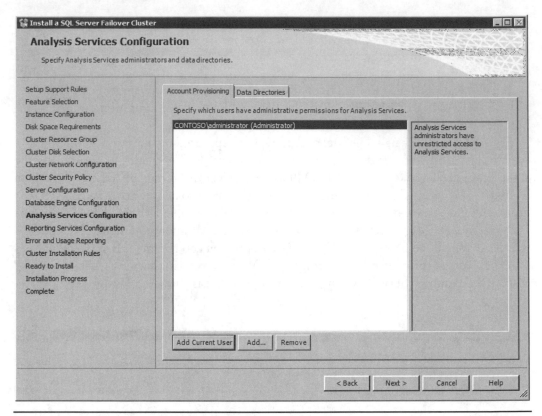

Figure 4-24   *Install a SQL Server Failover Cluster: Analysis Services Configuration*

As you might expect, the Analysis Services Configuration dialog box is only displayed if you have elected to install Analysis Services. On the Account Provisioning tab, you can assign Analysis Services administrators. To add the current user, click Add Current User, and the current administrators account will be added as an Analysis Services administrator, as you see in Figure 4-24. If you want to change the default Analysis Services directories, you can do that on the Data Directories tab. After configuring Analysis Services, click Next to configure Reporting Services.

In Figure 4-25 you can see the Reporting Services Configuration dialog box. Like the earlier Analysis Services Configuration dialog box, the Reporting Services Configuration dialog box is only displayed if you elect to install Reporting Services in the initial features selection dialog box. The stand-alone installation allows you to install a default Reporting Services configuration. However, that option is not present in the Failover Cluster installation. Reporting Services must be configured using the Reporting Services Configuration Manager after the installation has completed. Clicking Next displays the Error and Usage Reporting dialog box that you can see in Figure 4-26.

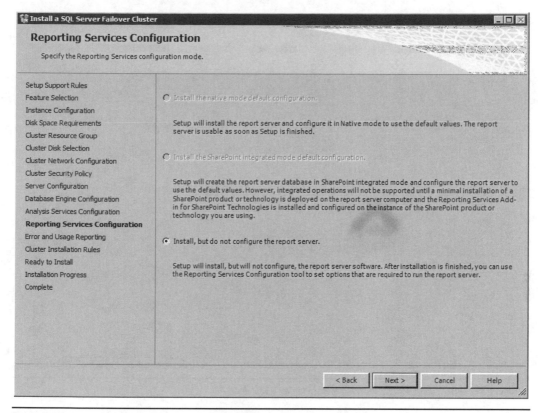

Figure 4-25 *Install a SQL Server Failover Cluster: Reporting Services Configuration*

SQL Server 2008's Error and Usage Reporting screen enables you to optionally report errors in the SQL Server database service and other subsystem service errors to Microsoft. Likewise, the usage report shows Microsoft how you use the product. Microsoft does not collect any personal information from these reports. Microsoft just uses this information to better understand how SQL Server is used as well as to identify and resolve problems that are encountered. SQL Server 2008's error reports send the following information to Microsoft:

► The status of the service when the error occurred

► The operating system version

► The basic hardware configuration

► SQL Server's Digital Product ID (which is used to identify your license)

► The server's IP address

► Information about the process that caused the error

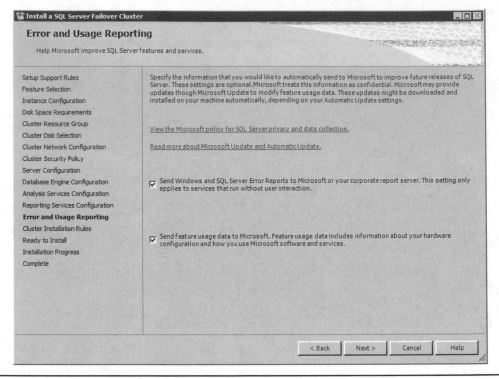

Figure 4-26 *Install a SQL Server Failover Cluster: Error and Usage Reporting*

Participating in Microsoft's error and usage reporting is completely optional. Clicking Next displays the Cluster Installation Rules dialog box that is shown in Figure 4-27.

The Cluster Installation Rules dialog box performs a final check for any conditions that might cause an error in the installation process. If any error condition is found, it will be shown in the Cluster Installation Rules dialog box with a red *x*. If all of the items have green check marks as shown in Figure 4-27, then the installation is ready to proceed. Clicking Next displays the Ready To Install dialog box shown in Figure 4-28.

The Ready to Install dialog box enables you to confirm your choices. If you need to change any of the values, you can use the Back button to page back through the previous installation configuration screens. Clicking Install begins the installation process for SQL Server 2008 on the first node of the failover cluster. The installation itself will take several minutes depending on the hardware that you're using and the installation media. As the installation program runs, the current status is shown in the Installation Progress window that you can see in Figure 4-29.

When the SQL Server 2008 installation on the first cluster node has completed, you'll see the Complete dialog box as shown in Figure 4-30.

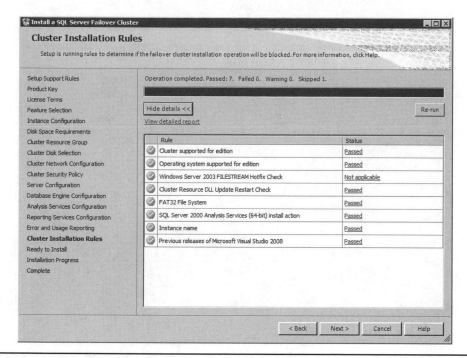

Figure 4-27   *Install a SQL Server Failover Cluster: Cluster Installation Rules*

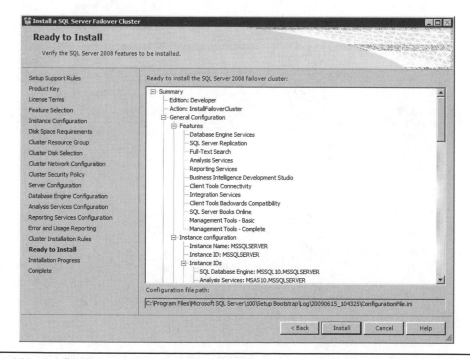

Figure 4-28   *Install a SQL Server Failover Cluster: Ready to Install*

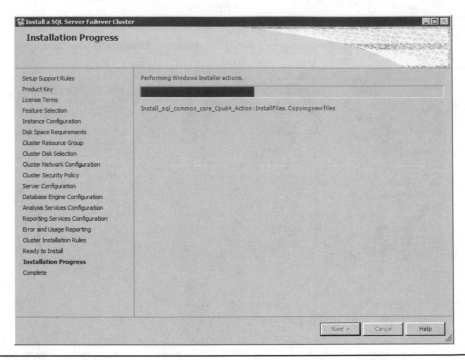

Figure 4-29 *Install a SQL Server Failover Cluster: Installation Progress*

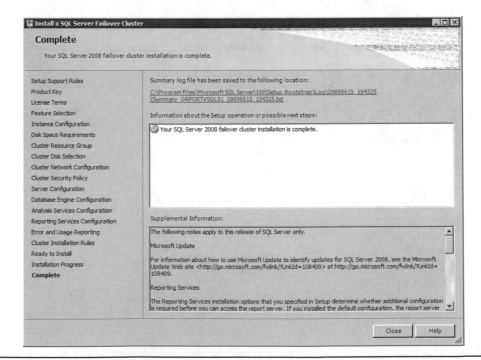

Figure 4-30 *Install a SQL Server Failover Cluster: Complete*

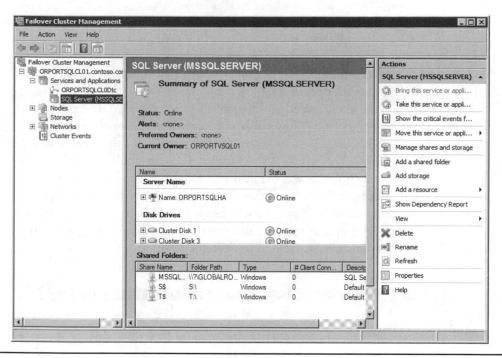

Figure 4-31   *Failover Cluster Management: SQL Server application*

When the installation of SQL Server 2008 on the first cluster node has completed, you'll see the Complete window like the one shown in Figure 4-30. At this point SQL Server 2008 is fully functionally on the first node. Clients can connect to it, and databases can be installed and accessed. However, because the second node has not been added, there is no high availability. In other words, at this point you have a one-node cluster and no nodes that you can failover to.

If you open the Failover Cluster Management console on the first node, it will appear like the screen shown in Figure 4-31.

Expanding the Services and Applications node shows that SQL Server is now listed as a clustered application. To make it a highly available installation, you need to add another node to the cluster.

Installing Server 2008 on the Second Cluster Node

After you've successfully installed SQL Server 2008 on the first cluster node, the next step is to install SQL Server 2008 onto the second node and to add that node to the cluster. To add the second node to the cluster, go to the second node in the cluster, and run the SQL Server 2008 installation program. After the SQL Server Installation Center starts, click the Installation link to display the installation options that you can see in Figure 4-32.

To install SQL Server 2008 on your second cluster node, select the "Add node to a SQL Server failover cluster" option. This option assumes that a Windows failover cluster has been previously configured and that an instance of SQL Server 2008 has already been created on the cluster. You saw how to create a failover cluster using Windows Server 2008 in Chapter 3, and the previous section in this chapter illustrated how to install SQL Server 2008 on the first cluster node. Clicking the "Add node to a SQL Server failover cluster" link will begin the installation process on the second cluster node and will display the Setup Support Rules dialog box that you can see in Figure 4-33. As with the installation of the first cluster node, if you haven't previously installed SQL Server 2008 on the second cluster node, you will probably be prompted to update the Windows Installer and the .NET Framework.

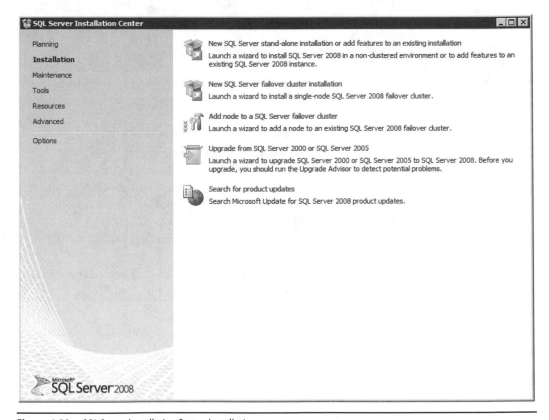

Figure 4-32 *SQL Server Installation Center: Installation*

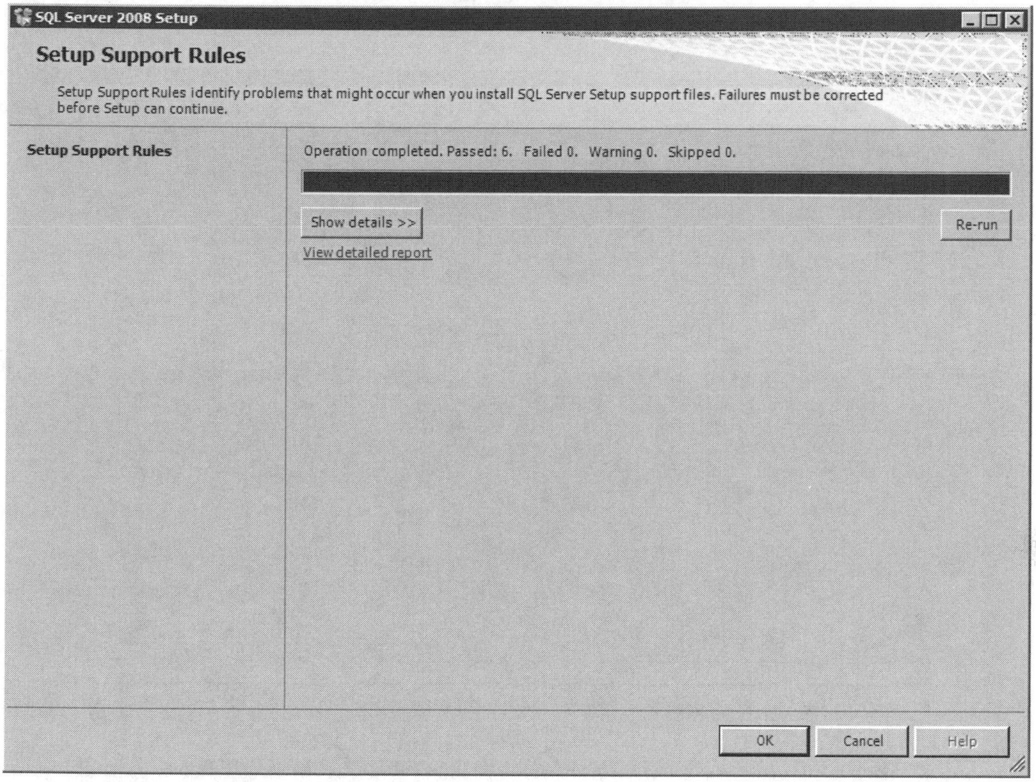

Figure 4-33 *SQL Server 2008 Setup: Setup Support Rules*

The Setup Support Rules dialog box checks your system for problems that might prevent the successful installation of SQL Server 2008. Exactly the same as in node one, the Setup Support Rules dialog box tests for six different system requirements including for the minimum operating system level, administrative privileges, and if the WMI (Windows Management Instrumentation) service is running. Clicking OK displays the Product Key dialog box that you can see in Figure 4-34.

The Product Key screen in the SQL Server 2008 setup process prompts you to enter your SQL Server product key. Select the "Enter the product key" radio button; then type in the product installation key and click Next. This will display the End User License Agreement (EULA) in the License Terms dialog box that you can see in Figure 4-35.

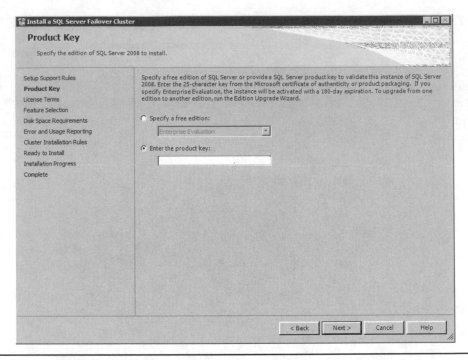

Figure 4-34 *Install a SQL Server Failover Cluster: Product Key*

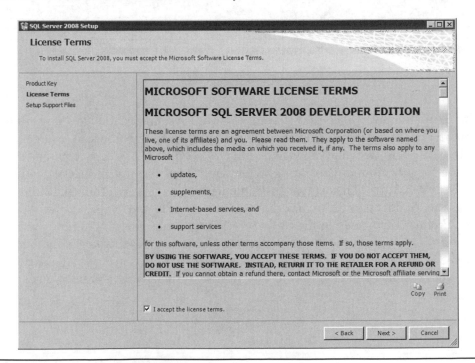

Figure 4-35 *SQL Server 2008 Setup: License Terms*

You need to accept the SQL Server 2008 license agreement to proceed with the installation. Accept the license agreement by choosing the "I accept the license terms" box. Clicking Next will display the Setup Support Files dialog box that's shown in Figure 4-36.

You use the Setup Support Files dialog box to copy the setup components onto node two. Clicking Install copies the required setup files to the system and displays the SQL Server 2008 Setup Support Rules dialog box that you can see in Figure 4-37.

The Setup Support Rules dialog box performs a second set of tests to determine if there will be any problems running the setup program. A green check mark indicates that the installation can proceed, while a red *x* notifies you of any problems that must be corrected. If all of the items have green check marks like you see in Figure 4-37, then you can click Next to continue with the installation, which will display the Cluster Node Configuration screen that you can see in Figure 4-38.

The Cluster Node Configuration screen prompts you for the name of the failover cluster that you want to add the node to. This example has only one other existing cluster, and it is displayed by default in the SQL Server Instance Name shown at the top of the screen.

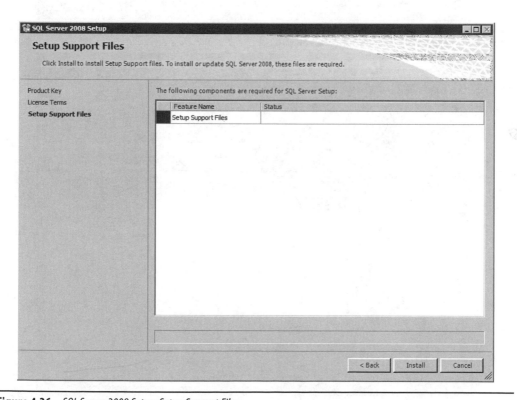

Figure 4-36   *SQL Server 2008 Setup: Setup Support Files*

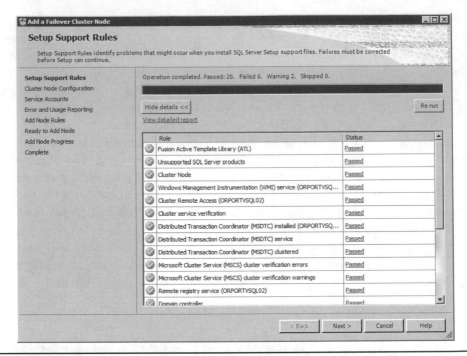

Figure 4-37   *Add a Failover Cluster Node: Setup Support Rules*

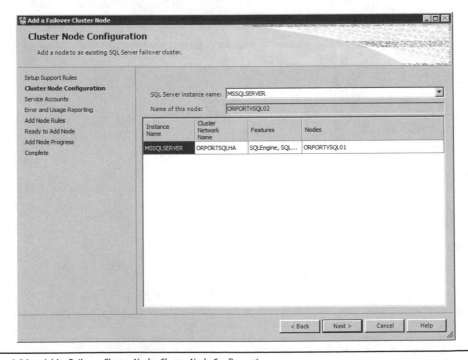

Figure 4-38   *Add a Failover Cluster Node: Cluster Node Configuration*

If you had additional clustered SQL Server instances, they would be listed here as well. In this example, you can see that I selected the existing MSSQLSERVER instance name. For reference, you can see where this value was initially configured in Figure 4-15. Clicking Next displays the Service Accounts configuration dialog box that is shown in Figure 4-39.

The Service Accounts dialog box enables you to specify the accounts that each of the SQL Server services will run under on node two. As with node one, the SQL Server services on node two should run under a domain account that doesn't have administrator privileges. Here again, Microsoft recommends that you run each of the services using a separate account. In Figure 4-39 you can see that the SQL Server services are being started using the SQLServiceUser account, which is a domain account in the CONTOSO domain. This is the same account that was used on node one. The startup type for the SQL Server Database Engine and SQL Server Agent are fixed with the value of Manual, which is normal for clustered installations. There is no need to configure the Database Engine, Analysis Services, or Reporting Services, as node two will adopt the values that were previously configured on the first node. Clicking Next will display the Error and Usage Reporting dialog box shown in Figure 4-40.

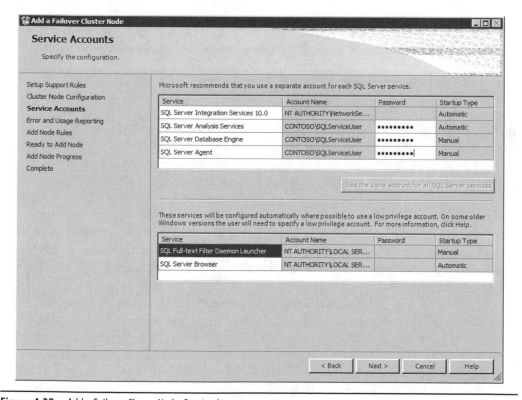

Figure 4-39   *Add a Failover Cluster Node: Service Accounts*

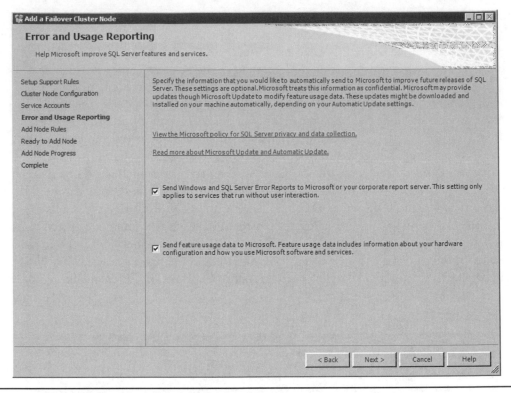

Figure 4-40   *Add a Failover Cluster Node: Error and Usage Reporting*

SQL Server 2008's Error and Usage Reporting screen enables SQL Server to report to Microsoft the errors in the SQL Server database service and other subsystem services. Error and usage reporting are optional. In Figure 4-40 you can see that I elected to turn them on. Clicking Next displays the Add Node Rules dialog box that you can see in Figure 4-41.

The Add Node Rules dialog box checks for any issues that might cause the installation process to fail. If an error condition is found, it will be indicated with a red *x*. If all of the items have green check marks as they do in Figure 4-41, then you can proceed with the installation by clicking Next. This will display the Ready to Add Node dialog box that you can see in Figure 4-42.

The Ready to Add Node dialog box lets you review your configuration choices. You can use the Back button to page back and change values from the previous installation configuration screens. If all of the values look good, clicking Install begins the installation process for SQL Server 2008 on the second cluster node. The installation itself will take some time depending on the speed of the server systems that you're using and the installation media. The Add Node Progress dialog box that you can see in Figure 4-43 shows the status of the installation.

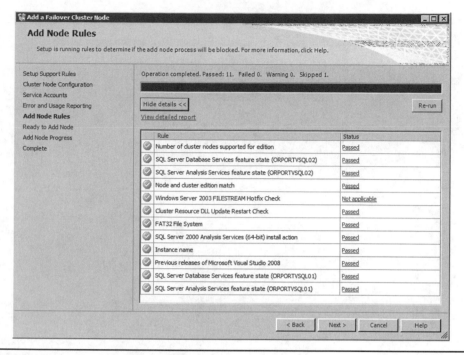

Figure 4-41   *Add a Failover Cluster Node: Add Node Rules*

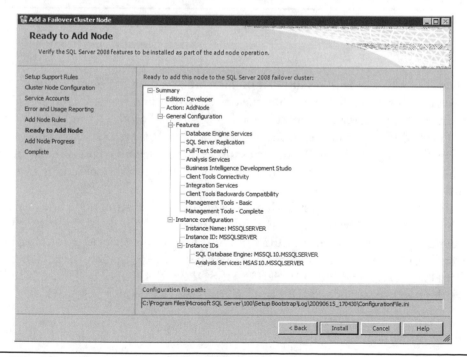

Figure 4-42   *Add a Failover Cluster Node: Ready to Add Node*

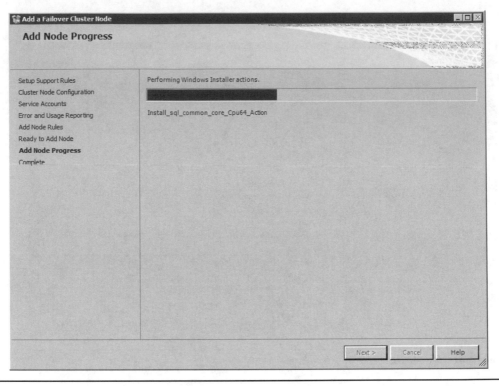

Figure 4-43   *Add a Failover Cluster Node: Add Node Progress*

When the SQL Server 2008 installation has completed on the second cluster node, you'll see the Complete dialog box like the one shown in Figure 4-44.

When the SQL Server 2008 installation has completed on the second cluster node, SQL Server 2008 is fully clustered and highly available. If there is a server failure on node one, then SQL Server will failover to the second node and begin running in the time that it takes SQL Server to roll back any uncommitted transactions and roll forward all of the committed transactions.

If you open the Failover Cluster Management console on either node one or node two, it will appear like the screen shown in Figure 4-45.

In Figure 4-45, you can see the ORPORTSQLCL01 failover cluster running in the Failover Cluster Management console. The Services and Applications node lists both the MS DTC service and the SQL Server MSSQLSERVER service. Under Nodes you can see the two cluster nodes: ORPORTVSQL01 and ORPORTVSQL02.

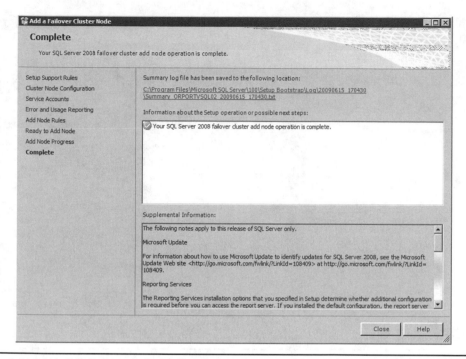

Figure 4-44   *Add a Failover Cluster Node: Complete*

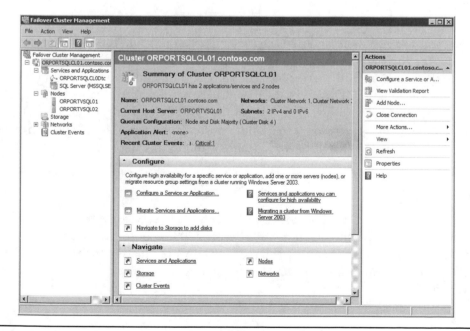

Figure 4-45   *Managing the cluster with the Failover Cluster Management console*

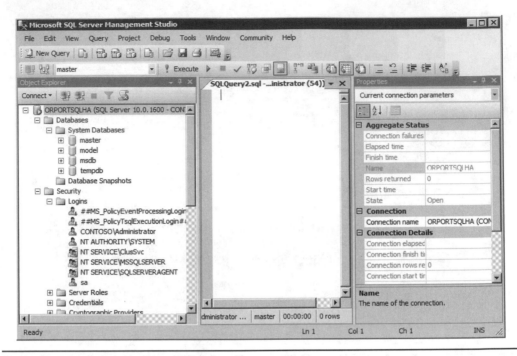

Figure 4-46   *Connecting to the clustered SQL Server*

If you want to add more nodes to the cluster later, you would follow the same steps as you did for adding node two.

Using the clustered SQL Server installation is very much like using a stand-alone SQL Server installation. The primary difference is that the clients connect to the SQL Server cluster name. In this example that is ORPORTSQLHA. You can see SQL Server Management Studio connected to the cluster in Figure 4-46. More information about using the clustered SQL Server instance is found in Chapter 5.

Summary

In this chapter you first saw how to set up the MS DTC service on the cluster. Then you saw how to set up and configure SQL Server 2008 on both the first and second cluster nodes. In the next chapter, you'll see how network clients connect to the cluster as well as how to manage the failover cluster including how to manually initiate and failover and failback.

Chapter 5

Managing Failover Clustering

In This Chapter

► **Managing the Cluster**
► **Backing Up the Cluster**

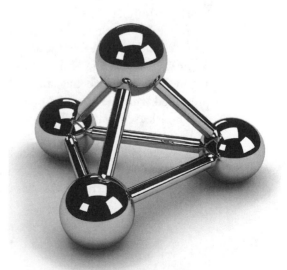

I
n Chapters 3 and 4, you saw how to set up a Windows Server 2008 failover cluster and then how to install SQL Server 2008 on that cluster, enabling SQL Server to quickly and automatically recover from unplanned downtime. In this chapter you learn about some of the basic techniques for managing the clustered SQL Server service. In the first part, you'll see some basic cluster management techniques like how to take the cluster service on- and offline as well as how to pause and resume the service and how to initiate a manual failover. In the second part of this chapter, you'll see how to back up the cluster for disaster recovery.

Managing the Cluster

While a Windows failover cluster provides high availability in the event of unplanned downtime, at times you may need to bring the clustered application offline to perform troubleshooting or other infrastructure maintenance activities. In addition, managing a clustered application has different aspects than managing a regular application. For example, you can pause and resume clustered applications without stopping them. Additionally, if you want to perform planned maintenance on one or more of the cluster nodes, you can manually initiate a failover, switching the support for the application from the primary node to one of the backup nodes.

Bringing a Clustered Service Offline

Bringing a clustered service or application offline stops the application. No clients can connect to the application when it is stopped. You may want to stop the application in order to perform cluster maintenance or to implement a complete application update. To bring a clustered application offline, start Failover Cluster Management by choosing Start | Administrative Tools | Failover Cluster Management.

To take the clustered SQL Server offline, expand the cluster node, and then expand the Services and Applications node. Next, right-click the SQL Server (MSSQLSERVER) service, and select the "Take this service or application offline" option, as illustrated in Figure 5-1. After selecting the "Take this service or application offline" option, you are presented with the warning dialog box that you can see in Figure 5-2.

The Please Confirm Action dialog box warns you that if you continue, the clustered SQL Server service (MSSQLSERVER) will no longer be available. To proceed and take the service offline, select the Take SQL Server (MSSQLSERVER) offline option. This will stop the MSSQLSERVER service on the cluster, and no clients will be able to reconnect until the service has been brought back online.

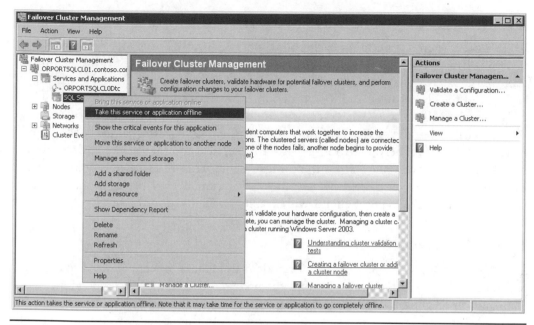

Figure 5-1 *Taking a clustered application offline*

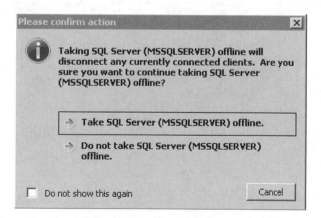

Figure 5-2 *Offline confirmation dialog box*

Bringing a Clustered Service Back Online

To bring a clustered application back online, start Failover Cluster Management by choosing Start | Administrative Tools | Failover Cluster Management. This will display Failover Cluster Management, as shown in Figure 5-3.

Expand the cluster node and then expand the Services and Applications node. The SQL Server (MSSQLSERVER) service should be displayed with a red down arrow. This indicates that the service is offline. To bring the SQL Server service back online, right-click the SQL Server (MSSQLSERVER) service, and then select "Bring this service or application online" from the context menu. After the service is online, it will be displayed in Failover Cluster Management with a small, gray gear icon indicating the service is active. At this point clients will be able to reconnect to the service.

Pausing a Node

Pausing and resuming a node is used for node maintenance where you need to apply software updates to a node but you want the node resources groups to stay online. Pausing a node allows the cluster resources to stay online, but additional resources cannot be brought online until the node is resumed. In this scenario you would typically pause the node, move the resources to another node, update the node, and then resume the node.

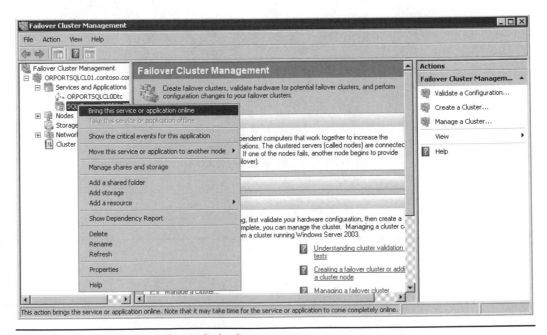

Figure 5-3   *Bringing the clustered service back online*

Figure 5-4   *Pausing a cluster node*

To pause a clustered node, start Failover Cluster Management; choose Start | Administrative Tools | Failover Cluster Management. This will display Failover Cluster Management, as shown in Figure 5-4.

Expand the cluster node, then expand Nodes, and right-click the node that you want to pause. From the context menu select Pause, as demonstrated in Figure 5-4. The node status displayed in the Summary pane will be changed to Paused.

Resuming a Node

To resume the node, choose Start | Administrative Tools | Failover Cluster Management to start Failover Cluster Management. Expand the cluster node, expand Nodes, and right-click the node that you want to resume. From the context menu select Resume, as demonstrated in Figure 5-5.

Performing a Manual Failover

Performing a manual failover enables you to test your failover cluster configuration. It can also enable you to take a cluster node offline to perform hardware or software maintenance on the node. To perform a manual failover, start Failover Management; select Start | Administrative Tools | Failover Cluster Management. Failover Cluster Management will be displayed as you can see in Figure 5-6.

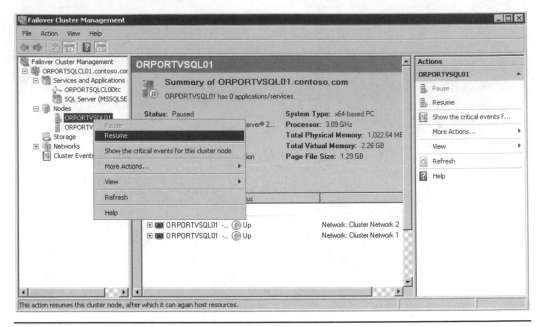

Figure 5-5 *Resuming a node*

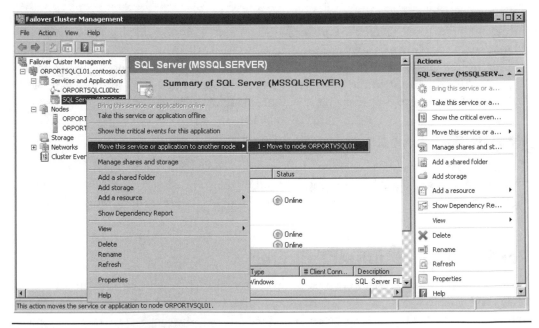

Figure 5-6 *Initiating a manual failover*

After Failover Cluster Management is displayed, expand the cluster node, and then open the Services and Applications node. Then right-click the SQL Server (MSSQLSERVER) service, and select "Move this service or application to another node" from the context menu. If there are multiple nodes, they will all be displayed in the submenu. In this example two-node cluster, there is only one other node. To initiate the failover, select the "Move to node ORPORTVSQL01" node as illustrated in Figure 5-6. This will display the configuration dialog box that you can see in Figure 5-7.

The Please Confirm Action dialog box warns you that you are about to perform a failover. Click the "Move SQL Server (MSSQLSERVER) to ORPORTVSQL01" option to start the failover. When you perform the failover, any clients that are currently connected will be disconnected. They can reconnect as soon as the failover has completed.

Performing a Manual Failback

Performing a manual failback is much like performing a manual failover. The only real difference is that you select the original node as the target for the failover option. In Failover Cluster Management, either right-click the SQL Server (MSSQLSERVER) service, or select that service and then click the "Move this service or application" link (obscured in the Actions pane shown in Figure 5-8). Both options are different ways of performing the same task.

After you select the "Move this service or application" link, the Please Confirm Action dialog box shown in Figure 5-9 will be displayed.

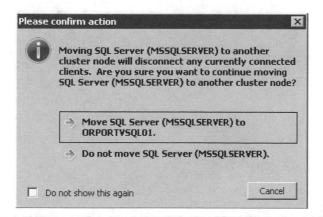

Figure 5-7   *Confirming the failover*

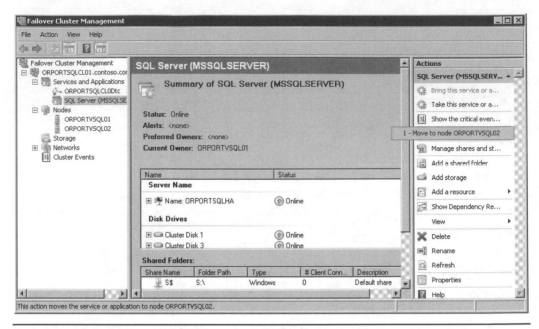

Figure 5-8 *Confirming the manual failback*

The Please Confirm Action dialog box warns you that you are about to perform a failover. In this case it is actually a failback to the original node. Click the "Move SQL Server (MSSQLSERVER) to ORPORTVSQL02" option to start the failover. Since a failback is essentially a failover, as before, any clients that are currently connected will be disconnected. They can reconnect as soon as the failback has completed.

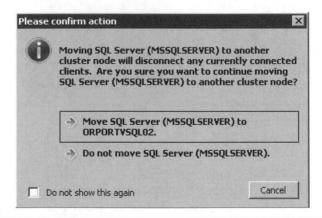

Figure 5-9 *Performing a manual failback*

Configuring for Automatic Failback

If you can have a specific cluster node that you prefer to run the clustered SQL Server service, you can set up a preferred owner for the clustered service. This will enable the clustered service to run on the preferred node. In the event of a failure on the preferred node, failover clustering will failover the service to one of the backup nodes. Later when the node that has been designated as the preferred one comes back online, failover clustering will automatically failback the clustered service to the preferred owner node.

To set up a node as the preferred owner, choose Start | Administrative Tools | Failover Cluster Management to open Failover Cluster Management, as shown in Figure 5-10.

To specify a node as the preferred owner, expand the cluster, expand the Services and Applications node, right-click the SQL Server (MSSQLSERVER) service, and select Properties from the context menu. This will display the cluster's properties dialog box, which you can see in Figure 5-11.

To set a node as the preferred owner, open the Properties dialog box's General tab, and select the node on the Preferred Owners list that you want to act as the preferred owner of the SQL Server service. In Figure 5-11 you can see that I selected node ORPORTVSQL01 to be the preferred owner of the service.

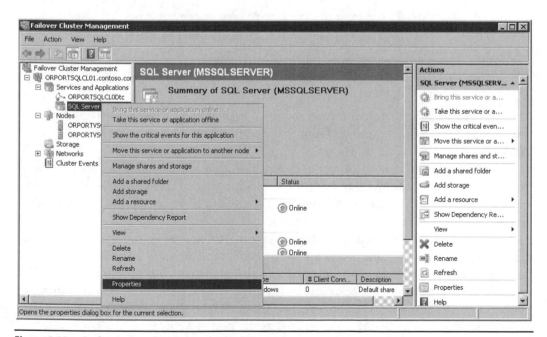

Figure 5-10   *Configuring a preferred owner for the cluster service*

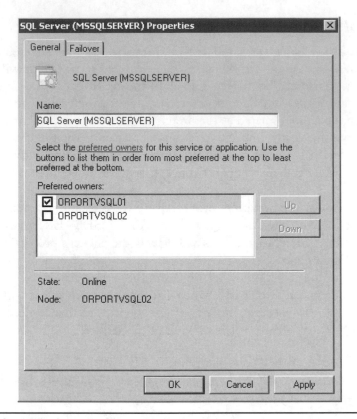

Figure 5-11   *Configuring the cluster properties*

After selecting the preferred owner, you need to click the Failover tab to configure
the clustered service's failover and failback properties. You can see the Failover tab in
Figure 5-12.

The Failover portion in the upper half of the window allows you to set up a
maximum number of failovers to occur in a certain period. This is essentially to prevent
some spurious event or aberration from causing the cluster to repeatedly failover and
failback when there isn't a true system failure.

The settings that allow you to control automatic failback are in the lower half of the
dialog box. The default value is set to Prevent Failback, which will not allow automatic
failback to occur even if you have selected a preferred owner. To enable automatic
failback, click the Allow Failback radio button, and then select either the Immediately
option or the Failback Between option. The Immediately option causes failback to
occur as soon as the node that is designated as the preferred owner is available. The
Failback Between option sets a period in hours for a delayed failback. In Figure 5-12,

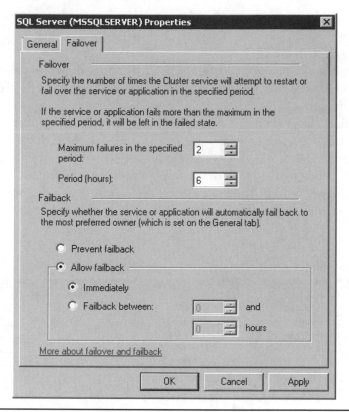

Figure 5-12   *Configuring the cluster failback properties*

you can see the SQL Server (MSSQLSERVER) service has been set to failback as soon as the preferred owner node is available.

NOTE

If you manually initiate a failover, failover clustering recognizes that this is not an unplanned failure, and it will not automatically perform a failback even if you have configured the clustered service for automatic failback. Automatic failback only occurs when the failover is not manually initiated.

Monitoring Failover Events

One of the strengths of failover clustering is that it automatically handles unplanned failures. It can perform this function without any operator intervention. However, this can also mean that the administrator may be unaware of the failover events that have occurred. To alert the administrator about any important recent activity, Failover Cluster Management displays the most recent cluster events on the cluster summary screen as you can see in Figure 5-13.

In the Summary of Cluster ORPORTSQLCL01 panel shown in the center of Figure 5-13, you can see the Recent Cluster Events field contains a flag for one critical event. This is the message that appears after the cluster has performed a failover operation. To view the event detail, you can either click the Cluster Events node shown in the Failover Cluster Management pane, or you can click the Critical 1 link. This will display the Cluster Events pane shown in Figure 5-14.

The Cluster Events pane lists all of the recent events for the cluster. A failover event like the one in Figure 5-14 is listed as a critical event. You can find more information about each event in the Event Details pane shown in the lower part of the screen.

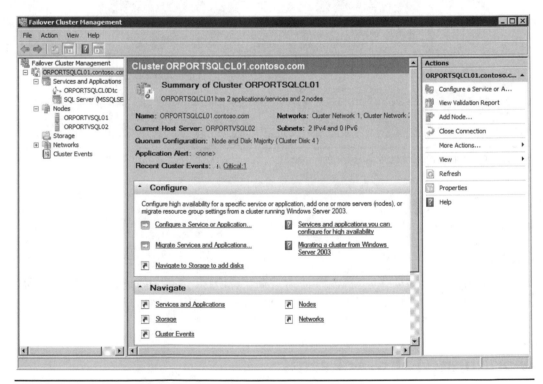

Figure 5-13   *Displaying recent cluster events*

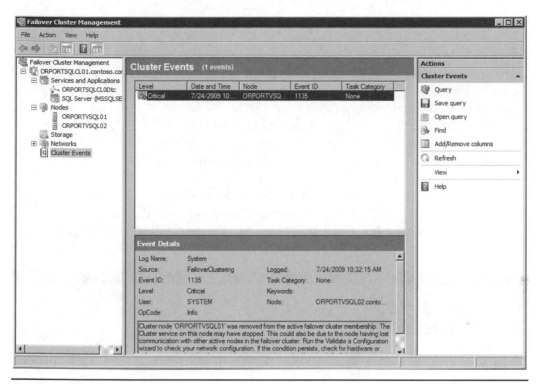

Figure 5-14   *Displaying cluster events*

Backing Up the Cluster

For protection against major disasters, you should always be sure to implement a backup procedure for your clusters. In fact, before using your cluster in production, you should test your backup and recovery procedures to be certain that you can restore the cluster. You can back up the cluster using Windows Server 2008's built-in backup, Microsoft Data Protection Manager, or a number of other third-party backup products. In the next section of this chapter, you see how to perform a basic cluster backup using the Windows Server Backup program.

Adding the Windows Backup Feature

Windows Server Backup is not installed by default in Windows Server 2008. You need to use Server Manager to add the Windows Server Backup feature to all the nodes that you want to back up using Windows Server Backup. To add the Windows Server

Backup feature, run Server Manager by selecting Start | Administrative Tools | Server Manager. This will start Server Manager and display the Server Summary screen that you can see in Figure 5-15.

To add the Windows Server Backup feature, click the Features node in the Server Manager pane shown on the left side of the screen. This will display the Features Summary window that you can see in Figure 5-16.

The Features Summary window shows the features currently installed in Windows Server 2008. To add Windows Server Backup, click the Add Features link shown on the right side of the Features Summary screen. This will display the Select Features window that you can see in Figure 5-17.

Scroll through the list of features shown in the Select Features window until you see Windows Server Backup Features. To add the Windows Server Backup feature, select the Windows Server Backup check box. If you want to install the command-line tools,

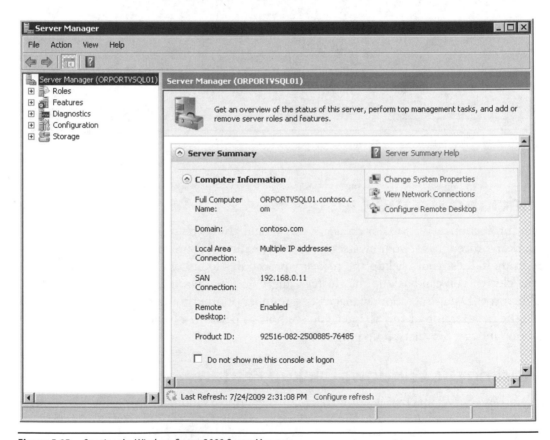

Figure 5-15   *Starting the Windows Server 2008 Server Manager*

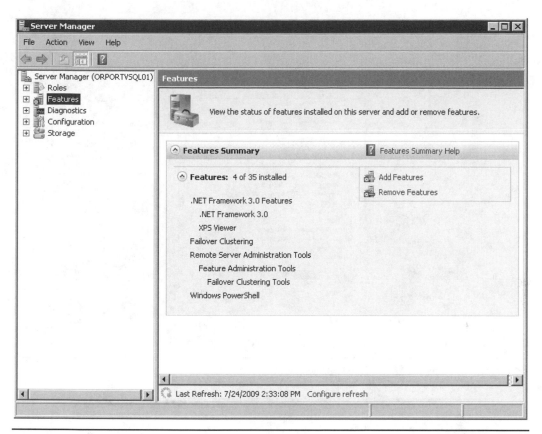

Figure 5-16   *Adding the Windows Server Backup feature*

select the Command-line Tools check box. Clicking Next will display the Confirm
Installation Selections screen that you can see displayed in Figure 5-18.

The Confirm Installation Selections dialog box confirms that you have elected to
install the Windows Server Backup feature. To proceed with the installation, click
Install. This will take a few minutes as the wizard installs the binary files for the
Windows Server Backup feature on the system. After the installation has completed,
the results dialog box that you can see in Figure 5-19 will be displayed.

The Installation Results screen reports the success or failure of the installation.
If the feature installation failed, you will see a red *x* along with the message that the
feature installation failed. If the installation of the Windows Server Backup feature
succeeded, you will see a green check mark followed by an "Installation succeeded"
message as shown in Figure 5-19. Clicking Close ends the Add Features Wizard, and
the Windows Server Backup feature is ready to use.

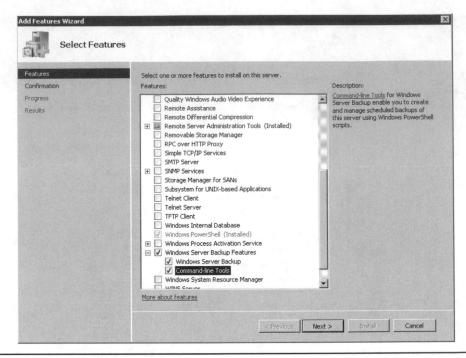

Figure 5-17   *Selecting the Windows Server Backup feature*

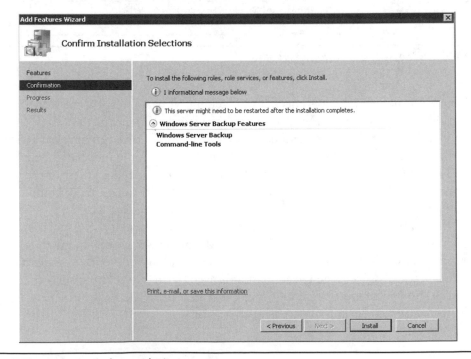

Figure 5-18   *Confirming the feature selections*

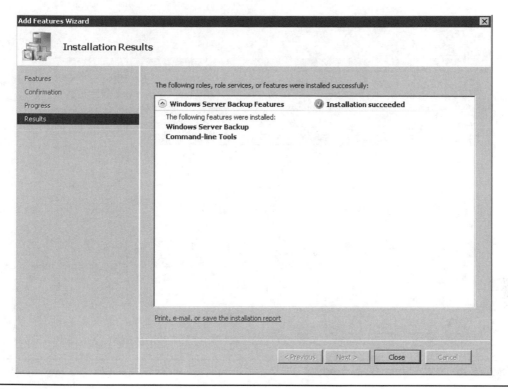

Figure 5-19   *Feature installation results*

Backing Up a Cluster Node

To successfully back up a cluster node, you need to be sure to back up each node's local disk and system state. In addition, you should be sure to back up the cluster quorum and all clustered application storage. Be sure that all of the disks that are used by the cluster node are online before the backup begins. Only disks that are online and owned by the cluster will be backed up.

To back up the cluster node, start the backup program by choosing Start | Administrative Tools | Windows Server Backup. This will start the Windows Server Backup program that you can see in Figure 5-20.

You can use the Windows Server Backup Wizard either to create a new scheduled backup or to perform a one-time backup. In this example, you'll see how to perform a one-time backup. Once your cluster is in production, you should be sure to set up a regularly scheduled backup routine.

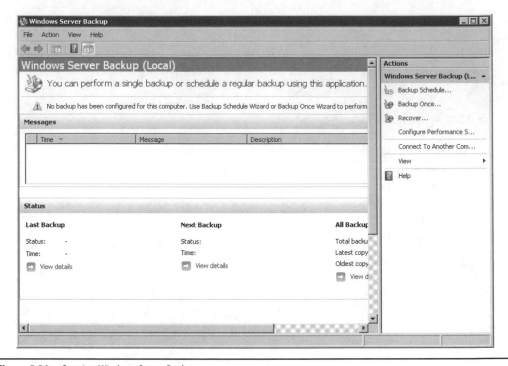

Figure 5-20 *Starting Windows Server Backup*

To start the backup wizard for a one-time backup, click the Backup Once link shown in the Actions pane of the Windows Server Backup program. This will start the Backup Once Wizard that you can see in Figure 5-21.

If you have previously created a scheduled backup, you can elect to use that backup's settings as the basis for this backup operation. This example has no previously scheduled backup, so choose the Different Options button. This will allow you to specify all of the backup settings that you need. Clicking Next displays the Select Backup Configuration dialog box that is shown in Figure 5-22.

The Select Backup Configuration screen enables you to choose the type of backup that you want to perform. The Full Server Backup will back up the server, all of the local drives, and the contents of online attached drives that are on a SAN. In this case the server is connected to some SAN drives that should not be included in the backup, so I've selected the Custom option. Clicking Next displays the Select Backup Items dialog box that you can see in Figure 5-23.

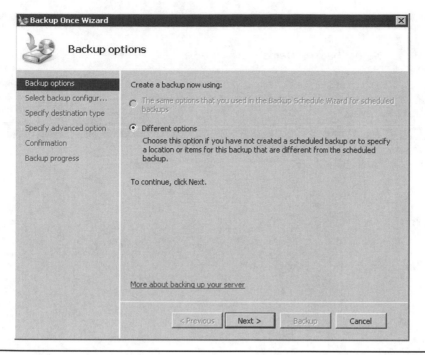

Figure 5-21   *Backup options*

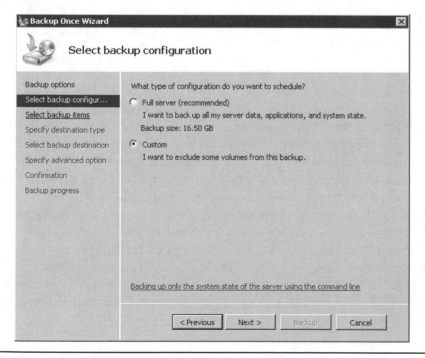

Figure 5-22   *Select backup configuration*

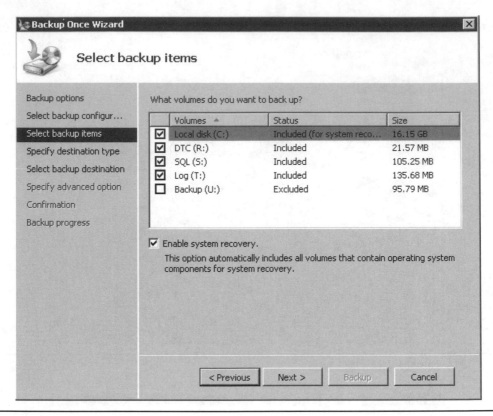

Figure 5-23 *Select backup items*

The Select Backup Items dialog box enables you to choose which volumes will be backed up. In Figure 5-23, you can see that the Local disk (C:) will be backed up, as will the three different clustered storage drives DTC (R:), SQL (S:), and Log (T:). The Backup (U:) drive is not included because it is used to store backups from a number of networked systems. It's important to note that the Enable System Recovery box is selected. This will instruct the backup program to save the node's system state. Clicking Next will display the backup wizard's destination screen, which you can see in Figure 5-24.

The Specify Destination Type dialog box lets you choose where you want the backup data to be written. The Local Drives option allows you to save the backup file to one of the local drives that is visible to the local system's Disk Management. The Remote Shared Folder option allows you to save the backup file to a network share. In this case the backup will be written to one of the local drives, so the Local Drives option has been selected. Clicking Next will allow you to choose the local drive that you want to use for the backup, as you can see in Figure 5-25.

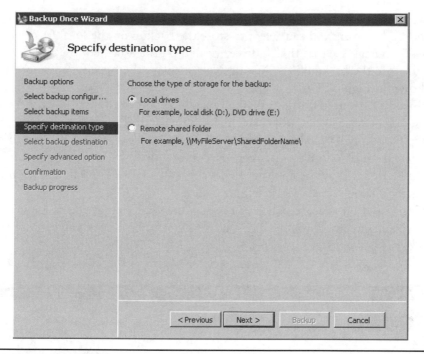

Figure 5-24   *Specify destination type*

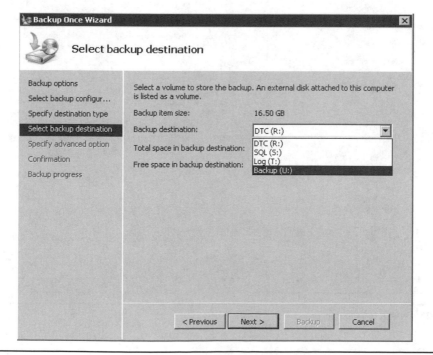

Figure 5-25   *Select backup destination*

The Select Backup Destination screen only lists the external disks that are attached to the node. This mean you can't elect to store the backup on the local C: drive. In Figure 5-25 you can see that the U: drive, located on the attached iSCSI, has been selected to store the backup file. Clicking Next displays the Specify Advanced Option screen shown in Figure 5-26.

The Specify Advanced Options dialog box allows you to choose how the Volume Shadow Copy Service (VSS) will treat the backup. In most cases the clustered SQL Server application will be using its own application-level backup, so it's best to select the default option of VSS Copy Backup (Recommended). This allows the application's log files to be updated by the application-level backup. Click Next to display the Confirmation dialog box, shown in Figure 5-27.

The Confirmation dialog box lets you review the choices that you made in the previous wizard screens. If you need to change any of the choices, you can use the

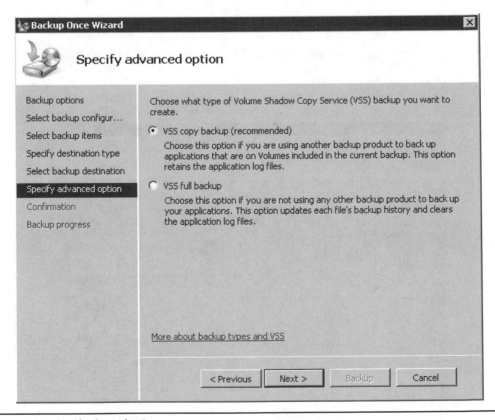

Figure 5-26 *Specify advanced option*

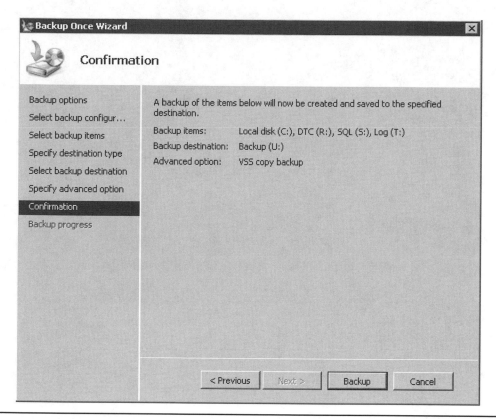

Figure 5-27   *Confirmation*

Previous button to page back through the earlier backup wizard screens. Clicking Backup begins the backup process, and the Backup Progress dialog box that you can see in Figure 5-28 will be displayed until the backup has completed.

Restoring a Cluster Node

You should always be sure to test your ability to restore each cluster node from the node's backup. You can perform two basic type of restores for a cluster node. Either you can select to perform a non-authoritative restore, which restores just the cluster node, or you can select to perform an authoritative restore, which will enable you to replace the cluster configuration.

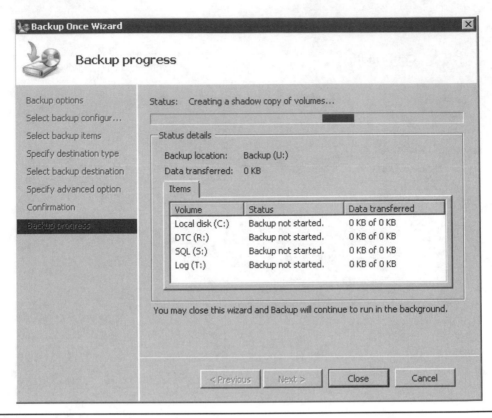

Figure 5-28 *Backup progress*

Non-Authoritative Restore

The non-authoritative restore is used to restore a failed cluster node. Here the cluster and the other cluster nodes are operating correctly. After a non-authoritative restore completes and the cluster node has rejoined the cluster, the current cluster configuration will be automatically replicated to the node.

Authoritative Restore

An authoritative restore is used when you want to replace the current cluster configuration with the configuration saved in the backup. The authoritative restore is used when the cluster itself needs to be repaired. To perform an authoritative cluster restore, all of the cluster nodes must be taken offline before beginning the restore process.

NOTE

When you restore backed-up data to a failover cluster node, be sure to note which disks are online. Data can only be restored to disks that are online and owned by the cluster node that performed the backup.

Summary

In this chapter you learned about some of the basic Windows Server Failover Cluster Management techniques. In the first part of the chapter, you saw how to take the cluster service offline and then bring it back online. Then you saw how to pause and resume a clustered service. Next you saw how to manually initiate failover and failback operations as well as how to configure the cluster for automatic failback. In the last part of this chapter, you saw how to back up the cluster by using Windows Server Backup.

Part II

Implementing Database Mirroring

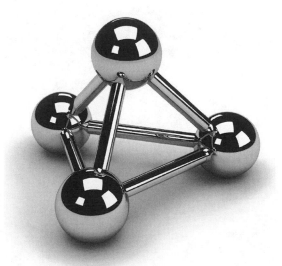

Chapter 6

Database Mirroring Architecture

In This Chapter

- ► **Database Mirroring Requirements**
- ► **Database Mirroring Architecture**
- ► **Database Mirroring Modes**
- ► **Client Failover**
- ► **Using Database Snapshots for Reporting**
- ► **Combining Database Mirroring and Failover Clustering**

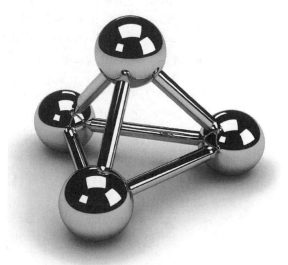

SQL Server 2008's Database Mirroring feature protects against database or server failure by providing very rapid database failover. In the event that the primary database fails, the database mirror enables a standby, or mirror, database to be available in about 2–3 seconds. Database mirroring provides zero data loss, and the mirrored database will always be up-to-date with the current transaction that's being processed on the primary database server. The impact of running database mirroring on transaction throughput is zero to minimal. Database mirroring works with all of the standard server systems that support SQL Server—there's no need for special systems. In addition, the primary or principal server and the mirrored server do not need to be identical. In addition, unlike in high-availability clustering solutions, there's no need for any shared storage between the principal server and the mirrored server.

Database Mirroring Requirements

Database mirroring in SQL Server 2008 has the following requirements:

▶ **SQL Server 2008 Standard or Enterprise editions**   Database mirroring is only supported in the SQL Server 2008 Standard and Enterprise editions. The SQL Server 2008 Standard Edition is limited to synchronous mirroring mode. The SQL Server 2008 Enterprise Edition supports both synchronous and asynchronous modes. More information about mirroring components and modes is presented in the next section. The SQL Server 2008 Express Edition can function only as a witness.

▶ **Full recovery model**   All mirrored databases must use the Full recovery model. You cannot mirror a database that uses the Simple or Bulk recovery models.

▶ **Single mirror target**   Database mirroring is limited to use between two systems. You cannot set up multiple database mirroring targets. If you need to send database transactions to multiple targets, then you must use log shipping.

▶ **User databases only**   You can set up database mirroring only for user databases. You cannot mirror any of the system databases including the master, model, msdb, or tempdb. In addition, only databases are mirrored. Other database entities such as logins that may be required by applications are not mirrored. To support full automatic failover, you must manually add logins to the mirror system.

Database Mirroring Architecture

Database mirroring works by reading the transactions from the principal (primary) server and then forwarding them across the network to the mirror server. You can see an overview of the database mirroring architecture in Figure 6-1.

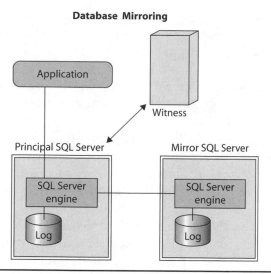

Figure 6-1   *The database mirroring architecture*

Database mirroring is implemented using three systems: the principal server, the mirroring server, and the witness. The *principal server* is the name of the system currently providing the database services. All incoming client connections are made to the primary server. The *mirror server's* job is to maintain a copy of the primary server's mirrored database. The mirror server is not restricted to just providing backup services; other databases on the secondary server can be actively supporting other unrelated applications. Depending on the mirroring mode that is in use, the principal server and the mirror can seamlessly failover, and the mirror server can become the principal server. The *witness* essentially acts as an independent third party that determines which system will act as the principal server.

Database mirroring can be set up with a single database, or it can be set up for multiple databases. Database mirroring is initialized by taking a backup of the database that you want to mirror on your principal server and then restoring that backup to your mirroring server. This puts the underlying database data and schema in place on both the principal and the mirror servers. In other words, the mirrored database must exist on the mirror server before the mirroring process can begin. The backup and restore process can use any of SQL Server's standard media types, including tape or disk.

Database mirroring works by capturing transaction logs on the principal server and sending them on to the mirror server. So in essence, the database mirroring is a real-time log shipping application. When a client system writes a transaction on the principal server, that transaction actually gets written to the principal server's transaction log file before it is written into the data file. Next, database mirroring monitors the transaction log, pulling out transaction records for the mirrored databases and sending them to the mirror server. The mirror server receives the transaction where it gets written to the mirroring server's transaction log. To keep its data files up-to-date, the mirroring server is essentially in a state of continuous recovery, taking the data from the log and updating the data file.

After the mirroring server has written the record to its log, it sends an acknowledgment to the principal server that the record has been received. For synchronous mirroring mode operations, the principal server waits to receive an acknowledgment from the mirroring server before sending its response back to the client, telling it the operation is completed. For asynchronous mode the principal does not wait for a response from the mirror before replying to the client and allowing the client to continue. More information about database mirroring modes is presented in the next section of this chapter.

Database mirroring can be set up so database failover can be performed either automatically or manually. Automatic failover is only supported for asynchronous database mirroring. A third system that acts as a witness is also required for automatic failover. Each system gets a vote as to who will be the primary server. It takes two votes to decide on the primary server. This is important because it's possible that the communications between the primary server and the mirror server could be cut off, in which case each system would elect itself to function as the primary server. The witness casts the deciding vote.

Database Mirroring Modes

Database mirroring can operate in one of two modes depending on the level of performance and data protection that's required: high *safety* mode or high *performance* mode. The database mirroring mode is controlled by the Transaction Safety database property. When the Transaction Safety property is set to OFF, database mirroring operates in high performance asynchronous mode. If Transaction Safety is set to FULL, then database mirroring will operate in high safety synchronous mode. You can set the Transaction Safety property using the ALTER DATABASE command on the principal server as illustrated in the following listings:

```
-- Turn on high performance mode
ALTER DATABASE <database> SET PARTNER SAFETY OFF

-- Turn on high safety mode
ALTER DATABASE <database> SET PARTNER SAFETY FULL
```

High Safety Mode

As its name suggests, high safety mode provides the highest level of data protection by ensuring that transactions are committed on both the principal and the mirror servers. High safety mode uses synchronous database mirroring, and it supports two different types of operation depending on the availability of the witness.

High Safety Mode Without a Witness

If there is no witness, then database mirroring operates in high safety mode without automatic failover. In this case if the principal database is unavailable, the mirror is suspended, but service can be manually forced to the mirror. If the mirror becomes unavailable, then the principal continues to run.

High Safety Mode with a Witness

If the witness is present, then the synchronous mode operates in high safety mode with automatic failover. In this mode, database availability is the highest priority, and the database will be available as long as two of the three database mirroring components (principal, mirror, witness) are present. If the principal server becomes unavailable, the mirror will initiate an automatic failover and will assume the role of the principal. If the mirror server becomes unavailable, then operation continues unaffected on the principal server. If the witness becomes unavailable, then operation continues unaffected on the principal server, but no failover can happen until the witness is returned and a quorum can be reestablished.

Synchronous Mode Database Mirroring Data Flow

Synchronous mode database mirroring utilizes the following data flow:

1. The principal server writes a transaction to the transaction log.
2. The principal server concurrently writes the transaction to the database and sends the log data to the mirror server.
3. The principal server waits for an acknowledgment from the mirror server.
4. The mirror server hardens the log data by writing it to disk.
5. The mirror server returns an acknowledgment to the principal server.
6. After receiving the acknowledgment, the principal server sends a confirmation message to the client that originally enacted the transaction.

High Performance Mode

High performance mode operates asynchronously, and as its name implies, it provides the highest level of performance. With high mode, database transactions made on the principal are immediately committed without waiting for any acknowledgment from the mirror server. High performance mode does not support automatic failover. If the principal server becomes unavailable, service can be manually forced to the mirror, but data loss can occur. If the mirror becomes unavailable, the principal continues to operate. High performance mode does not require a witness. High performance mode is designed for disaster recovery scenarios when the mirror server may be some distance from the principal and when there may be a high amount of latency in sending the transaction data from the principal to the mirror.

Asynchronous Mode Database Mirroring Data Flow

Asynchronous mode database mirroring utilizes the following data flow:

1. The principal server writes a transaction to the transaction log.
2. The principal server concurrently writes the transaction to the database and sends the log data to the mirror server.
3. The principal server sends a confirmation message to the client that enacted the transaction.

Client Failover

To facilitate high availability for client applications, database mirroring works in conjunction with the SQL Native Client to provide transparent client redirection. *Transparent client redirection* enables applications to be automatically redirected to the mirror server when the principal server becomes unavailable.

Keywords in the application's connection string enable the client application to be aware of both the principal and the mirror servers. If the client application loses its connection to the principal server, then the client will make one attempt to reconnect to the principal server. If that connection attempt fails, then the client will automatically redirect the next connection attempt to the mirror server. You'll see how to set up the client for transparent redirection in Chapter 7.

Using Database Snapshots for Reporting

The database on the mirror server is normally in recovery mode, so it cannot be used for active database operations. However, by using database snapshots of the mirror, you can create a reporting server using the snapshot's point-in-time copy of the database.

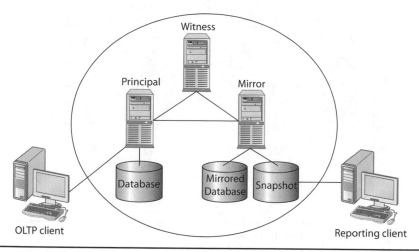

Figure 6-2   *Using database mirroring and database snapshots to create a read-only reporting server*

You can see an overview of using database snapshots and database mirroring to create a read-only reporting database in Figure 6-2.

In Figure 6-2, you can see the principal database is populated with data from the organization OLTP line-of-business application. Database mirroring is used to create a mirrored copy of that database on a remote server. Then database snapshots are used on the mirror database to create a read-only copy of the mirrored database. That database snapshot can be freely accessed in read-only mode by queries and reporting applications.

Combining Database Mirroring and Failover Clustering

Windows failover clustering and database mirroring are high-availability solutions that are designed to address different levels of system availability. Windows failover clustering is designed to provide server-level protection. Failover clustering uses multiple servers to provide protection from server failure by allowing the workload of the failed server to be automatically assumed by one of the other servers. Windows failover clustering can provide protection from both planned and unplanned downtime. Database mirroring is a database-level solution. More information about Windows failover clustering can be found in Chapter 2. Database mirroring enables data protection by sending transaction log records of a primary database to a standby database.

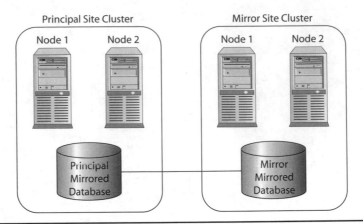

Figure 6-3   *Failover clustering and database mirroring*

While Windows failover clustering and database mirroring can be used separately, they can also be used together. Combining these technologies can provide a more complete level of overall system protection. Database mirroring can be used to enhance the availability provided by Windows failover clustering by providing protection from site and disk failures for mission-critical databases. Figure 6-3 shows an example of using Windows failover clustering in conjunction with database mirroring for site-level protection of your vital databases.

Summary

In this chapter, you learned about the different database mirroring components as well as the architecture used by database mirroring. In addition, you learned about the two different modes that you can use for database mirroring. In the next chapter, you'll see how to put this background to work by stepping through the setup of a highly available asynchronous database mirroring configuration.

Chapter 7

Configuring Database Mirroring

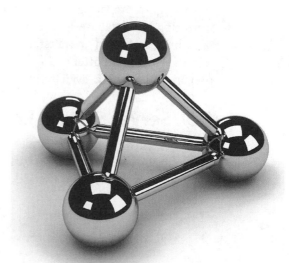

I n this chapter, you see how to configure database mirroring for high availability. In the last chapter, you saw that SQL Server 2008's database mirroring has two modes: a synchronous mode, which provides high safety, and an asynchronous mode, which provides high performance. To recap, the high performance mode operates asynchronously, and it enhances performance at the expense of availability. High performance essentially means that the principal server does not wait for an acknowledgment from the mirroring server after forwarding transactions to the mirror server. In high safety synchronous mode, the principal server does wait for an acknowledgment from the mirror server. The primary difference is that high safety mode is designed to maximize that availability of your data. In the synchronous high safety mode, if the principal server is unavailable, then database mirroring can automatically failover, making the database available on the mirror server. As you saw in the previous chapter, automatic failover requires the presence of a third server called the witness.

In this chapter, you'll see how to set up SQL Server 2008 database mirroring for high availability with automatic failover. In the first part of this chapter, you'll learn about some of the server and infrastructure requirements for using database mirroring in high-availability mode. Next, you'll get a walkthrough of the specific steps required to configure database mirroring on the principal, mirror, and witness servers. In the last part of the chapter, you'll see how to set up the network clients in order to take advantage of the transparent client redirection to automatically reconnect to the mirror server after a failover.

Database Mirroring Requirements

Before you set up database mirroring for high availability, you need to be sure that your supporting infrastructure will meet the requirements for synchronous database mirroring. In preparing your environment it's important to remember that database mirroring is a database-level feature. It is also limited to user databases. Likewise, there is no built-in facility to transfer logins or other system-level information between servers. For true unattended failover, you'll need to manually set up user logins in preparation for high-availability database mirroring.

SQL Server System Requirements

Database mirroring can be implemented on all editions of the Windows Server 2003 and Windows Server 2008 operating systems that support SQL Server 2008. Database mirroring is supported on the following editions of SQL Server 2008:

- ▶ SQL Server 2008 Standard Edition (synchronous mode only)
- ▶ SQL Server 2008 Enterprise Edition

NOTE

The mirror server must use the same edition of SQL Server as the principal server. In addition, it's a good idea to make sure that the principal and the mirror are comparable systems and that the mirror can handle the disk requirements and workload from the principal server's mirrored databases. Microsoft recommends that the mirror server have a CPU utilization rate of 50 percent or lower.

The witness server can be any edition of SQL Server 2008 including the SQL Server 2008 Express Edition, the SQL Server 2008 Workgroup Edition, the SQL Server 2008 Standard Edition, and the SQL Server 2008 Enterprise Edition.

For the best performance, use a dedicated network connection between the principal and the mirror servers.

SQL Server Database Server Requirements

It's important to remember that database mirroring is a database-level technology and therefore is influenced by a number of server-level settings. In particular the following settings should be the same on the principal server and the mirror server:

- ► System drive letters
- ► Data and log file path locations
- ► Master code page
- ► Collation

There are a few other considerations before implementing database mirroring. On 32-bit servers, you can mirror only a maximum of ten databases per server. In addition, database mirroring does not support databases with FILESTREAM data.

NOTE

Be sure that the SQL Server service is running under a domain account. This will make your setup much easier. If you attempt to use database mirroring when the SQL Server service is started using the LocalSystem or the Network Service account, then you must register the service SPN for Kerberos authentication.

Initializing Database Mirroring

Before you begin to use database mirroring, you need to set up your database servers. The first task you need to do is to make sure that your database has been set to use the Full recovery model. This enables SQL Server to capture all transactions in the transaction log. Next, you need to back up the database that will be mirrored and to restore a copy of that database to the mirror server.

Setting the Database Recovery Mode to Full

Before you can begin using database mirroring, you need to be sure that the database that you intend to mirror is using the Full recovery model. This is required because you need to make sure that SQL Server is capturing all of the transactions for the database. To set the recovery model of the database to full, first open SQL Server Management Studio (SSMS) and connect to the Database Engine. Then use Object Explorer to navigate to the appropriate SQL Server instance, click the Databases node, and select the database that you want to use with database mirroring. For this example, I'll use the Microsoft sample database AdventureWorks.

NOTE

AdventureWorks is not supplied as part of the SQL Server base installation. You can download the sample AdventureWorks databases from http://msftdbprodsamples.codeplex.com/Release/ProjectReleases .aspx?ReleaseId=18407.

Right-click the AdventureWorks link, and then select Properties, as shown in Figure 7-1.

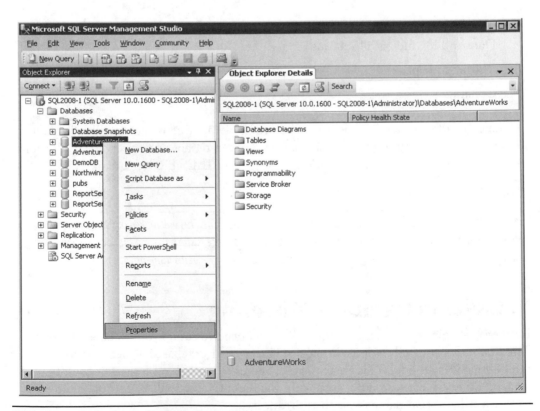

Figure 7-1   *Configuring the database properties of the principal server*

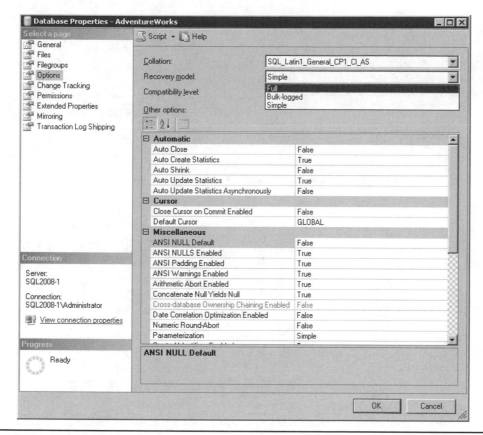

Figure 7-2   *Setting the database recovery model to Full*

This opens the AdventureWorks Database Properties dialog box that you can see in Figure 7-2.

To change the database to use the Full recovery model, go to the Options page of the Database Properties dialog box, and then use the "Recovery model" drop-down list as shown in Figure 7-2. The current model will be displayed in the "Recovery model" list box. To change to the Full recovery model, select Full from the list, and then click OK.

Perform a Full Database Backup on the Principal Server

The next step to setting up database mirroring is to perform a full database backup of the database that you want to mirror. To back up the database, open the SSMS, and then select the database that you want to use as the Principal for database mirroring.

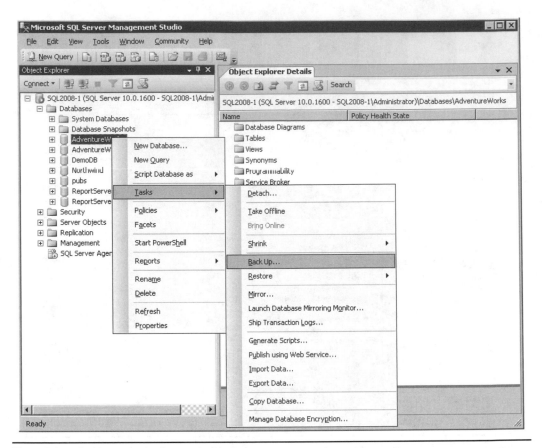

Figure 7-3 *Backing up the database on the Principal*

Select the AdventureWorks database. Next, right-click the selected database, and then from the context menu choose Tasks | Back Up as shown in Figure 7-3.

This will display the Back Up Database dialog box that you can see in Figure 7-4. Make sure that you select Full in the "Backup type" drop-down list. By default the backup will be saved to the AdventureWorks.bak file in the C:\Program Files\Microsoft SQL Server\MSSQL10.MSSQLSERVER\MSSQL\Backup directory, as you can see in Figure 7-4.

To do a complete backup, you need to select the "Backup type" as Full. You have the choice of backing up by Database or by "Files and filegroups." For the purposes of setting up database mirroring it's simpler to choose to back up the Database. You can also elect to back up by "Files and filegroups," but if you do, you need to be sure to select all of the files and file groups that compose the database.

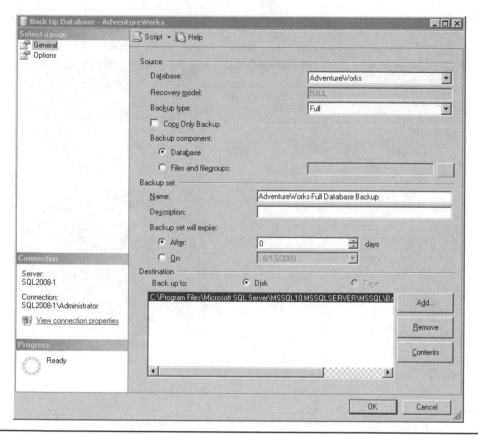

Figure 7-4   *Select backup destination*

After the database has been backed up, users can connect to the database and perform queries and post transactions. All these transactions will be captured in a subsequent backup of the transaction log.

Next, move the AdventureWorks.bak file to the mirror server where it can be restored.

Restore the Database Backup to the Mirror Server with NORECOVERY

To restore the database backup on the mirror server, open up SSMS and connect to the SQL Server instance that will act as the mirror server. Right-click the Databases node, and then select Restore Database from the context menu as illustrated in Figure 7-5.

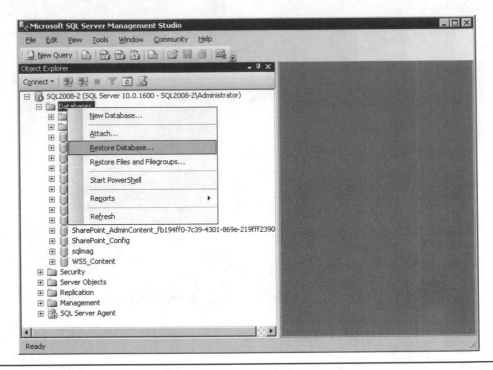

Figure 7-5 *Restoring the database to the mirror server*

NOTE

Be sure the mirroring server has adequate disk space before restoring the database.

Selecting the Restore Database option displays the Restore Database dialog box like the one shown in Figure 7-6.

On the Restore Database dialog box, you first enter the name of the database that will be restored. In this case the database name will be AdventureWorks. Then you specify where the restore process can find the backup file that contains the database data to restore. If the database is new to the mirror server, then you will need to click the "From device" radio button as shown in Figure 7-6.

NOTE

It's best to have the path to the restored database use the same path that was used on the mirrored server. In other words, if the database on the principal server resided on c:\Program Files\Microsoft Server\MSSQL10 .MSSQLSERVER\MSSQL\Data, then the restored database on the mirror server should use this path as well.

Then you must tell the Restore Database dialog box where to find the backup file by clicking the browse ("…") button at the end of the "From device" option to open the Specify Backup dialog box that you can see in Figure 7-7.

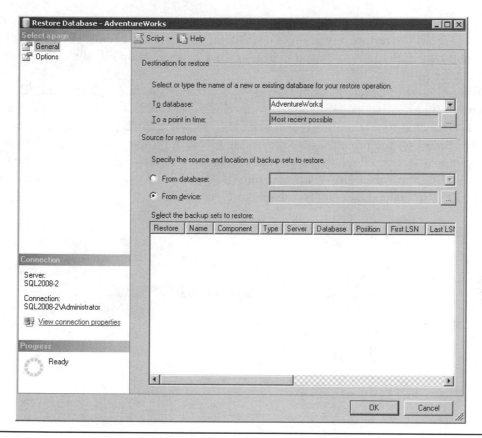

Figure 7-6   *Restoring the database to the mirror server*

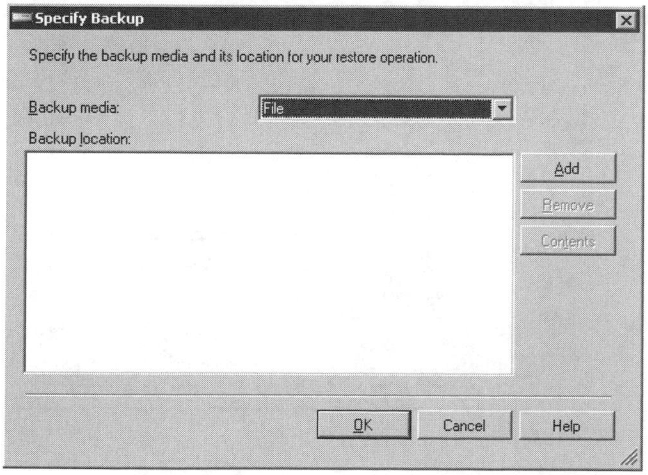

Figure 7-7   *Specify the backup media location*

In the Specify Backup dialog box, use the "Backup media" drop-down list to select File. This tells the restore operation that it will be restoring the database from the file system. Then click the Add button to display the Locate Backup File dialog box that you can see in Figure 7-8.

You can use the Locate Backup File dialog box to navigate through the local file system to find the database backup that you want to restore. In Figure 7-8 you can see that I've selected the AdventureWorks.bak file. This is the database backup that was created earlier on the principal server. Clicking OK returns you to the Specify Backup dialog box, where you'll see the AdventureWorks file added to the "Backup location" list. Selecting the AdventureWorks file from the list and then clicking OK returns you to the Restore Database dialog box shown in Figure 7-9.

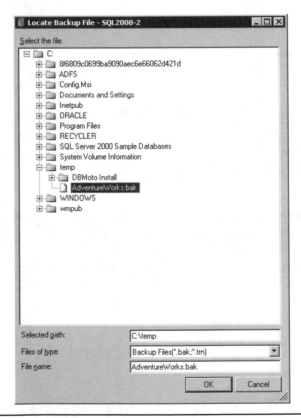

Figure 7-8   *Locate the backup file*

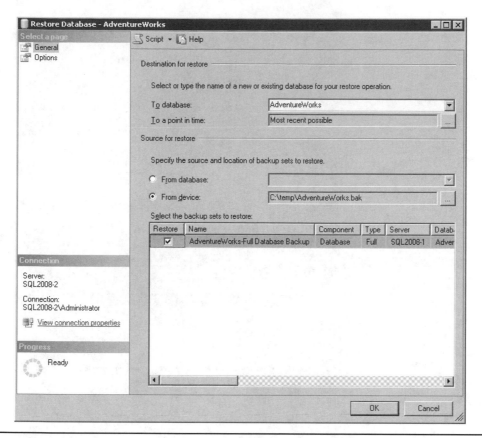

Figure 7-9   *Restore the database*

After locating the backup file, the next step is to make sure that you select the NORECOVERY option for the backup. This restores the database in recovery mode, which will allow you to later apply any transactions to the restored database. To specify the NORECOVERY option, click Options. This will display the Restore Database— Options page that you can see in Figure 7-10.

For the "Restore options," move down to the "Recovery state" section. The "Recovery state" options control the state that the database will be left in following the restore operation. To implement database mirroring, select RESTORE WITH NORECOVERY. The database will be restored, and if a prior version of the database exists, it will be overwritten. Uncommitted transactions are not rolled back. This option restores the

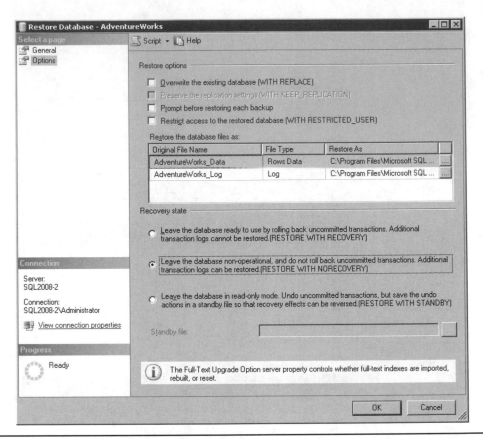

Figure 7-10 *Specify RESTORE WITH NORECOVERY*

database, but the database is not in a usable state. It will be left in a recovering state. Further transaction backups can be restored to the database, which is usually required in order to capture the latest changes to the original database. After selecting the RESTORE WITH NORECOVERY option, click the General page to finish the restore operation. On the General page be sure to select the Restore box as illustrated in Figure 7-11, and then click OK to restore the AdventureWorks database to the mirror server.

At this point the AdventureWorks database has been restored to the mirror server, and it is in recovery mode.

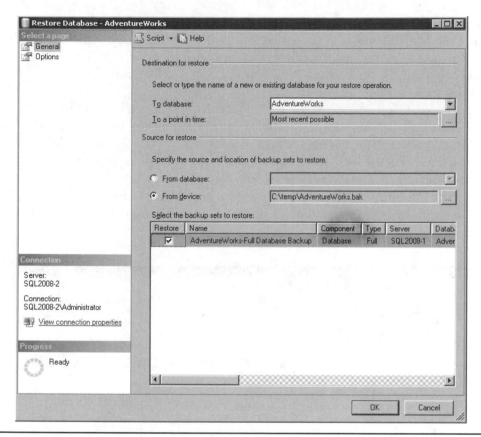

Figure 7-11   *Restoring the database on the mirror server*

Perform a Transaction Log Backup on the Principal Server

Just before you're ready to initiate database mirroring between the principal and the mirror server, you should perform a transaction log backup on the principal server to capture the most recent changes to the database that's being mirrored. Then you need to apply the transaction log backup to the database on the mirror server.

> ### NOTE
> *You would usually perform a log backup to capture the most recent transactions to the database. However, performing a log backup is not always necessary. For example, if the database was newly created just before the backup and has not been used, then you would not need to back up the transaction log.*

To back up the transaction log, go to the principal server and start SSMS. Then expand the Databases node as illustrated in Figure 7-12. Then right-click the database that you want to mirror, and then choose Tasks | Back Up from the context menu.

Choosing the Backup option will display the Back Up Database dialog box that you see in Figure 7-13.

On the Back Up Database dialog box be sure that you select Transaction Log in the "Backup type" drop-down list. By default the backup will be saved to the AdventureWorks.bak file in the C:\Program Files\Microsoft SQL Server\MSSQL10 .MSSQLSERVER\MSSQL\Backup directory—the same place as the previous full database backup. You can rename the backup file if you want to.

Clicking OK performs the transaction log backup. After the backup completes, the next step is to move the transaction log backup to the mirror server where you will restore it.

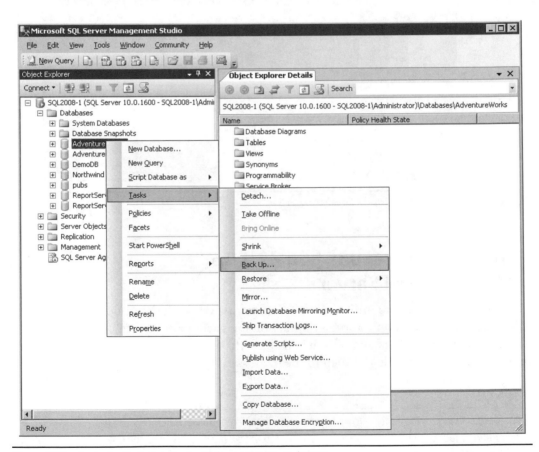

Figure 7-12 *Beginning the transaction log backup on the principal server*

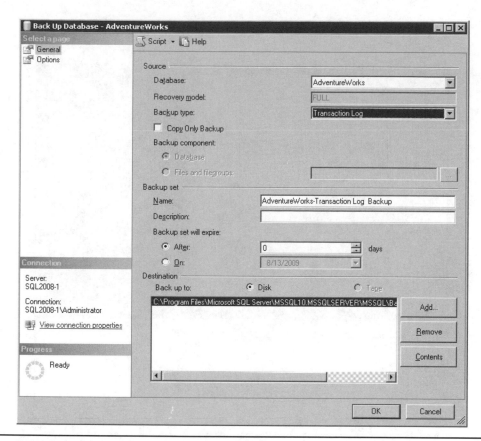

Figure 7-13   *Backing up the transaction log on the principal server*

Restore the Log Database Backup on the Mirror with NORECOVERY

To restore the transaction log backup to the mirror server, start SSMS and connect to the SQL Server instance that will act as the mirror server. Right-click on the Databases node, and then select Restore Database from the context menu as shown in Figure 7-14.

Selecting the Restore Database option displays the Restore Database dialog box that you can see in Figure 7-15.

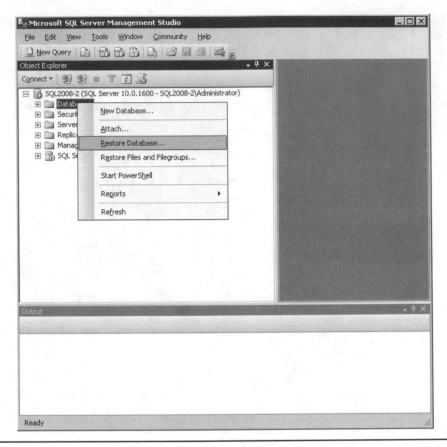

Figure 7-14   *Beginning to restore the transaction log backup to the mirror server*

On the Restore Database dialog box enter the name of the database that the transaction log will be restored to. In this example, the database name will be AdventureWorks. Then you specify where the restore process can find the backup file that contains the database data to restore. To restore from a file-based backup, choose the "From device" radio button as shown in Figure 7-15. The Specify Backup dialog box, which you can see in Figure 7-16, appears.

In the Specify Backup dialog box, use the "Backup media" drop-down list to select File. This tells the restore operation that it will be restoring the database from a file-based backup. Then click the Add button to display the Locate Backup File dialog box that you can see in Figure 7-17.

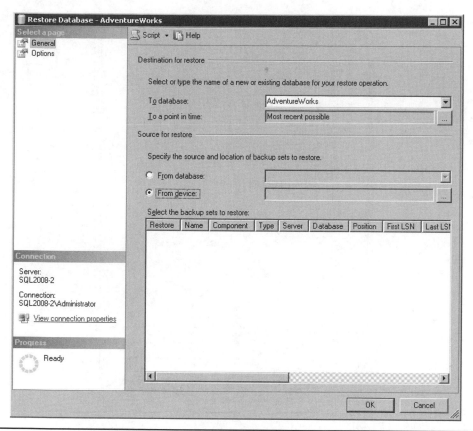

Figure 7-15   *Restoring the transaction log backup to the mirror server*

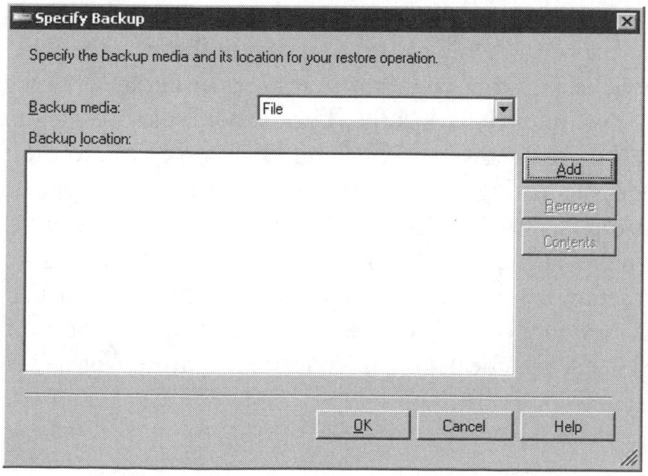

Figure 7-16   *Specify the backup media location.*

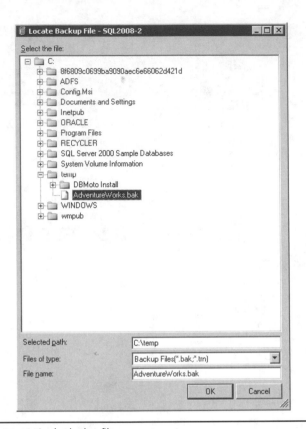

Figure 7-17 *Locate the transaction log backup file.*

Use the Locate Backup File dialog box to navigate through the local file system to find the database backup that you want to restore. In Figure 7-17 you can see that I've selected the AdventureWorks.bak file. This is the transaction log backup that was created earlier on the principal server. Clicking OK returns you to the Specify Backup dialog box shown earlier in Figure 7-16, where you'll see the AdventureWorks_Log file added to "Backup location". Select the AdventureWorks file from the list, and then click OK to return to the Restore Database dialog box shown in Figure 7-18.

Next, the transaction log needs to be restored to the mirror by using the NORECOVERY option. To set the NORECOVERY option for the transaction log restore operation, select the check box in front of AdventureWorks-Transaction Log

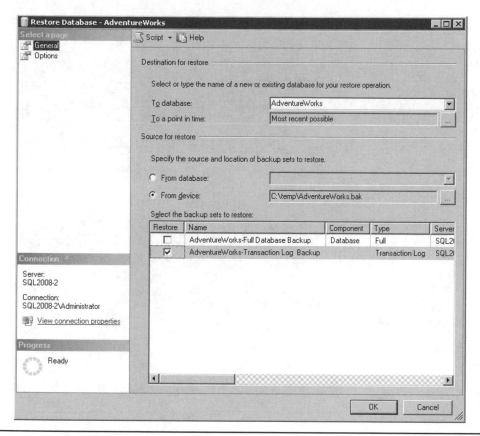

Figure 7-18   *Restore the transaction log backup on the mirror server.*

Backup, and then click Options shown on the left side of the screen. This will display the Restore Database—Options page dialog box, as you can see in Figure 7-19.

To restore the transaction log with the NORECOVERY option, select the option "Leave the database non-operational, and do not roll back uncommitted transactions. Additional transaction logs can be restored (RESTORE WITH NORECOVERY)." You want to restore the transaction log with the NORECOVERY option because this allows database mirroring to continue to restore the mirrored transaction log data to the database on the mirror server. Clicking OK will restore the transaction log backup.

This completes the preparation for database mirroring. At this point you're ready to go ahead and create the specific database mirroring configuration.

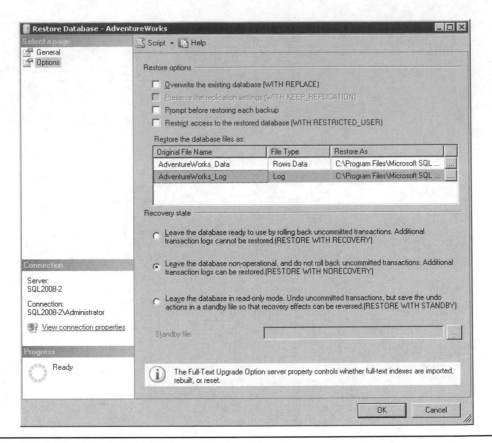

Figure 7-19 *Select the RESTORE WITH NORECOVERY option.*

Configuring Mirroring on the Principal Server

Once the requisites are out of the way, you begin the process of configuring database mirroring. To get started with the database mirroring configuration, first open SSMS, and then select the SQL Server instance that will act as the principal server in the database mirroring connection. Next, expand the Databases node, right-click the database that you want to mirror, and select Tasks | Mirror from the context menu as shown in Figure 7-20. In this example, you can see that I've selected the AdventureWorks database.

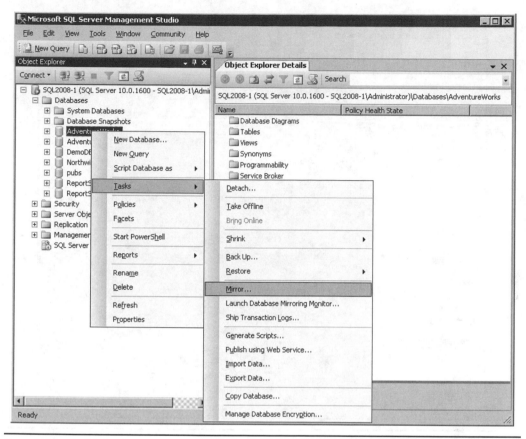

Figure 7-20   *Configuring database mirroring on the principal server*

This will open the Database Properties window that you can see in Figure 7-21.

The Database Properties window shows you the current configuration settings that apply to the database. In Figure 7-21 since database mirroring is not set up yet, all of the database mirroring configuration values are initially blank. To begin setting up database mirroring, you must first click the Configure Security button. This starts the database mirroring configuration process and displays the Configure Database Mirroring Security Wizard as shown in Figure 7-22.

To run the Configure Database Mirroring Security Wizard, click Next. This will display the Include Witness Server dialog box that you can see in Figure 7-23.

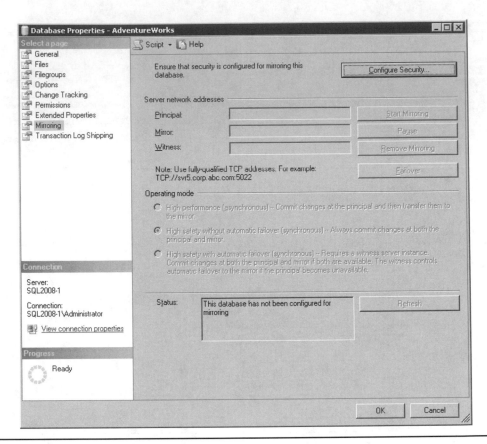

Figure 7-21 *Database Properties—Mirroring page*

The Configure Database Mirroring Security Wizard's Include Witness Server dialog box essentially controls the type of database mirroring mode that you are going to use. The Witness server is required in order to configure database mirroring in high-availability mode. Select the Yes radio button in response to the "Do you want to configure security to include a witness server instance?" prompt. Then click Next to display the "Choose Servers to Configure" dialog box as shown in Figure 7-24.

The dialog box in Figure 7-24 allows you to select where to save the database mirroring connection and security information. If you're using database mirroring in high-availability mode with a witness server, then the security information will be saved on the witness server by default. Make sure the check box before "Witness server instance" is selected, and then click Next to display the next Configure Database Mirroring Security Wizard screen shown in Figure 7-25.

Figure 7-22   *Running the Configure Database Mirroring Security Wizard*

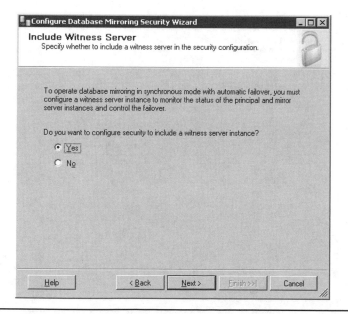

Figure 7-23   *Configure Database Mirroring Security Wizard—Include Witness Server*

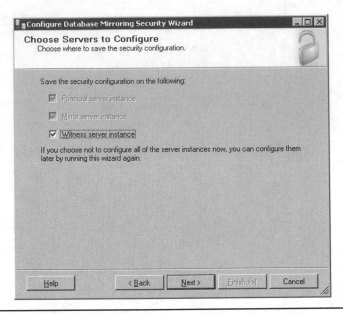

Figure 7-24 *Configure Database Mirroring Security Wizard—Choose Server to Configure*

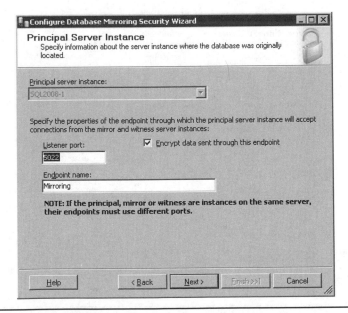

Figure 7-25 *Configure Database Mirroring Security Wizard—Principal Server Instance*

The Principal Server Instance dialog box shown in Figure 7-25 enables you to specify the SQL Server instance that will function as the principal server. By default the Principal server instance prompt will be filled in with the server name from SSMS. In Figure 7-25 you can see that in this example the principal server is a system named SQL2008-1. The "Listener port" identifies the TCP port that the principal server will use to connect to the mirror server and the witness. The data that is transmitted can be in plaintext or encrypted. If the principal and the mirror server are linked over a shared network, then you should be sure to keep the default setting of "Encrypt data sent through this endpoint." This will encrypt the data stream between the principal and the mirror server and will prevent network monitors or other systems from making use of the data. If the principal and the mirror server are connected on a private network that isn't shared with other systems, then you can safely uncheck the "Encrypt data sent through this endpoint" check box. The "Endpoint name" is used to identify the TCP/IP Endpoint used by database mirroring. The default value is Mirroring, but you can change it if you want to. Clicking Next displays the configuration screen for the mirror server shown in Figure 7-26.

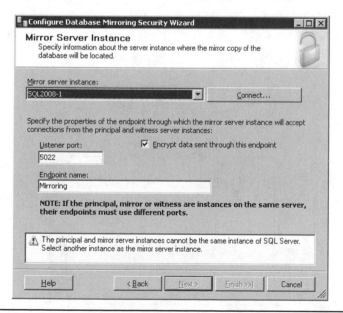

Figure 7-26   *Configure Database Mirroring Security Wizard—Mirror Server Instance*

You use the Mirror Server Instance dialog box shown in Figure 7-26 to specify the SQL Server instance that will function as the mirror server. You use the drop-down list to select the SQL Server instance that will be the mirror. Initially the "Mirror server instance" drop-down list contains the name of the principal server. Clicking the drop-down arrow displays the other SQL Server systems that have been recently used in the SMSS Connection dialog box. If the mirror is shown in the list, select it. If the mirror server is not shown in the list, click the Connect button to display the "Browse for Servers" dialog box that you can see in Figure 7-27.

For high availability, the server instance selected for the mirror server needs to be on a different server than the one used by the principal server. On the "Browse for Servers" dialog box click the Network Servers tab. The additional SQL Server systems that can be located on the network will be displayed. Select the system that you want to act as the mirror server and then click OK. This will return you to the Mirror Server Instance configuration dialog box and will fill in the name of the selected mirror server as shown in Figure 7-28.

The example in Figure 7-28 shows that the mirror system is a SQL Server system named SQL2008-2. As you saw with the configuration for the principal server, the "Listener port" identifies the TCP/IP port that the mirror server will communicate on, and the "Endpoint name" supplies a server endpoint name. These values do not need to match the values supplied on the configuration for the principal server. Clicking Next displays the Witness Server Instance configuration dialog box that you can see in Figure 7-29.

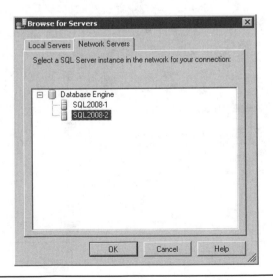

Figure 7-27   *Browsing to locate the mirror server*

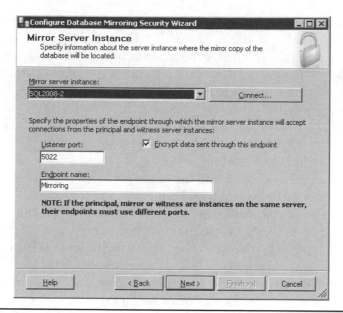

Figure 7-28   *Configure Database Mirroring Security Wizard—Mirror Server Instance*

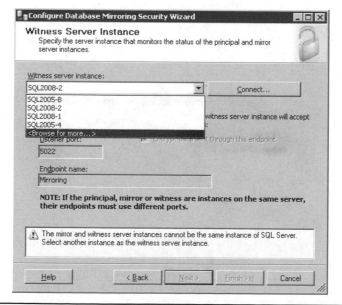

Figure 7-29   *Configure Database Mirroring Security Wizard—Witness Server Instance*

As with the previous two wizard screens, where you configured the principal and mirror servers, you use the Configure Database Mirroring Security Wizard—Witness Server Instance screen to configure the SQL Server instance that will act as the witness server. While the witness doesn't share data with the principal or the mirror server, it is required to implement database mirroring in high-availability mode. Use the drop-down list to select the SQL Server instance that will act as the witness server. If the system you want to act as the witness isn't shown, click the <Browse for more…> option at the bottom of the drop-down list. This will display the "Connect to Server" dialog box that you can see in Figure 7-30.

The "Server name" drop-down list in the "Connect to Server" dialog box shows all of the SQL Server instances that have been recently used in the SSMS Connect dialog box. If the system you want to use as the witness is shown in the list, go ahead and select it. If the desired witness system is not shown in the list, select the <Browse for more…> option at the bottom of the list. This will display the "Browse for Servers" dialog box that you can see in Figure 7-31.

On the "Browse for Servers" dialog box, click the Network Servers tab. The additional SQL Server systems that can be located on the network will be displayed. Select the system that you want to act as the witness server. In Figure 7-31 you can see that I selected a server named SQL2008-3. Clicking OK will return you to the "Connect to Server" dialog box, and the name of the selected witness server will be filled in as shown in Figure 7-32.

In Figure 7-32 you can see that the SQL Server system named SQL2008-3 has been selected. Clicking Connect will complete the connection to the witness server and will return you to the Witness Server Instance dialog box shown in Figure 7-33.

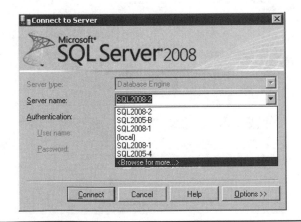

Figure 7-30 *Connect to the witness server.*

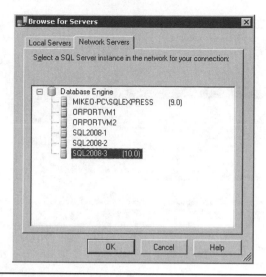

Figure 7-31   *Browsing for the witness server*

In Figure 7-33 you can see that for this example, the SQL Server system named SQL2008-3 will act as the witness server. As you saw in the principal and mirror instance configuration screens, you also need to set the TCP/IP "Listener port" that is used as well as the "Endpoint name." In Figure 7-33 you can see this configuration is using the default values of 5022 for the "Listener port" and Mirroring for the "Endpoint name." Clicking Next displays the Service Accounts configuration dialog box that you can see in Figure 7-34.

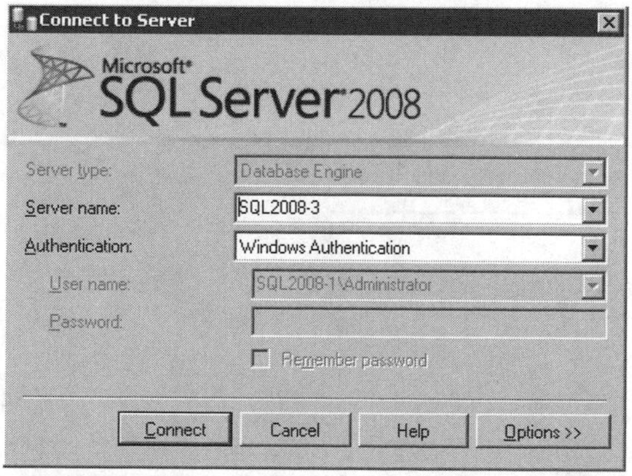

Figure 7-32   *Connecting to the witness server*

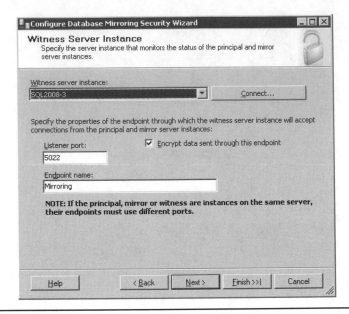

Figure 7-33 *Configure Database Mirroring Security Wizard—Witness Server Instance*

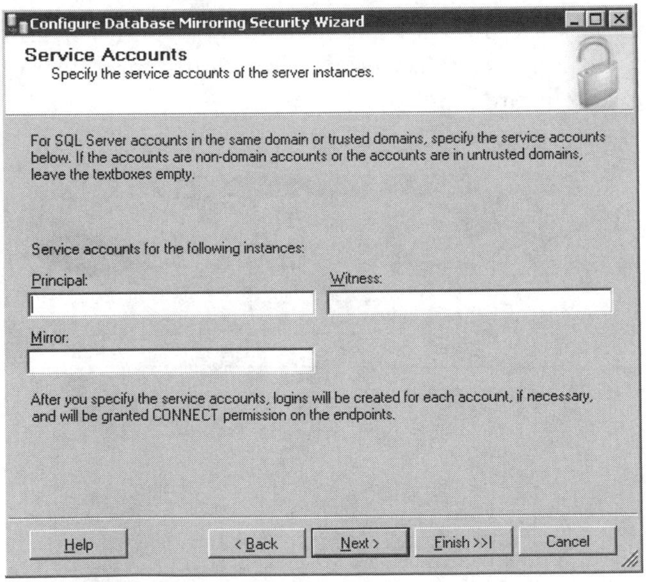

Figure 7-34 *Configure Database Mirroring Security Wizard—Service Accounts*

The Service Accounts screen lets you specify service accounts for running mirroring when the instance servers are running under different accounts. If you enter values here, the database mirroring wizard will create logins for each of these accounts on the target systems. In this example, all of the servers are in the same local domain, and they are using the same account, so all of the account values should be left blank. Clicking Next will display the Complete The Wizard screen as you can see in Figure 7-35.

The "Complete the Wizard" dialog box enables you to verify the choices you made on the earlier wizard screens. In Figure 7-35 you can see that the principal server is named SQL2008-1. The mirror server is named SQL2008-2, and the witness is named SQL2008-3. All three systems will use the endpoint named Mirroring, the TCP port 5022, and the data stream will be encrypted. If you need to make a change, you can click Back to page back through the previous dialog boxes. If the settings look good, then clicking Finish will configure database mirroring, and the Configuring Endpoints dialog box will be displayed, as shown in Figure 7-36.

If the Configure Database Mirroring Security Wizard was able to successfully create the endpoints on all three of the systems, then you will see green check marks for the principal, the mirror, and the witness. Warnings will be displayed with a yellow triangle. Warning errors allow you to continue on. A failed configuration is indicated with a red *x*. If there are errors, you will need to rerun the Configure Database Mirroring Security Wizard. Clicking Close displays the Database Properties dialog box shown in Figure 7-37.

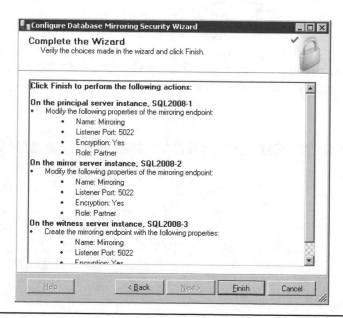

Figure 7-35   *Configure Database Mirroring Security Wizard—Complete the Wizard*

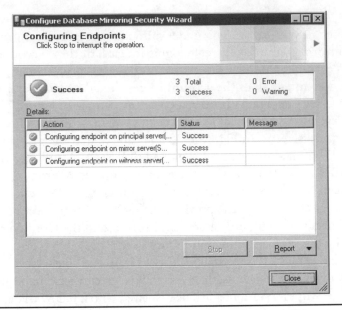

Figure 7-36 *Configure Database Mirroring Security Wizard—Configuring Endpoints*

The Database Properties dialog box is shown at the end of the database mirroring configuration process. The configuration values for the principal, the mirror, and the witness servers are displayed along with the type of mirroring that is being configured. In Figure 7-37, you can see that database mirroring will be run in synchronous high safety mode, which allows for automatic failover. Clicking Start Mirroring will initiate database mirroring, and the database mirroring properties will be displayed as you can see in Figure 7-38.

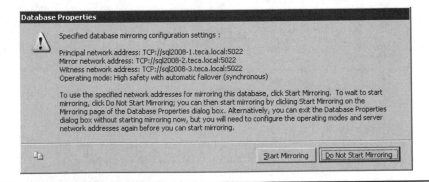

Figure 7-37 *Starting database mirroring*

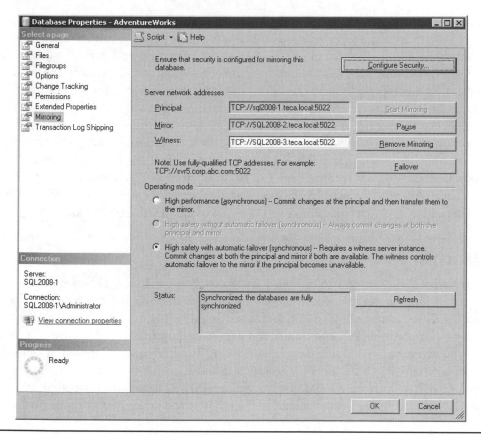

Figure 7-38 *Running database mirroring*

The Database Properties dialog box displays the database mirroring status and also allows you to manage database mirroring. More information about managing database mirroring is presented in Chapter 8. The Status box at the bottom of the window shows that database mirroring is active and that both the principal and the mirror are fully synchronized.

Configuring the Client for Failover

Synchronous database mirroring with the presence of a witness enables the database on the principal server to automatically failover to the mirror server. However, the mirror server uses a different IP address and host name than the principal server. To enable the networked client application to use the transparent client redirection, use the following:

```
"Server=SQL2008-1; FailoverPartner=SQL2008-2; Database=AdventureWorks;
Network=dbmssocn"
```

The `Server` keyword identifies the principal server. The `FailoverPartner` keyword identifies the mirror server. The `Database` keyword identifies the database that the application will connect to. The `Network=dbmssocn` keyword pair indicates that the TCP/IP protocol will be used to connect the client application to the server. You can find a complete list of SQL Server Native Client Connection keywords at http://technet.microsoft.com/en-us/library/ms130822.aspx.

If the client applications connection is lost, the application needs to be aware of connection failures and must have logic to retry the connection. If the client cannot reconnect to the principal, it will be automatically redirected to the mirror server. More information about client reconnection can be found at http://technet.microsoft.com/en-us/library/ms366199.aspx. In addition, details about the connection retry algorithm can be found at http://technet.microsoft.com/en-us/library/ms365783.aspx.

Summary

In this chapter, you saw how to configure database mirroring for SQL Server 2008. In the first part of this chapter, you learned about the requirements for implementing database mirroring. Next, you saw how to initialize database mirroring on the mirror server by installing a database backup and transaction log file backup from the principal server. Then you saw how to configure database mirroring by running the Configure Database Mirroring Security Wizard. Finally, you saw how to set up the client application to be aware of database mirroring by adding the FailoverPartner keyword to the application's connection string. In the next chapter, you'll learn how to manage database mirroring.

Chapter 8

Managing Database Mirroring

In This Chapter

- ► **Managing the Mirroring Session**
- ► **Monitoring Database Mirroring**
- ► **Verifying Your Database Mirroring Configuration**

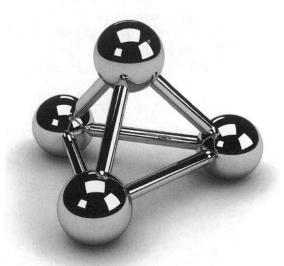

I n Chapters 6 and 7, you learned about SQL Server 2008's database mirroring architecture and saw how to prepare a database for mirroring and then how to configure database mirroring. In this chapter, you'll see how to perform the basic management for database mirroring.

Managing the Mirroring Session

Database mirroring provides high availability for SQL Server databases while it is online. However, for maintenance purposes, you might elect to pause mirroring or to initiate a manual failover. In this section, you'll see how to pause and resume a database mirroring session as well as how to perform a manual failover and failback.

Pausing Mirroring

Pausing database mirroring temporarily stops the sending of transactions from the principal server to the mirror server. The principal database remains available, but the mirror database is set to suspended. To pause database mirroring, start SSMS on the principal server by choosing Start | All Programs | Microsoft SQL Server 2008 | SQL Server Management Studio. After SSMS has started, right-click the database that is being mirrored, and select Properties from the context menu. This will display the Database Properties window. Select the Mirroring page on the left side of the screen. This will display the Database Properties—Mirroring window like the one in Figure 8-1.

The current database mirroring configuration is displayed in the "Server network addresses" section of the screen. In Figure 8-1 you can see that the Principal is SQL2008-1. The Mirror is SQL2008-2, and the Witness is SQL2008-3. When you pause database mirroring, the principal server stops sending database transactions to the mirror server.

To pause database mirroring, click Pause. This will display the "Are you sure you want to pause mirroring of this database?" prompt that you can see in Figure 8-1. Clicking Yes will pause database mirroring.

Resume Mirroring

After database mirroring has been paused, you must tell it to resume when you want database mirroring to start again. To resume mirroring, open the Database Properties page on the principal server for the mirrored database that has been paused. This will display a screen that looks like the one you can see in Figure 8-2.

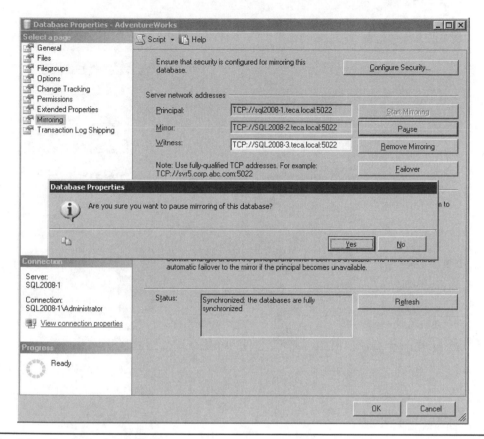

Figure 8-1   *Pausing database mirroring*

In Figure 8-2 you can see that database mirroring has been paused by examining the entry in the Status field. To restart database mirroring, click Resume. Database mirroring will be resumed, and the Database Properties dialog box will be refreshed as shown in Figure 8-3.

After database mirroring has been resumed, the Pause button will be enabled, and the Status field will be updated with the message "Synchronizing: data is being transferred from the principal database to the mirror database."

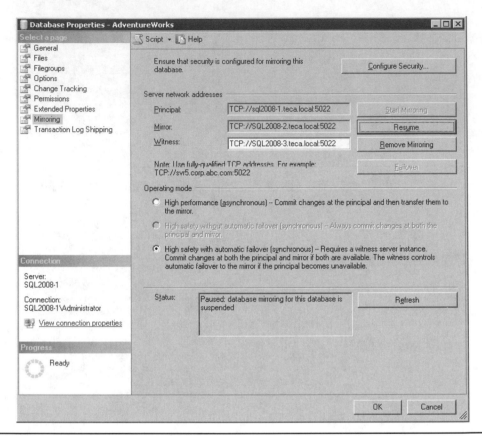

Figure 8-2 *Resuming database mirroring*

Performing a Manual Failover

You can initiate a manual database mirroring failover if you need to perform maintenance on the principal server or if you want to test database mirroring failover operation. To perform a manual failover, start SSMS on the principal server by choosing Start | All Programs | Microsoft SQL Server 2008 | SQL Server Management Studio. Figure 8-4 shows the state of the principal and mirror databases before performing the failover operation.

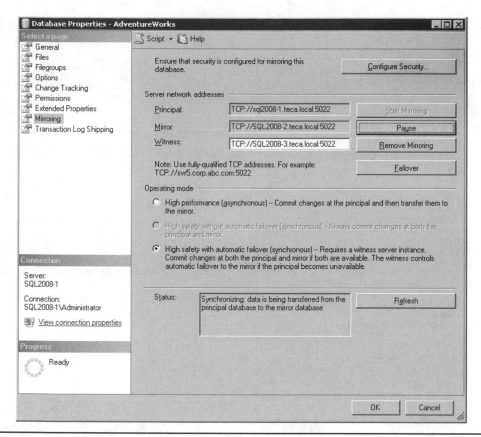

Figure 8-3   *Updated Database Properties after resuming database mirroring*

After SSMS has started, right-click the database that is being mirrored, and select Properties from the context menu. This will display the Database Properties window. Select the Mirroring page on the left side of the screen. This will display the Database Mirroring Properties window like the one you can see in Figure 8-5.

To initiate a manual failover, click the Failover button on the right portion of the screen. This will display the Database Properties prompt that you can see in Figure 8-5. This prompt warns you that you are about to perform a failover for the mirrored database. When the failover completes, the mirror database will become the new principal, and

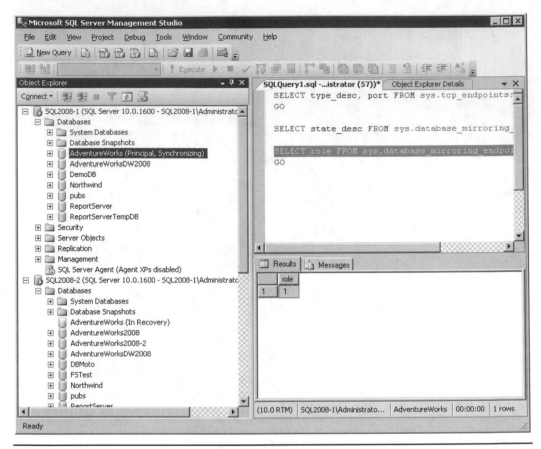

Figure 8-4   *Opening the properties of the mirroring database on the principal server*

the current principal will become the mirror. Clicking Yes starts the database mirroring failover and returns you to the SSMS Object Explorer like you can see in Figure 8-6.

While the manual database mirroring failover is running, the AdventureWorks database on what was the principal will show the status of "(Restoring…)" as you can see in Figure 8-6. After it has completed, the server that was acting as the mirror will show the status of Principal (Synchronized).

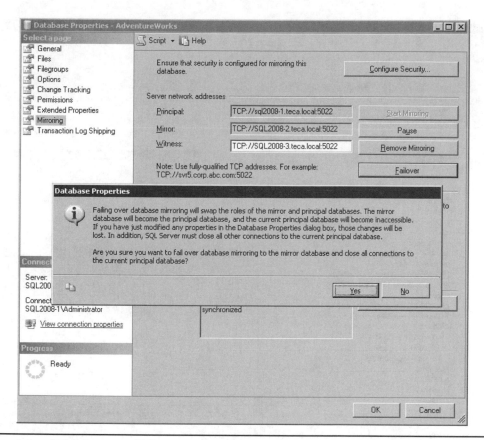

Figure 8-5 *Performing a manual failover*

Performing a Manual Failback

Database mirroring has no facility for performing automated failback. After you've completed maintenance on the server that was the principal server and you want it to resume operations as the principal once again, you need to perform a manual failback. Initiating a failback is exactly like performing a manual failover, except you

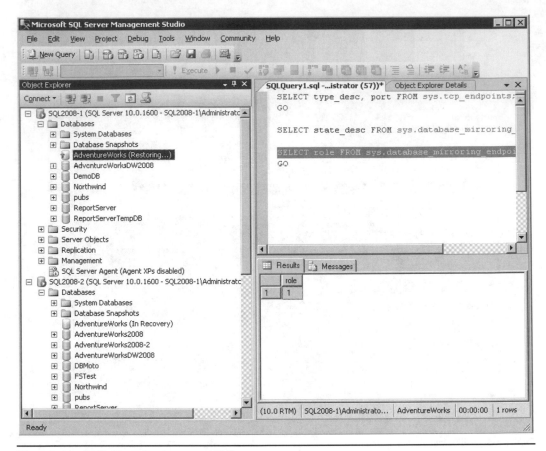

Figure 8-6   *SSMS after performing a manual failover*

must perform it on the server that was formerly acting as the mirror but that is now acting as the principal. In this example, that would be SQL2008-2. To perform the manual failback, start SSMS on the principal server (SQL2008-2) by choosing Start | All Programs | Microsoft SQL Server 2008 | SQL Server Management Studio. The mirrored database will be displayed as shown in Figure 8-7.

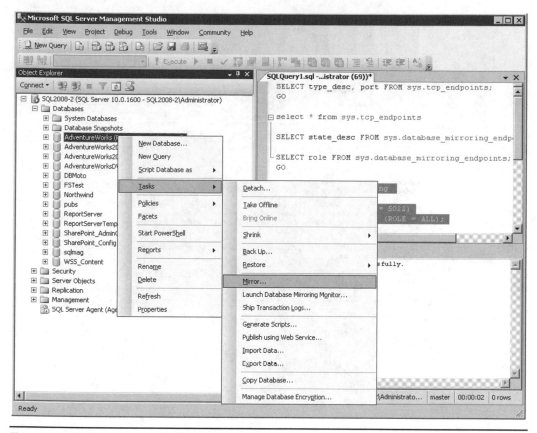

Figure 8-7   *Performing a manual failback*

Expand the Databases node and right-click the database that is being mirrored. Then select Tasks | Mirror from the context menu. This will display the Database Properties—Mirroring page as you can see in Figure 8-8.

To failover back to the original principal server, click the Failover button on the right portion of the screen. This will display the Database Properties prompt that you can see in Figure 8-8. This prompt warns you that you are about to perform a failover for the mirrored database. When the failover completes, the mirror database will become the new

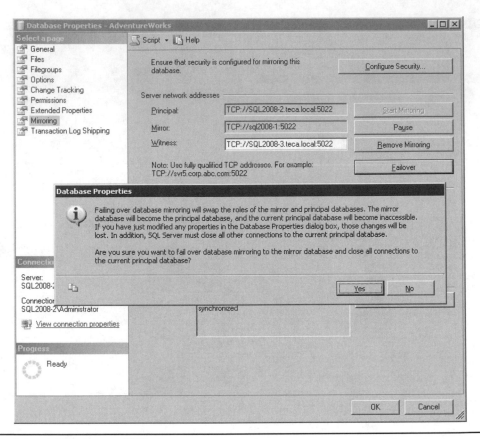

Figure 8-8   *Initiating a manual failback*

principal, and the current principal will become the mirror. In this example, that means that SQL2008-1 will become the principal once again and that SQL2008-2 will become the mirror. Clicking Yes starts the database mirroring failover and returns you to the SSMS Object Explorer as you can see in Figure 8-9.

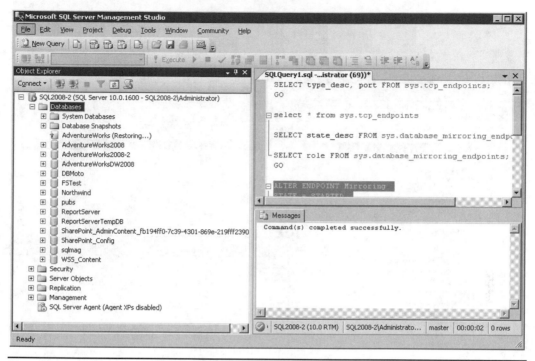

Figure 8-9   *SSMS on the mirror after performing a manual failback*

After the manual database mirroring failover has completed, the AdventureWorks database SQL2008-2 will show the status of "(Restoring…)". This indicates that the database is now functioning as the mirror.

Opening SSMS on the server named SQL2008-1 shows that it is now functioning as the principal as indicated in Figure 8-10 by the status of "(Principal, Synchronized)" next to the AdventureWorks database.

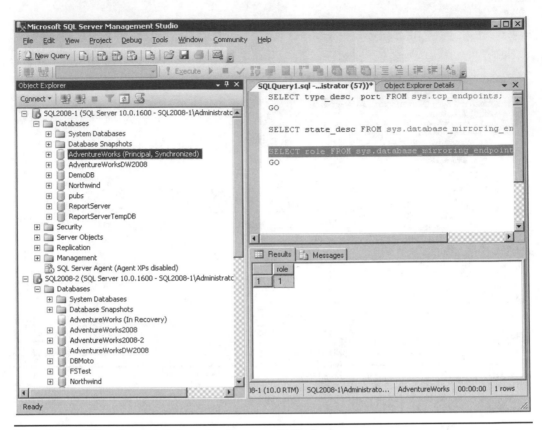

Figure 8-10   *SSMS on the principal after performing a manual failback*

Monitoring Database Mirroring

In addition to pausing and resuming database mirroring, SSMS also has a monitoring capability that can allow you to view the current database mirroring status.

Using the Database Mirroring Monitor

To start the Database Mirroring Monitor, choose Start | All Programs | Microsoft SQL Server 2008 | SQL Server Management Studio to start SSMS. Then expand the Database node, and right-click on the database that is being mirrored as you can see in Figure 8-11.

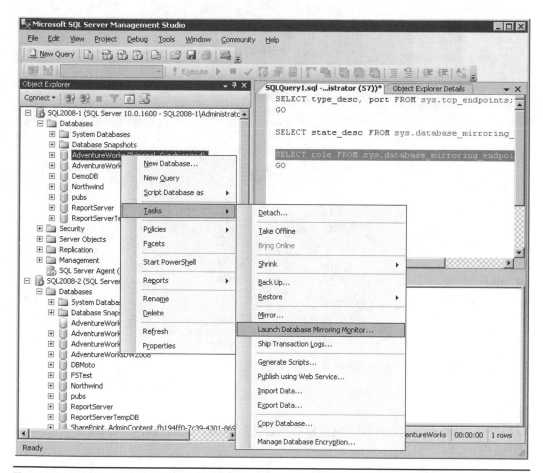

Figure 8-11   *Starting the Database Mirroring Monitor*

Choose Tasks | Launch Database Mirroring Monitor to start the Database Mirroring Monitor. The Database Mirroring Monitor is shown in Figure 8-12.

The Database Mirroring Monitor lists all of the database mirroring connections that are active on the server. For each connection, the Status tab shows the current status of the connection between the principal and the mirror. It lists the current rate of transactions that are being sent from the principal to the mirror. It also lists the address of the witness server.

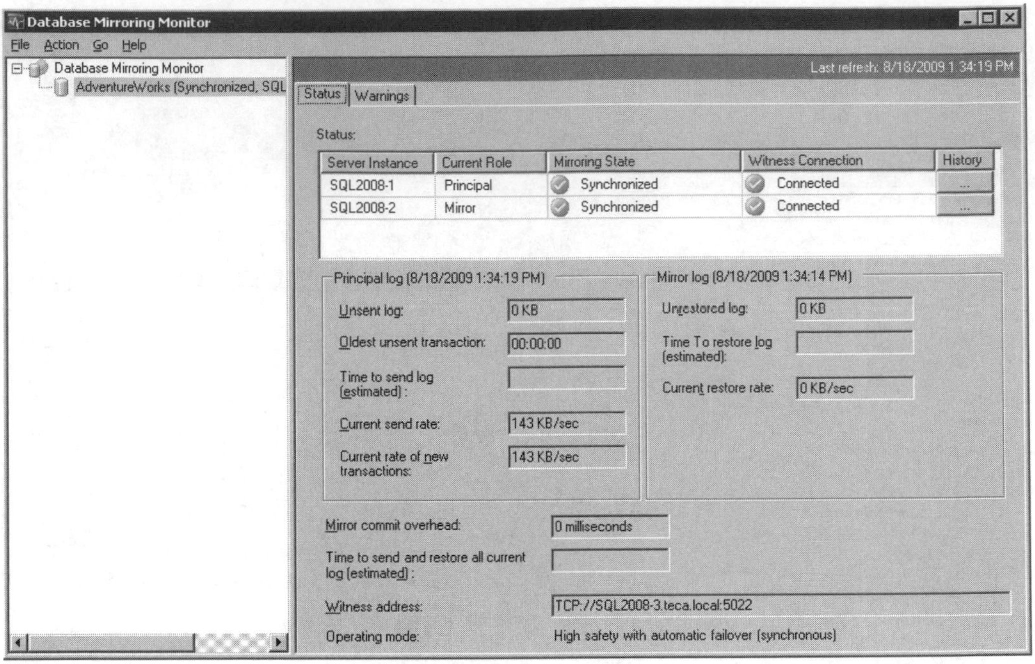

Figure 8-12   *The Database Mirroring Monitor*

Using the sp_dbmonitorresults Stored Procedure

You can also monitor the database mirroring status on your system by running the sp_dbmmonitorresults stored procedure. The sp_dbmmonitorresults stored procedure accepts the name of the mirrored database as a parameter, and it must be run from the msdb database as illustrated by the following:

```
use msdb
exec sp_dbmmonitorresults 'Adventureworks'
```

The partial results of the sp_dbmonitorresults stored procedure are shown next:

```
database_name   role mirroring_state witness_status unsent_log send_rate
--------------- ---- --------------- -------------- ---------- --------
Adventureworks 1    4               1               0          0
```

The name of the mirrored database is listed in addition to the role the database is using and the mirror and witness states. The role of 1 indicates the database is the principal, and the state of 4 indicates the database is synchronized. Other information is also provided that is not shown in the results. You can find a complete explanation of the sp_dbmonitorresults stored procedure at http://msdn.microsoft.com/en-us/library/ms366320.aspx?ppud=4.

Verifying Your Database Mirroring Configuration

SQL Server 2008 also provides a number of dynamic management views (DMVs) that can provide you with information and that can help you troubleshoot connection problems.

Listing SQL Server Endpoints

To see the TCP endpoints that have been configured on the system, you can query the sys.tcp_endpoints view as follows:

```
SELECT name, port FROM sys.tcp_endpoints;
```

This query lists the name of the configured endpoints and ports they are using as you can see next:

```
name                                  port
------------------------------------- -----------
Dedicated Admin Connection            0
TSQL Default TCP                      0
Mirroring                             5022

(3 row(s) affected)
```

You can see more information about the columns in sys.tcp_endpoints view at http://msdn.microsoft.com/en-us/library/ms177572.aspx.

Listing the Mirroring Endpoint Information

You can also query the sys.database_mirroring_endpoints view for more information about the status of your database mirroring configuration.

The following query shows how to retrieve the database mirroring role of the current system.

```
SELECT role FROM sys.database_mirroring_endpoints;
```

You can see some sample results in the following:

```
Role
----
1


(1 row(s) affected)
```

The value of 0 indicates none. The value of 1 indicates the system is a mirroring partner. The value of 2 indicates the witness, and the value of 3 indicates all.

You can also use the sys.databasemirroring_endpoints view to discover the current status of database mirroring on the system as you can see in the following:

```
SELECT state_desc FROM sys.database_mirroring_endpoints
```

The sample results are shown next. In this example, the current state of database mirroring is started. This means database mirroring is currently active.

```
state_desc
---------------------
STARTED


(1 row(s) affected)
```

You can see more information about the columns in sys.database_mirroring_endpoints view at http://msdn.microsoft.com/en-us/library/ms190278.aspx.

Summary

In this chapter, you learned about the basic techniques for managing database mirroring. Here you saw how to start, pause, and resume mirroring as well as how to perform manual database mirroring failover and failback operations. You also saw how to monitor database mirroring using the Database Mirroring Monitor as well as the T-SQL sp_dbmmonitorresults stored procedure. Finally, you saw how to query some of the SQL Server 2008 DMVs to get information about your system's database mirroring configuration.

In the next section of this book, you'll learn how virtualization can be used to increase SQL Server availability.

Part III

Implementing Hyper-V Virtualization and Live Migration

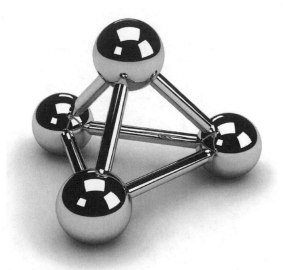

Chapter 9

Virtualization and Live Migration Architecture

In This Chapter

▶ **An Overview of Virtualization**

▶ **High Availability and Virtualization**

▶ **Live Migration Architecture**

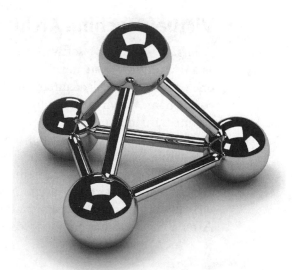

Virtualization is one of the most rapidly adopted technologies in IT today. Virtualization can address a number of different issues facing IT including increasing hardware utilization, more rapid server deployment, and reduced IT costs. While virtualization can address all of these issues, it can also be used to improve business continuity by increasing system availability in a number of different ways.

In this chapter, you'll get an overview of server virtualization and how it can be used for higher levels of availability. In the first section of this chapter, you'll get a basic understanding of server virtualization technology and Microsoft's Hyper-V virtualization technology. In the second section of this chapter, you'll see some of the ways that virtualization can be used to achieve higher levels of availability. Here you'll see how virtualization can be used to facilitate deployment and disaster recovery, as well as how Hyper-V's Quick Migration and Live Migration features can be used to address the issue of unplanned downtime. In the last section of this chapter, you'll learn about the requirements for Live Migration as well as get a deeper understanding of how Live Migration works.

An Overview of Virtualization

In this section, you'll get an introduction to the basic concepts of virtualization. Here you'll learn about the fundamental concepts of virtualization. You'll get an understanding of what a virtual machine is, and then see an overview of the different components that compose a virtual machine. Next, you'll dive in deeper and get an understanding of Microsoft's Hyper-V server virtualization technology. You'll see an overview of the Hyper-V architecture, and then you'll learn about the requirements for using Hyper-V.

Virtual Machine Architecture

A *virtual machine* is a software entity that is designed to appear to an operating system as a real physical system. Like a physical system, a virtual machine has a CPU, RAM, one or more network adapters, and hard drives. However, for the virtual machine, these components are virtual not physical. You can see an overview of the virtual machine architecture in Figure 9-1.

The physical server that runs the virtualization software is typically referred to as the *host*, while each virtual machine is referred to as a *guest*. Multiple virtual machines can be created on the host. Each virtual machine requires its own operating system (OS), and each guest operating system is completely separate and isolated in each of the guest virtual machines. The guest operating system thinks it is running on a "real" system. After a guest OS has been loaded on the VM, applications are installed exactly as you

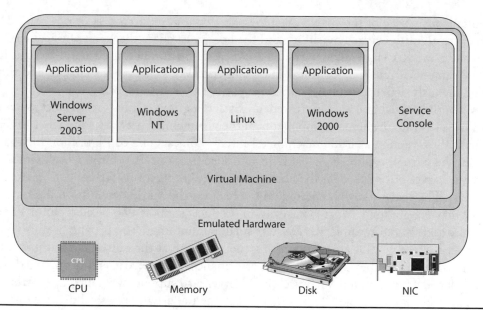

Figure 9-1   *Virtual machine overview*

would install them on a physical system. For example, in Figure 9-1, you can see that four different guest operating systems are simultaneously active. Each guest operating system is then running its own applications. If a failure occurs in one of the virtual machine guests, it will not affect the operation of the other virtual machines. The exact types of guest operating systems that are supported depend on the capabilities of the virtualization software.

Virtual machines can have one or more virtual CPUs. The actual number depends on the number of physical processor cores in the host server and the capabilities of the virtualization software. Microsoft's Hyper-V is capable of supporting guest virtual machines with up to four virtual CPUs per virtual machine.

NOTE

You cannot have more virtual CPUs in your virtual machines than you have physical processor cores in your host system. Likewise, you cannot allocate more RAM to a virtual machine than the amount of physical RAM in your host.

Another important point to understand is that the physical RAM on the host must be shared by all active guest virtual machines. For example, if the host system has 4GB of RAM, you could probably only run a maximum of three virtual machines simultaneously if all of the virtual machines were configured to use 1GB of RAM. This is because all of the virtual machines and the host must share the same physical RAM. Increasing the RAM available in the host increases the number of virtual machines that can be run concurrently. The limit to the number of VMs that can be created and run simultaneously depends primarily on the capacity of the host server.

When the virtual machine is created, it exists as a group of files on the host system's hard drive. While the actual components of the virtual machine vary somewhat for each virtualization vendor, a virtual machine essentially consists of a configuration file that defines the virtual machine's virtual hardware specifications. In addition, each virtual machine carves out a space on the host system's hard drive for its virtual hard drives (VHDs). The space actually required on the host for the VHD depends on the type of VHD that's configured. Most virtualization products support two basic types of VHDs: dynamic and fixed. Dynamic VHDs start small but automatically expand as more space is required. Fixed VHDs are created using their full size at the outset, but because they don't need to resize, they provide better performance. For scenarios requiring maximum performance, Hyper-V and VMware's ESX server also support what are called *raw* or *linked* VHDs, where the VHD is mapped to the underlying physical drive. Most production virtual machine installations use fixed VHDs. This is because dynamic hard drives incur a system performance penalty when they are dynamically expanded. Fixed VHDs avoid this performance hit, and they still retain the flexibility and portability offered by the VHD format.

No matter which type of hard drive you use, the space required on the host can be considerable—it is the same space that would be required if you were running on a physical system. A VHD requires a minimum of a 2–4GB for a basic installation up to hundreds of gigabytes for production server installation. The actual amount depends on the requirements of the applications and services running on the virtual machine.

Microsoft Hyper-V Architecture

Hyper-V is Microsoft's second-generation server virtualization platform. Hyper-V is Microsoft's first hypervisor-based virtualization platform, and it was introduced with Windows Server 2008. Hyper-V replaced Microsoft's older Virtual Server 2005 hosted virtualization product. Designed to compete directly with VMware's ESX Server, Microsoft's Hyper-V virtualization product uses an all-new microkernel-based hypervisor architecture. The older Virtual Server 2005 product used a hosted virtualization model, where the virtualization support was handled by virtualization management software that was installed on top of a host operating system. This type of virtualization is termed *hosted* because of the requirement for a host operating system. The new Hyper-V virtualization software runs directly on the system hardware with no intervening host operating system. This model is similar to the model used by

VMware's ESX server and XEN. It is termed *hypervisor–based virtualization* because the virtualization support is provided by a hypervisor that runs directly on the system hardware. There is no intervening host operating system. You can see an overview of the new Windows Server 2008 Hyper-V architecture in Figure 9-2.

The new Hyper-V architecture consists of the microkernel hypervisor that runs directly on the host server's hardware. In addition, Hyper-V requires two types of partitions: parent and child.

▶   **Parent partition**   All Hyper-V installations have one parent partition. The parent partition is used to manage the Hyper-V installation, and it is the only partition that has direct access to the physical hardware. The Windows Server Virtualization console runs from the parent partition. Device drivers used by the virtual machines running in the other child partitions reside in the parent partition. In addition, the parent partition is used to run threads supported by legacy hardware emulation virtual machines. These emulation-based virtual machines use a similar architecture as the virtual machines that would run under a hosted virtualization product like Virtual Server 2005.

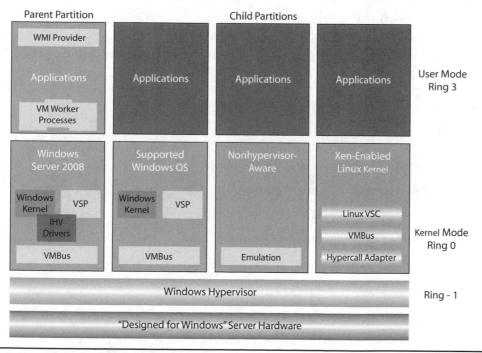

Figure 9-2   *Hyper-V Architecture*

▶ **Child partitions**   Hyper-V child partitions are where the guest virtual machines run. There are two types of virtual machines supported in Hyper-V's child partitions: high performance VMBus-based virtual machines or hosted emulation virtual machines. VMBus-enabled virtual machines have operating system drivers that can take advantage of the new VMBus architecture. The new VMBus architecture is essentially a high performance in-memory pipeline that connects Virtual Service Clients (VSCs) in the guests with the Virtual Service Provider (VSP) running in the parent partition in order to provide high performance access to physical host resources. VMBus-enabled guest operating systems virtual machines include Windows Server 2008, Windows Server 2003, Windows 7, the Vista business editions, and SUSE Linux. Future support for more VMBus-enabled Linux distributions is likely, as Microsoft has released the VMBus code as open source. Hosted emulation virtual machines provide support for guest operating systems that do not include support for the new VMBus architecture. This includes Windows 2000, Windows NT, and most Linux distributions. The virtual machines for these run as worker processes in the parent partition.

The Windows Server 2008 Hyper-V Role

Windows Server 2008 Hyper-V virtualization requires an x64-based system that has either the Intel-VT or AMD-V processor assisted virtualization support. In addition, the host system's CPU must have Data Execution Protection enabled (the Intel XD bit or the AMD NX bit).

Microsoft provides Hyper-V virtualization with the following versions of Windows Server 2008:

▶ Windows Server 2008 Standard Edition

▶ Windows Server 2008 R2 Standard Edition

▶ Windows Server 2008 Enterprise Edition

▶ Windows Server 2008 R2 Enterprise Edition

▶ Windows Server 2008 Datacenter Edition

▶ Windows Server 2008 Datacenter Edition

▶ Windows HPC Server 2008

The Windows Server 2008 Standard and Windows Server 2008 R2 Standard editions allow one additional virtual instance with no addition licensing costs. The Windows Server 2008 Enterprise and Windows Server 2008 R2 Enterprise editions allow up to four virtual Windows instances with no additional licensing costs. The Windows Server 2008 Datacenter and Windows Server 2008 R2 Datacenter editions allow an unlimited number of virtual Windows instances with no additional licensing costs. Hyper-V virtualization can be used with either the full Windows Server 2008 installation, or it can be used with a minimal Server Core installation for any of the Windows Server 2008 editions.

Regarding high availability it's notable that Windows Server 2008 R2 supports Live Migration and Quick Migration. The base Windows Server 2008 product does not support Live Migration. It only supports Quick Migration. More information about Live Migration and Quick Migration is presented later in this chapter. You can find more information about Windows Server 2008 R2's Hyper-V role and Microsoft's Hyper-V Server 2008 R2 at http://www.microsoft.com/windowsserver2008/en/us/default.aspx.

Hyper-V Server 2008

In addition to including Hyper-V as an option in the Windows Server 2008 operating system, Microsoft also provides the following free stand-alone Hyper-V products:

▶ Hyper-V 2008 Server

▶ Hyper-V 2008 R2 Server

The stand-alone Hyper-V Server products are based on the same hypervisor as the one used in Windows Server 2008, and they also use a minimal version of the Windows Server 2008 operating system. The virtualization features that are supported are similar to those found in Windows Server 2008 Hyper-V role but there are differences. In terms of high availability, it's notable that Hyper-V Server 2008 R2 supports Live Migration and Quick Migration. The original Hyper-V Server 2008 product does not support Live Migration and only supports Quick Migration. You can find more information about Hyper-V Server 2008 and Hyper-V Server 2008 R2 at http://www.microsoft.com/hyper-v-server/en/us/default.aspx.

High Availability and Virtualization

Virtualization brings a number of benefits to the IT administrator. Some of the main benefits stem from the fact that the virtual machine's file-based storage abstract is from the underlying hardware platform. This lets you more rapidly deploy a new server as well as providing options for disaster recovery that aren't available for standard physical machines. Windows Server 2008 and Windows Server 2008 R2 provide a Quick

Migration feature that can be used to save and restart a virtual machine on different Hyper-V hosts. In addition, Windows Server 2008 R2's new Live Migration feature can be used to move virtual machines between Hyper-V hosts with no downtime. Quick Migration and Live Migration reduce planned downtime and lay the foundation for a dynamic IT infrastructure.

Deployment and Disaster Recovery

A couple of the main ways that virtualization can help availability is by speeding deployment of servers and the recovery of servers after a system failure. Because there is no need for any equipment procurement process and no need for bare metal installations, virtual machines can be deployed very rapidly to meet user demands. Virtual machines can make use of template or sysprep installation files, and deployment of a virtual machine can be as quick as the time it takes to copy the virtual machine files to the appropriate host server. In most cases, new virtual machines can be deployed in a few minutes rather than in the days or weeks it could take to deploy physical servers.

Disaster recovery has similar benefits. With virtualization there's no need to keep a cold, spare computer that you can use in case of hardware failure—even if your organization can afford keeping spare computer systems around. With virtualization you can back up your active virtual machine files using Volume Shadow Copy Service (VSS) or a storage snapshot technology, and then use Distributed File Services or a third-party replication product to automatically keep updated copies of your virtual machine files in a remote location. Then if the server in the location fails or worse, if there's a site-level failure, the offsite copies of the virtual machine files can be brought online in a matter of minutes.

Windows Failover Clustering and Virtualization

You can use Windows failover clustering to protect your virtualized infrastructure both at the server level and at the virtual machine level. You can see an overview of using failover clustering and virtualization in Figure 9-3.

Exactly as it is used with physical servers, Windows failover clustering provides protection against unplanned downtime. Windows failover clustering can be used at the host level to protect the Windows Server 2008 Hyper-V physical system, which is responsible for running the virtual machines, or it can be used at the virtual machine guest level to protect individual virtual machines on that server. You can see illustrations of each scenario in Figure 9-3. Using failover clustering to protect individual virtual machines is shown on the left side of Figure 9-3. At the virtual machine level, the virtual machine is a node in a failover cluster. If that virtual machine node fails, then the services or applications running on that virtual machine node will be assumed by

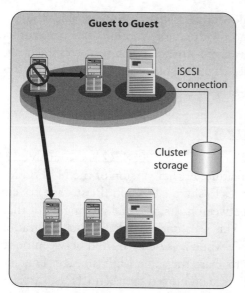 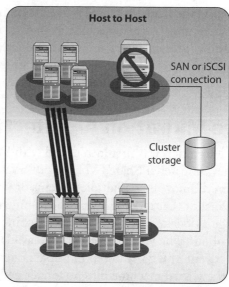

Figure 9-3   *Windows Failover Clustering and virtualization*

another virtual machine node in the cluster. The other virtual machine node could be on the same Hyper-V server, or it could be running on another Hyper-V server.

When Windows failover clustering protects the physical Hyper-V host, a failure at the host level will cause another physical Hyper-V node in the cluster to take over running all the virtual machines that were previously running on the failed node.

Quick Migration

Quick Migration is a high-availability feature that was introduced with the original release of Windows Server 2008 Hyper-V. Quick Migration enables the movement of Hyper-V virtual machines between Hyper-V hosts with minimal downtime. With Quick Migration a Hyper-V virtual machine's state is saved, and then its configuration and VHD files are moved to a new LUN, and the virtual machine's state is restored. The total downtime is typically a minute or so, depending on the speed on the network, the storage subsystem, and the size of the memory used in the virtual machine.

Live Migration

Live Migration is the newest high-availability option for Microsoft Hyper-V virtualization installations. Live Migration was first introduced with Windows Server 2008 R2, and it protects the virtual machine from planned downtime. Live Migration enables you to move a Hyper-V virtual machine to another host with no interruption of services and no downtime. This enables you to perform hardware or software maintenance on the host without any downtime for the end users of the virtual machines that are running on those hosts. More information about Live Migration is presented in the next section.

Live Migration Architecture

Live Migration was first introduced with Windows Server 2008 R2 and is enabled by the new Clustered Shared Volumes (CSV) feature. Earlier version of the NTFS file system did not allow multiple systems or nodes to share LUNs on the storage system. This meant that moving a virtual machine between hosts required moving all of the storage associated with the virtual machine. This is essentially what Quick Migration is all about. The virtual machine is unavailable while it is being moved between nodes. The advent of CSV allowed multiple nodes to share the same LUN storage. This meant that the virtual machine files no longer needed to be moved between LUNs. Instead the only thing that needed to be moved was the virtual machine's state. You can see an overview of Live Migration in Figure 9-4.

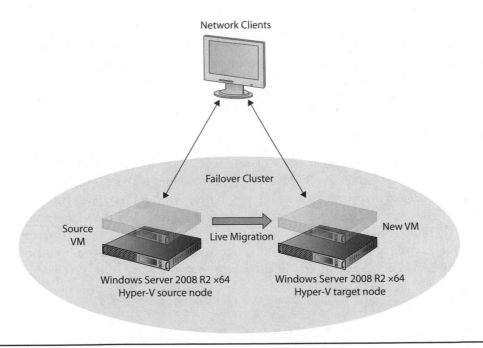

Figure 9-4   *Live Migration*

When you initiate a Live Migration, the source virtual machine starts a TCP connection to the target node. Then a skeleton virtual machine is created on the target node. Next, the virtual machine configuration data is send from the source node to the target node. Then the virtual machine's state is copied from the source node to the target node. Then as changes occur in the source virtual machine, deltas of the memory changes are sent from the source node to the target node. Live Migration will copy the memory changes in the source virtual machine to the target virtual machine until the target is the same as the source or the process has completed a predefined number of iterations. The source virtual machine remains available all the time this is occurring. When the memory copy process has completed, ownership of the storage is transferred to the target host. At this point the target host has the updated storage for the virtual machine and has control of the storage, so the target virtual machine is resumed, and the source virtual machine is shut down.

Requirements for Live Migration

To implement Live Migration, you must have the following components:

▶ **Two x64 server systems that are virtualization enabled and have compatible processors**   You need a minimum of two physical hosts to implement Live Migration. These hosts must have x64 processors. The processors can be either AMD or Intel, but they must be from the same manufacturer and family. They must have either AMD-V or Intel-VT virtualization support. You cannot mix AMD and Intel processors on hosts that will participate in Live Migration.

▶ **Three network adapters are recommended for each node**   One adapter is used to connect the Windows servers to shared storage. Another adapter is used to connect to the cluster. Another optional adapter is used to connect the cluster nodes for Live Migration.

▶ **One-gigabyte networking infrastructure**   Network connections between the nodes as well as any iSCSI network connections are recommended to be 1GB.

▶ **Windows Server 2008 R2 x64 Enterprise Edition or Datacenter Edition**   All hosts using Live Migration must be running Windows Server 2008 R2. The edition must have the Hyper-V role installed and the Failover Clustering feature.

▶ **Windows failover clustering**   A Windows failover cluster must be created, and the cluster must use the new CSV storage.

▶ **Shared storage infrastructure**   Both hosts must be connected to SAN infrastructure. The SAN can be either a Fibre Channel or an iSCSI SAN. If the SAN is an iSCSI SAN, it must implement the iSCSI-3 specifications that allow for persistent connections.

Summary

In this chapter, you learned the basics of server virtualization and saw some of the main ways the virtualization can be used to improve business continuity. In the first section of this chapter, you learned how virtual machines are created and the basics of Microsoft's Hyper-V virtualization technology. In the second section, you saw the primary ways that virtualization can provide improved availability for your IT resources. Finally, you learned how Live Migration works and the requirements for implementing Live Migration.

In the next chapter, you'll see how to configure Windows Server 2008 R2 to support Hyper-V and Live Migration.

Chapter 10

Configuring Hyper-V Live Migration

In This Chapter

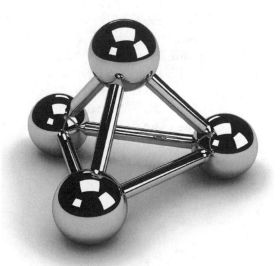

In the last chapter, you got a overview of how virtualization can contribute to high availability. In addition, you saw how Live Migration can address the question on planned downtime as well as getting an overview of the Live Migration requirements and architecture. In this chapter, you'll see how to set up a Live Migration environment for SQL Server using Windows Server 2008 R2 and Hyper-V R2. To take advantage of Live Migration, you need to utilize shared storage and Windows Server 2008 Failover Clustering. In this chapter, you'll learn about setting up a basic shared storage environment using an iSCSI SAN as well as Windows Server 2008 Failover Clustering. These requirements and this setup are similar to the setup used in Chapter 3. However, there are differences. In this chapter, you'll also see how to set up the Windows Server 2008 Hyper-V role as well how to configure the failover clustering to use the new Cluster Shared Volumes (CSV) that's required for Live Migration.

Configuring Windows Server 2008 Shared Storage

Using shared storage is a requirement for Windows failover clustering and Live Migration. In addition, Live Migration requires the Windows failover clustering. Shared storage is provided either by a Fibre Channel SAN or an iSCSI SAN and can be accessed by all of the nodes in the cluster. In this section, you'll see a sample Windows Server 2008 iSCSI Initiator connection to an iSCSI storage area network (SAN) that will provide the shared storage for Live Migration.

The iSCSI Connection

The iSCSI SAN connection needs to be on a completely separate network from your local client network. For best performance, network adapters used for the iSCSI network should run at a minimum of 1GB. For Live Migration, Microsoft also recommends the use of an additional network connection for node-to-node connectivity that is separate from both the client network and the SAN network. This example in this chapter will use two network connections.

The exact configuration steps of the SAN itself are highly dependent on each different vendor's hardware. The examples in this chapter were built using a LeftHand Networks SAS Starter SAN. The LeftHand Network Starter SAN is an iSCSI SAN. The example in this chapter uses two different SAN volumes:

▶ **Quorum** 100MB
▶ **VMs** 1TB

The quorum drive is required by the failover cluster. The VMs volumes will be used to store virtual machine VHD files. As you saw in Chapter 9, these files are accessed by multiple nodes in the cluster.

Configuring the Windows Server 2008 iSCSI Initiator

You need to configure the iSCSI Initiator on each of the Windows Server 2008 nodes. To configure the iSCSI Initiator, use the Start | Administrative Tools | iSCSI Initiator option. If you've never run the iSCSI Initiator option before, you'll see two prompts. The first prompt will alert you that the iSCSI service is not running. The second will ask you about unblocking the Windows Firewall. You will almost always want the iSCSI Initiator Service to automatically start when you start the computer. You can always change this option by manually configuring the iSCSI service using the Administrative Tools | Services option. The second prompt will ask you if you want to unblock the Microsoft iSCSI service so that it can communicate across the Windows Firewall. Again, you'll usually want to answer Yes. You can also manually configure this setting by taking the Control Panel | Windows Firewall option and unblocking port 3260. After you respond to these two prompts, the iSCSI Initiator will be displayed as you can see in Figure 10-1.

NOTE

Before connecting to the SAN, you may need to configure the SAN with the iSCSI Initiator name. The iSCSI Initiator Name can be found on the iSCSI Initiator's Configuration tab. The example presented here uses the name iqn.1991-05.com.microsoft:ws08r2-s1.contoso.com. The name used in your configuration will be different, depending on the system and domain names that are in use.

To configure the iSCSI Initiator to connect to your iSCSI SAN, click the Discovery tab and then click Discover Portal. This will display the Add Target Portal dialog box that you can see in Figure 10-2.

Using the Discover Target Portal dialog box, enter the IP address used by the SAN. In this example, the SAN address is 192.168.0.1 and it is using the default port of 3260. After entering the IP address, click OK; the iSCSI Initiator will discover the storage resources on the SAN and list them on the iSCSI Initiator's Target tab. Next, select each of the discovered targets and click Connect. This will display the Connect To Target dialog box, which will resemble the one in Figure 10-3.

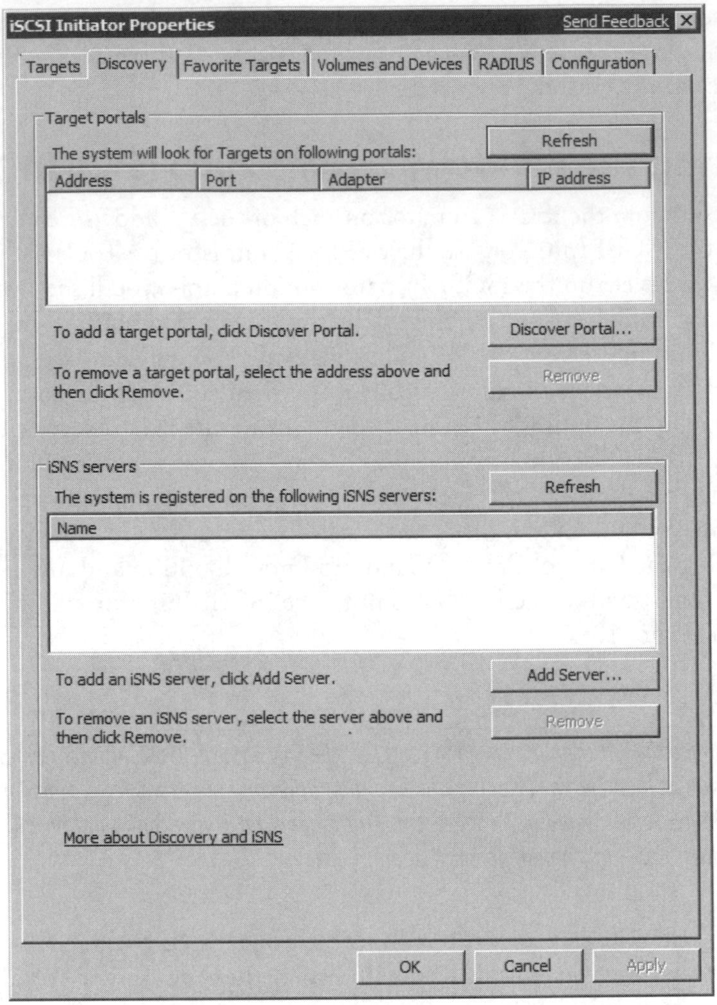

Figure 10-1 *Starting the iSCSI Initiator*

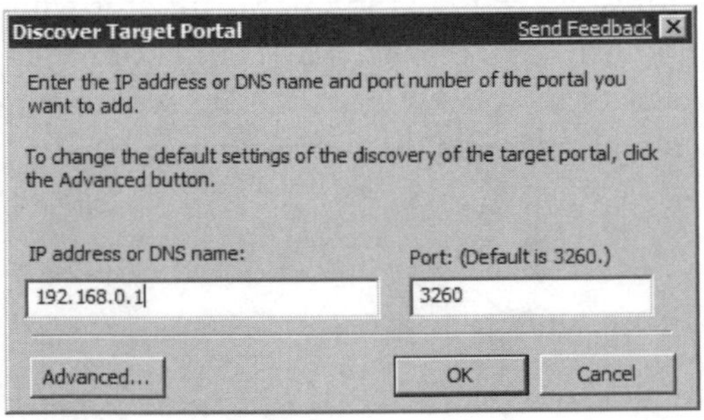

Figure 10-2 *iSCSI Initiator: Discover the Target Portal*

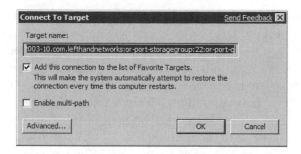

Figure 10-3   *iSCSI Initiator: Connect to Target*

The target name for each of the SAN resources will be listed in the Target Name field. Be sure that "Add this connection to the list of Favorite Targets" is checked. This will enable the Windows Server system to automatically connect to the storage when the system is started.

Before the storage can be used, you must initialize the volumes using Windows Server 2008's Disk Management. To start Disk Management, select Start | Administrative Tools | Server Manager. Then expand the Storage node and click Disk Management. This will display a screen like the one shown in Figure 10-4.

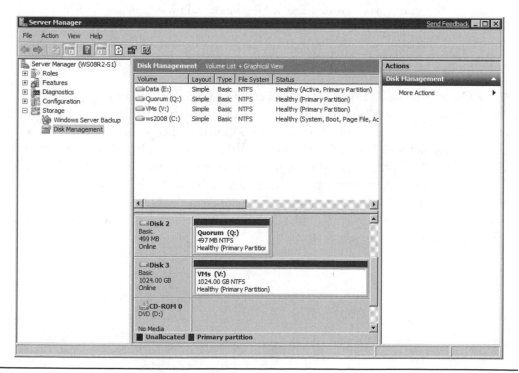

Figure 10-4   *Initializing iSCSI SAN storage using Disk Management*

In Figure 10-4, you can see the two iSCSI volumes shown as Disk 2 and Disk 3. Disk 2 has been assigned the drive letter Q and will be used as the failover cluster quorum. Disk 4 has been assigned the drive letter V and will be used for VHD storage. These drive letters do not have to be Q and V. You can choose other available drive letters. You assign drive letters by right-clicking each of the drives and selecting the Online option to bring the drives online. Then you can right-click the drive volume and select Change Drive Letter and Paths. The volumes must be formatted using the NTFS file system before you can use them.

After preparing the drives, be sure to bring them offline so that the Create Cluster Wizard can use them as storage. To bring the drives offline, right-click the disk portion and then select Offline from the context menu.

Adding the Hyper-V Role

After the shared storage has been configured, the next step to using Live Migration is to add the Hyper-V role and then the Failover Clustering feature. To add the Hyper-V role, open Server Manager, select the Roles node, and then click Add Roles to display the Select Server Roles window. In the Roles list, put a check next to the Hyper-V as you can see in Figure 10-5.

Any existing roles will be displayed with a gray check mark. Multiple roles can be installed on the same server. In this case a File Server role was previously installed. However, the File Server role is not required by Hyper-V or Live Migration.

Clicking Next displays a Hyper-V dialog box that displays a few informational links. Clicking Next again displays the Create Virtual Networks dialog box, which you can see in Figure 10-6.

The Create Virtual Network dialog box enables you to specify how Hyper-V's virtual networking capabilities will be connected to the network adapters present in the Hyper-V host server. Filling out this screen is optional at this point. You can always create a virtual network later using the Hyper-V administrator. In this example the host has two network adapters. One is being used for the connection to the iSCSI SAN. The other is used for client connectivity on the local area network. In Figure 10-6 you can see that the Local Area Connection network adapter on the host has been selected for use as a virtual external network. This will enable Hyper-V virtual machines to connect to the external business network.

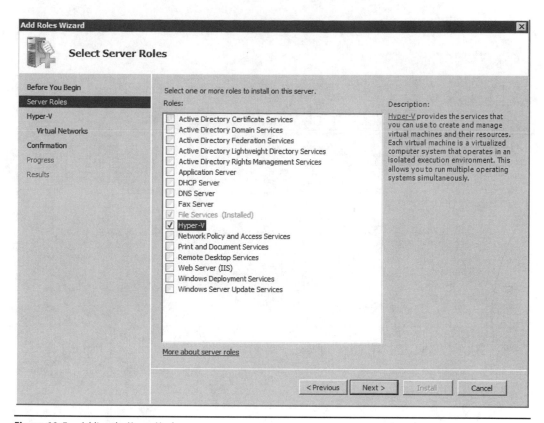

Figure 10-5 *Adding the Hyper-V role*

NOTE

In a production server consolidation environment, you would typically use many more host network adapters. Ideally, a one-to-one ratio of host NICs per VM would give your VMs the best performance, but you can also use less, depending on your network utilization requirements. In addition, a best practice is to reserve one host NIC for Hyper-V management.

After optionally creating the virtual network, clicking Next will install Hyper-V support. After the Hyper-V role has been installed on the system, you'll be prompted to reboot, as you can see in Figure 10-7.

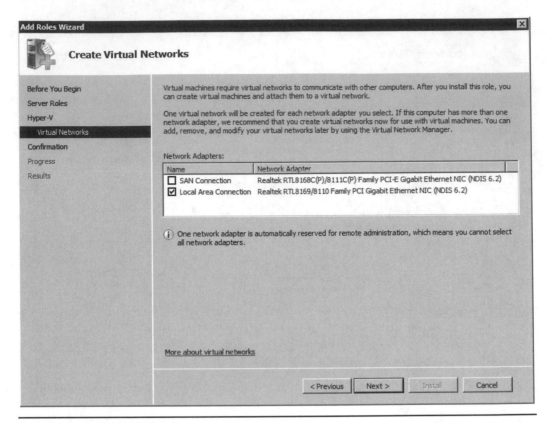

Figure 10-6 *Create Virtual Networks*

Installing the hyper-role requires that you reboot the system to allow the Hyper-V hypervisor to be installed and used. Clicking Next will reboot the system. After the system has restarted you'll see the Installation Results dialog box, shown in Figure 10-8.

At this point, the Hyper-V support is installed and available on the first node. You can create and manage virtual machines using the Hyper-V Manager, available from

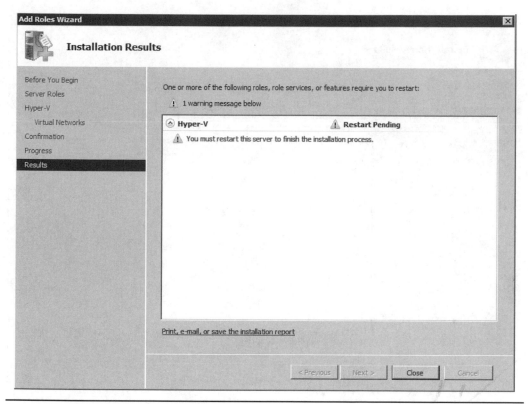

Figure 10-7   *Hyper-V Installation Results: Reboot*

the Administrative Tools menu. The Hyper-V role will also need to be installed on the other nodes in the cluster. For the example in this chapter, it will also be installed on another server, named WS08R2-S2.

Installing Hyper-V on both nodes will enable you to create virtual machines on both servers. However, you will not be able to use Live Migration until you have installed and configured Window Server 2008 R2 Failover Clustering.

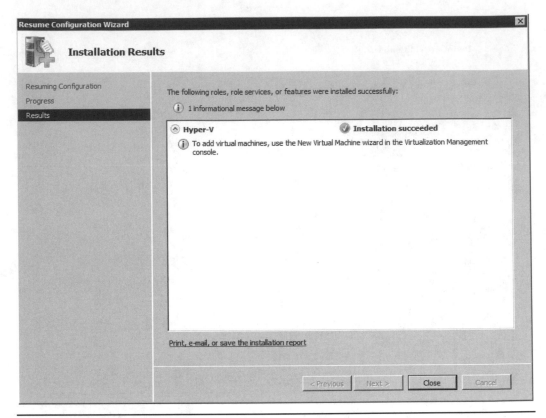

Figure 10-8 *Hyper-V Installation Results: Resume After Reboot*

Adding the Failover Clustering Feature

After adding the Hyper-V role, the next step is to add the Windows Server 2008 implements failover clustering feature. To add the Failover Clustering feature to Windows Server 2008, run Server Manager and select the Start | Administrative Tools | Server Manager option. Click the Features node in the Server Manager pane shown on the left side of the screen. This will display the Features Summary window, as you can see in Figure 10-9.

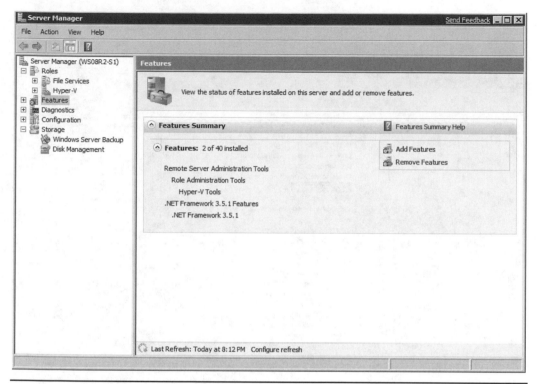

Figure 10-9 *Adding a feature using Server Manager*

The Features Summary window shows the currently installed features. To add the Failover Clustering feature, click the Add Features link shown on the right side of the Features Summary screen you can see in Figure 10-9. This will display the Select Features window, like the one you can see in Figure 10-10.

Scroll through the list of features shown in the Select Features window until you see Failover Clustering. To add the Failover Clustering feature, check the box in front of Failover Clustering and then click Next. This will display the Confirm Installation Selections screen, which you can see displayed in Figure 10-11.

The Confirm Installation Selections dialog box confirms that you have elected to install the Failover Clustering feature. To proceed with the installation, click Install. This will take a couple of minutes as the wizard copies the binary files that provide

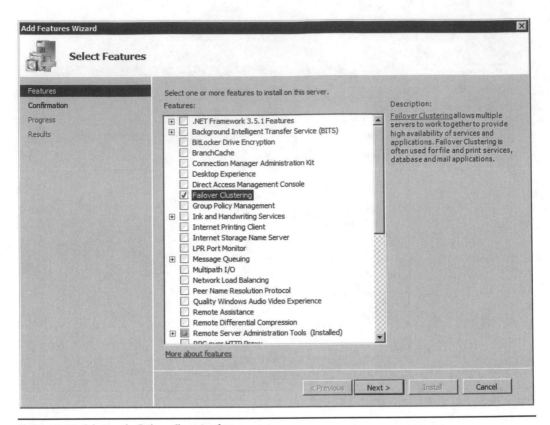

Figure 10-10 *Selecting the Failover Clustering feature*

failover clustering support onto the Windows Server system. Windows Server 2008 installs all of the binaries required for all of the roles and features as a part of the initial Windows Server installation. There's no need to find the original installation media. After the files required for failover clustering have been installed on the system, the Installation Results dialog box shown in Figure 10-12 will be displayed.

The Installation Results screen reports the success of failure of the installation. If the feature installation failed for some reason, you will see a red *x* along with the message indicating the feature installation failed. If the installation of the Failover Clustering

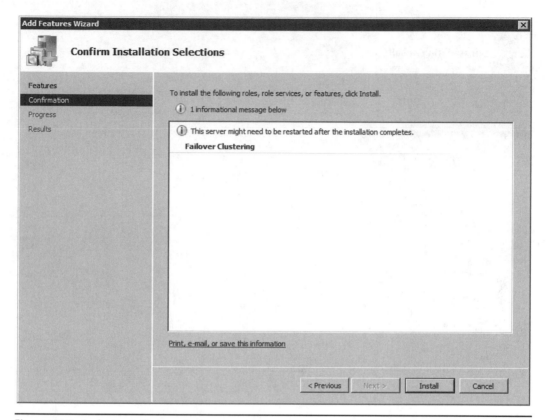

Figure 10-11 *Confirming the feature selection*

feature succeeded, you will see a green check mark followed by an "Installation succeeded" message like the one shown in Figure 10-12.

Clicking Close ends the Add Features Wizard, and the Server Manager's Feature Summary screen will be displayed. No reboot will be needed. After installing the Failover Clustering feature, you'll see the feature listing in the Server Manager Features Summary.

At this point, the basic support for failover clustering has been added to the first node in the Live Migration cluster. These same steps need to be performed for all of the servers that will participate in the Live Migration cluster.

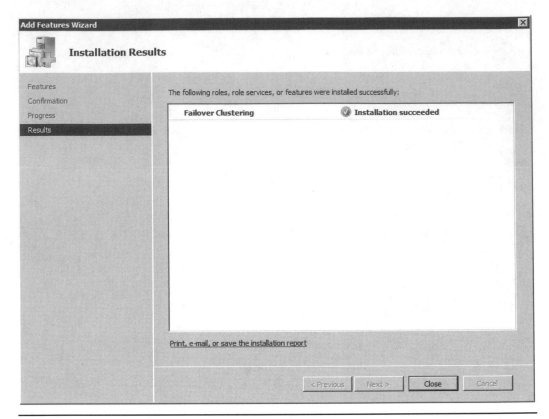

Figure 10-12 *Feature installation results*

Configuring Failover Clustering for Live Migration

After the Failover Clustering feature has been added to all of the nodes in the cluster, the next step is to configure failover clustering on the first cluster node. To configure failover clustering, you need to use the Failover Clustering Wizard.

Running the Failover Cluster Manager

Start the Windows Server 2008's Failover Clustering Wizard using the Start | All Programs | Administrative Tools | Failover Cluster Manager menu option. This will display the Failover Clustering Manager console. Before jumping straight into configuring the cluster, the first task that you should perform is to validate the cluster configuration.

Validate the Cluster Configuration

To validate the Windows failover clustering configuration, start the Failover Cluster Manager and then select the Validate A Configuration link that you can see in Figure 10-13.

Clicking the Validate a Configuration link starts the Validate a Configuration Wizard. The validation wizard must be run before creating a cluster; its purpose is to verify that all of the components in the cluster will work with Windows Server 2008 Failover Clustering. You can see the Select Servers or a Cluster dialog box of the Validate a Configuration Wizard displayed in Figure 10-14.

You can use the Validate a Configuration Wizard to test an existing cluster for compatibility with Windows Server 2008 Failover Clustering. To test the cluster nodes, enter each of the node names. In Figure 10-14 you can see that the first cluster node is named WS08R2-S1 and the second is named WS08R2-S2. Both nodes are part of the contoso.com domain. If your cluster has more than two nodes, you can enter the names of the other cluster nodes here. To begin the cluster configuration validation tests, click Next to display the Testing Options dialog box, which you can see in Figure 10-15.

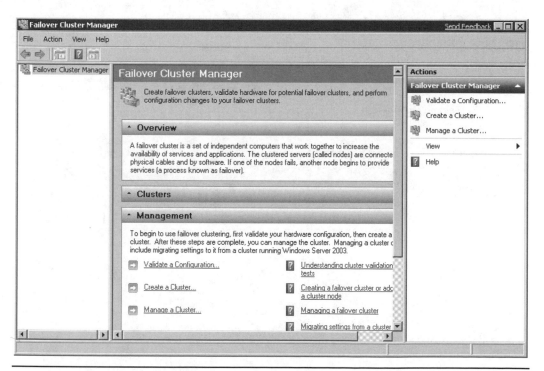

Figure 10-13 *Validating the cluster configuration*

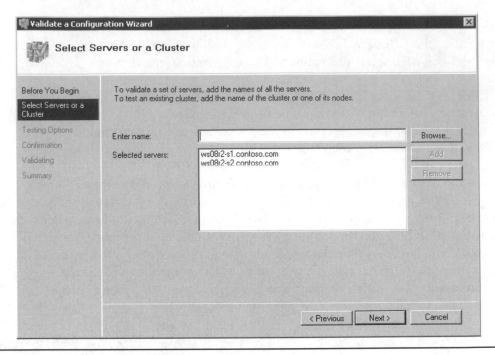

Figure 10-14 *Selecting the servers to validate*

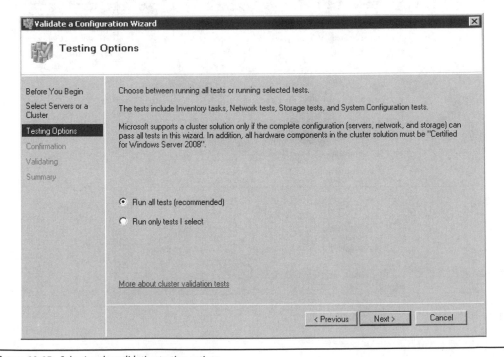

Figure 10-15 *Selecting the validation testing options*

The Testing Options screen lets you select the validation tests that you want to run. You can choose to run the entire battery of validation tests, or you can selectively run just the tests you choose. If this is a new failover cluster or if you are adding a new node to an existing cluster, then you should run all of the tests. Clicking Next displays the Confirmation dialog box, which you can see in Figure 10-16.

The Confirmation dialog box allows to you to verify the server nodes that the validation tests will be run on and the tests that will be run. Clicking Next runs the validation tests. The validation tests take several minutes, and the progress is displayed in the Validating dialog box. When the tests have completed, you'll see a Summary screen like the one shown in Figure 10-17.

The Summary dialog box shows the results of the set of failover cluster validation tests. You can scroll through the list to see the results for the tests that were run, or you can click View Report to display the results in the browser. You can find more information about each of the validation tests and its results by clicking the links next to each test. All the tests that are passed are marked with a green check mark. If a given test isn't passed, it's marked with a red *x*. Any warnings are marked with a yellow triangle. Clicking Finish ends the Validate a Configuration Wizard and returns you to the Failover Cluster Manager.

After the cluster nodes have been validated to support the Failover Clustering Feature, you can create the cluster.

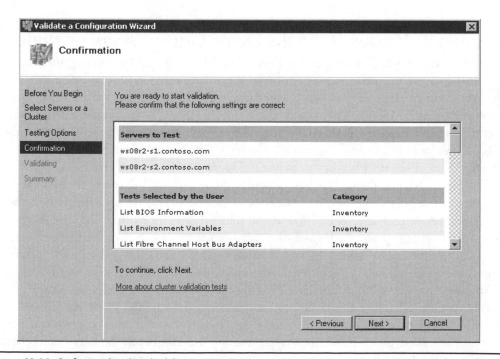

Figure 10-16 *Confirming the selected validation test options*

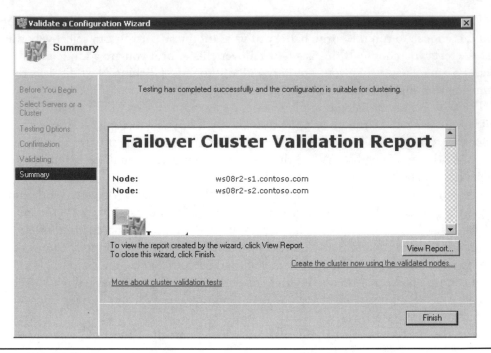

Figure 10-17 *Validation test results summary*

Creating the Cluster Using the Create Cluster Wizard on Node 1

To create the Failover Cluster open the Failover Cluster Manager by selecting the Start | Administrative Tools | Failover Cluster Manager menu option. This will display that Failover Cluster Manager that you saw earlier, in Figure 10-13. To create a new cluster, select the Create a Cluster link. This will start the Create Cluster Wizard. If this is the first time you've run the wizard, you'll see a Before You Begin dialog box that essentially tells you you're about to begin creating a cluster. Click Next to display the Create Cluster Wizard screen, which you can see in Figure 10-18.

The Select Servers dialog box lets you enter the names of the servers that will act as nodes in the failover cluster. You can either enter the server names directly into the Enter Server Name box or click Browse and select the server names using the Active Directory find dialog box. In Figure 10-18 you can see that the cluster will be created using servers named WS08R2-S1 and WS08R2-S2. Clicking Next displays the Access Point for Administering the Cluster dialog box, which you can see in Figure 10-19.

You use the Access Point for Administering the Cluster dialog box to name the cluster. In Figure 10-19 you can see that the cluster will be named WS08R2-CL01. Networked clients will use this name to connect to the cluster. The IP address must be manually assigned, and it should be unique and on same subnet as the networked clients. Clicking Next displays the Confirmation screen that you can see in Figure 10-20.

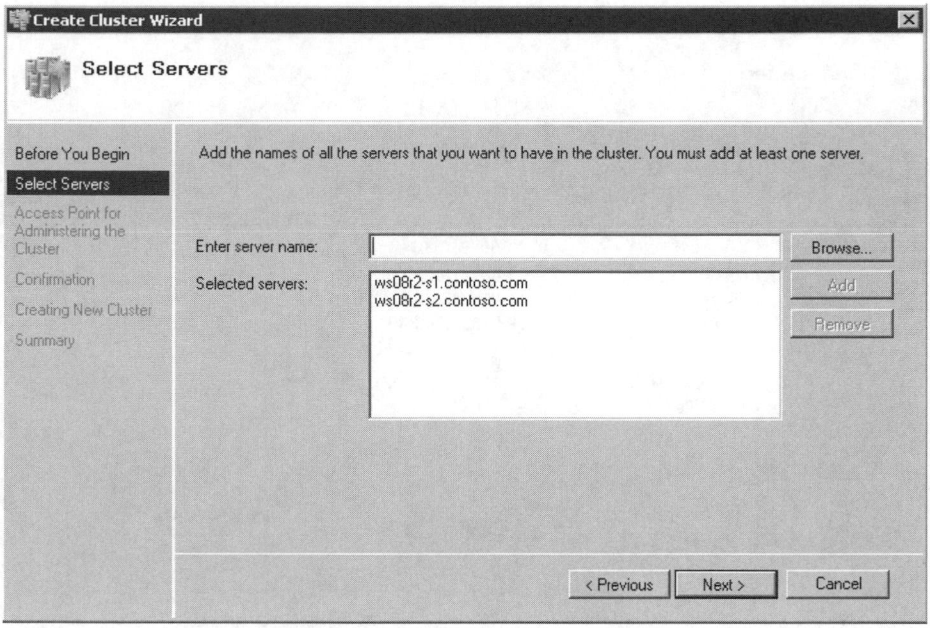

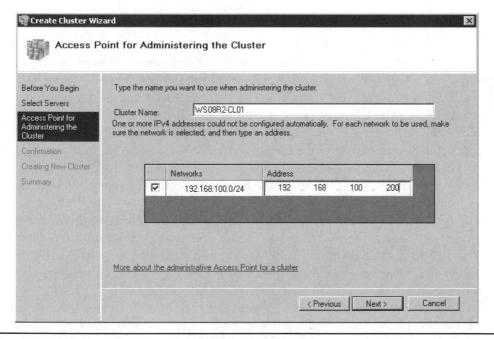

Figure 10-18 *Create Cluster Wizard: Selecting Servers*

Figure 10-19 *Create Cluster Wizard: Access Point for Administering the Cluster*

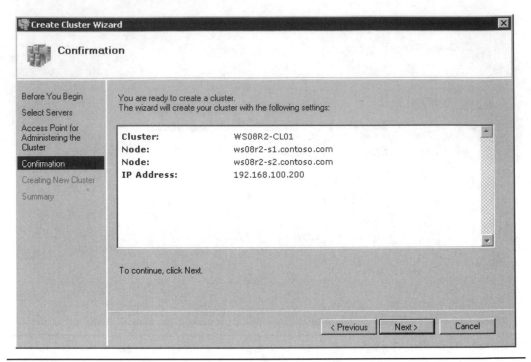

Figure 10-20 *Create Cluster Wizard: Confirmation*

The Confirmation screen presents a summary of the failover cluster configuration options that have been selected to this point. If you need to make changes to the values shown on the Confirmation dialog box, you can use the Previous button to page back through the previous wizard screens. Clicking Next will begin the cluster creation process. While Create Cluster Wizard is creating the cluster, the Creating New Cluster dialog box will be displayed. The process of creating a new failover cluster normally takes a couple of minutes. After the Create Cluster Wizard has successfully created the cluster, you'll see a Summary screen like the one shown in Figure 10-21.

The Create Cluster Wizard displays the Summary screen after the cluster has been successfully created.

While the Cluster Configuration Wizard does a great job of setting up the required services on all of the cluster nodes, it doesn't always select the correct quorum drive to use. The Create Cluster Wizard often selects the first shared drive available, and that's not always the drive that you want to use as the quorum. For more information about the cluster quorum drive, you can refer back to Chapter 2.

To change the quorum drive, you'll need to start the Failover Cluster Manager using Start | Administrative Tools | Failover Cluster Manager. This will start the Failover Cluster Manager, which you can see in Figure 10-22.

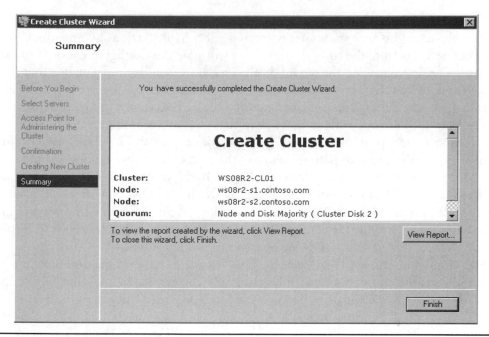

Figure 10-21 *Create Cluster Wizard: Summary*

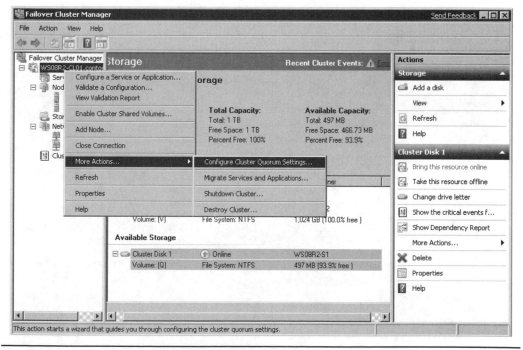

Figure 10-22 *Starting the Configure Cluster Quorum Wizard*

To use the Failover Cluster Manager to change the quorum drive used by your new failover cluster, right-click the cluster name and select More Actions | Configure Cluster Quorum Settings from the context menu. This will start the Configure Cluster Quorum Wizard. The first screen on the wizard displays a Before You Begin dialog box that basically warns you that you are about to reconfigure the cluster's quorum drive. Clicking Next displays the Select Quorum Configuration dialog box, shown in Figure 10-23.

The Select Quorum Configuration screen that you can see in Figure 10-23 allows you to choose the type of quorum used by your failover cluster. The Configure Quorum Configuration Wizard automatically chooses the type of quorum that best fits the number of nodes that are in the cluster. In Figure 10-23 you can see that the Configure Cluster Quorum Wizard recommends using the Node and Disk Majority cluster for a two-node cluster. (Chapter 2 describes the purpose of the different quorum types in more detail.) To continue the configuration of the cluster quorum, click Next to display the Configure Storage Witness dialog box, shown in Figure 10-24.

The Configure Storage Witness dialog box allows you to select the disk that you want to use as the cluster quorum. In Figure 10-24 you can see that Cluster Disk 1 has been selected. This was the drive that was previously assigned the letter Q. Clicking Next displays the Confirmation window. Clicking Next again reconfigures the cluster's quorum drive. When the configuration is complete, you'll see a Summary screen like the one shown in Figure 10-25.

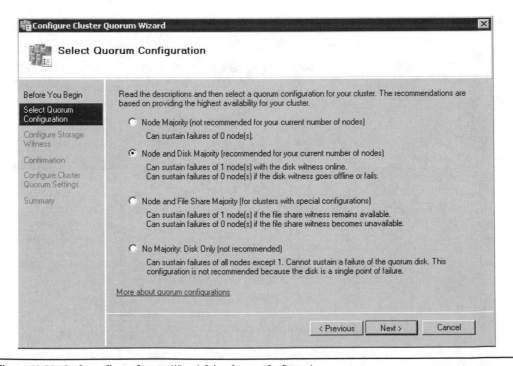

Figure 10-23 *Configure Cluster Quorum Wizard: Select Quorum Configuration*

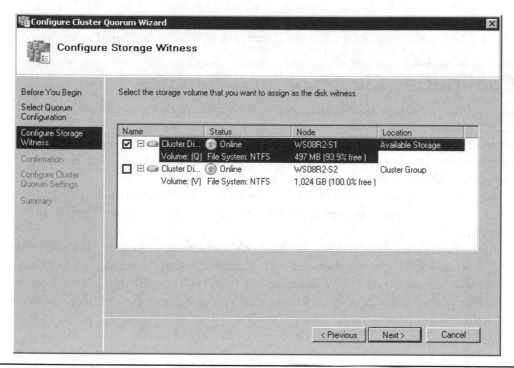

Figure 10-24 *Configure Cluster Quorum Wizard: Configure Storage Witness*

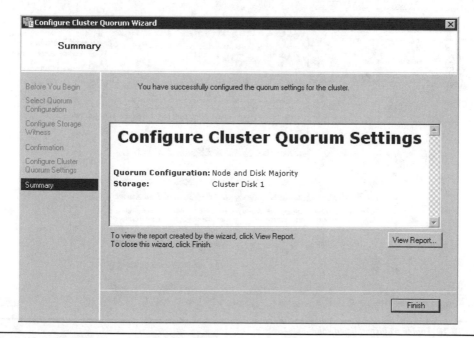

Figure 10-25 *Configure Cluster Quorum Wizard: Summary*

At this point the Windows Server 2008 failover cluster has been set up on both nodes. The next step is configuring the cluster to support cluster shared volumes.

Configuring Cluster Shared Volumes

Cluster Shared Volumes (CSV) help enable Live Migration. CSVs are a new feature in Windows Server 2008 R2; they essentially allow multiple virtual machines to have shared ownership of the same storage. This essentially allows two different virtual machines to have access to the same virtual hard disk (VHD) files stored in a CSV. More information about CSV can be found in Chapter 9.

To enable your cluster to use CSV, use the Start | Administrative Tools | Failover Cluster Manager option to start the Failover Cluster Manager, as you can see in Figure 10-26.

After the Failover Cluster Manager has been started, right-click the cluster that you want to enable CSVs on and then select the Enable Cluster Shared Volumes option, as you can also see in Figure 10-26. Selecting the Enable Cluster Shared Volumes option will initially display the Enable Cluster Shared Volumes dialog box, which you can see in Figure 10-27.

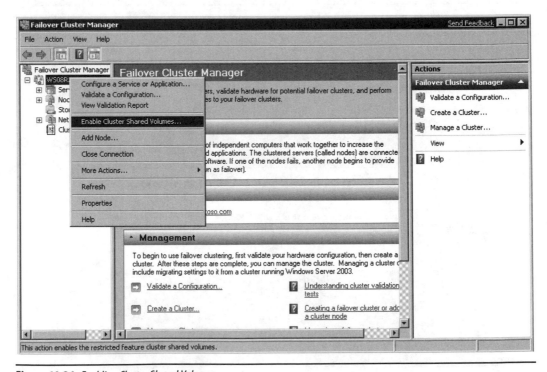

Figure 10-26 *Enabling Cluster Shared Volumes*

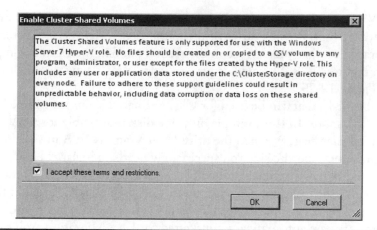

Figure 10-27 *Enable Cluster Shared Volumes*

The Enable Cluster Shared Volumes dialog box basically warns you that the CSV feature is only intended for use with Windows Server 2008 R2 Hyper-V virtual machines and should not be used for other purposes. To continue, check the "I accept these terms and restrictions" box and then click OK. This will add Cluster Shared Volumes support to the cluster and the Failover Cluster Manager will be displayed as you see in Figure 10-28.

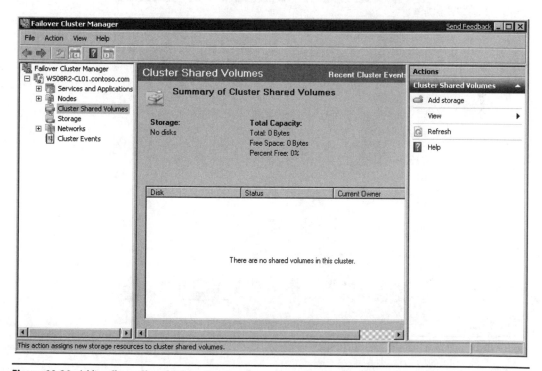

Figure 10-28 *Adding Cluster Shared Volume Storage*

After CSV support has been added to the cluster, the next step is add storage to the CSV. This storage must be previously visible to the cluster. To add CSV storage, click the Add Storage link that you can see in the Action pane in the right-hand portion of the screen in Figure 10-28. This will display an Add Storage window like the one that is shown in Figure 10-29.

The available disks that can be used for Cluster Shared Volumes will be listed in the Add Storage dialog box. In this example only one disk is available for CSV use. This is Cluster Disk 2. It has been assigned the drive letter V and is 1TB in size. You can use different drive letters, and the size you specify only needs to be large enough to hold the VHD files of the virtual machines that will take advantage of Live Migration. Check the box in front of the disk that you want to use and then click OK to add the cluster disk as CSV storage. At this point, the CSV storage has been added to the cluster.

Cluster networks are automatically configured for Live Migration. You can verify your cluster's networking configuration by opening the Failover Cluster Manager and then expanding the cluster node and then the Services and Applications node. Next, right-click the virtual machine and select Properties from the context menu. The networking configuration and preferred network adaptors for Live Migration are shown under the Network for Live Migration tab.

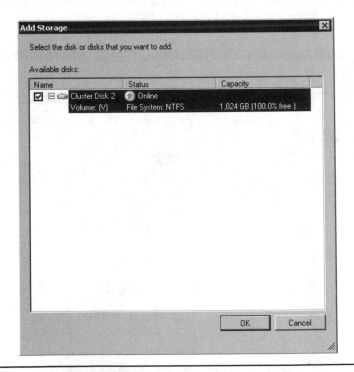

Figure 10-29 *Add Shared Cluster Volume Storage*

Summary

In this chapter, you went through the steps required to prepare your server infrastructure for Live Migration. In the first part of this chapter, you saw how to configure Windows Server 2008 R2 to use iSCSI storage. Then in the second section, you saw how to install the required Hyper-V Role and Failover Clustering feature to Windows Server 2008 R2. In the third part of this chapter, you saw how to configure a two-node failover cluster. Finally, in last part of this chapter, you saw how to add Cluster Shared Volumes support to the failover cluster. You can find more information about configuring Windows Server failover clusters for Live Migration at http://technet.microsoft.com/en-us/library/dd446679(WS.10).aspx.

In the next chapter, you'll see how to create a SQL Server virtual machine that uses this cluster for Live Migration.

Chapter 11

Configuring SQL Server with Hyper-V Live Migration

In This Chapter

- ► **Creating a Hyper-V VM with Live Migration**
- ► **Installing Windows Server 2008 on the VM**
- ► **Installing SQL Server 2008 on the VM**
- ► **Configuring the SQL Server VM for Live Migration**

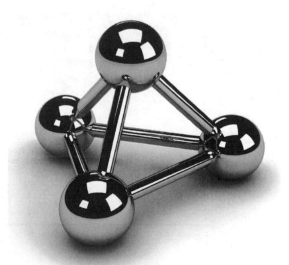

I n the last chapter, you saw how to set up Windows Server 2008 R2 to support Live Migration. In this chapter, you'll see how to create and configure a new Hyper-V virtual machine that can take advantage of Windows Server 2008 R2's Cluster Shared Volumes (CSV) and Live Migration. In the first part of this chapter, you'll see how to create and configure the Hyper-V virtual machine. Next, you'll see how to install the Windows Server 2008 operating system on the virtual machine. In the third part of the chapter, you'll see how to install SQL Server 2008 on the virtual machine. Finally, in the last part of this chapter, you'll see how to enable Live Migration for the SQL Server virtual machine.

Creating a Hyper-V VM with Live Migration

In Chapter 10, you saw how to install the Hyper-V role on the Windows Server 2008 R2 host. In this section, you'll see how to use the Hyper-V Manager to create a new virtual machine that is capable of Live Migration.

To create a new Hyper-V virtual machine, open the Hyper-V Manager using the Start | Administrative Tools | Hyper-V Manager option. This will start the Hyper-V Manager, which you can see in Figure 11-1.

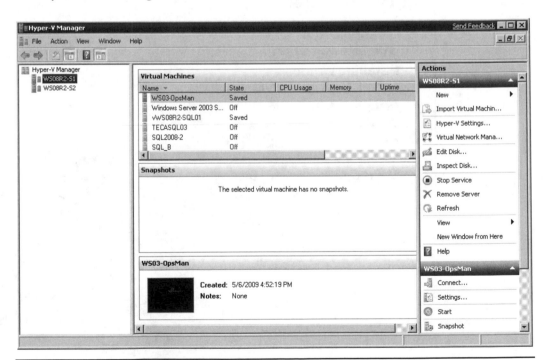

Figure 11-1   *Creating a new virtual machine*

To create a new Hyper-V virtual machine, select the New link in the Hyper-V Manager's Action pane. This will start the New Virtual Machine Wizard, which you can see in Figure 11-2.

The New Virtual Machine Wizard guides you through the steps to create a new virtual machine. The Name and Location boxes enable you to select the name that you want to use for the virtual machine and where the virtual machine configuration file will be created. In Figure 11-2 you can see that the virtual machine in this example will be named vWS08-SQL01. This name can be whatever value you choose. The important part of this dialog box is the Location prompt. By default the Hyper-V Manager will create virtual machines in the C:\ProgramData\Microsoft\Windows\Hyper-V folder. However, you can't use this location if you want the virtual machine to be able to use Live Migration. Instead, you need to specify the mount point that was created when you enabled CSV. By default the mount point is created at C:\ClusterStorage\Volume1. This is the value used in this example.

To find the mount point that's used by CSV, use the Start | Administrative Tools | Failover Cluster Manager option to start the Failover Cluster Manager, which you can see in Figure 11-3.

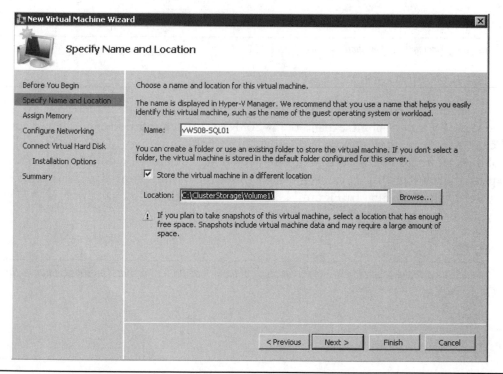

Figure 11-2   *New Virtual Machine Wizard: Specify Name and Location*

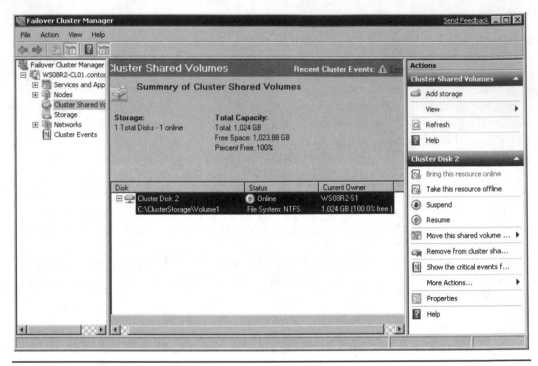

Figure 11-3 *Finding the Cluster Shared Volumes Mount Point*

In Chapter 10, you saw how the cluster named WS08R2-CL01 was created. To find the CSV mount point, expand the WS08R2-CL01 cluster node and then select the Cluster Shared Volumes node. This will display the Summary of Cluster Shared Volumes information that you can see in the middle portion of Figure 11-3. Then expand the Cluster Disk 2. You will be able to see the mount point directly under the Cluster Disk 2 heading. In Figure 11-3, you can see that the mount point is C:\ClusterStorageVolume1.

NOTE

To enable the virtual machine to use Live Migration, all of the virtual machine artifacts must be created on the CSV mount point.

After you've specified the virtual machine name and set the location of the virtual machine configuration file to the CSV mount point, click Next to view the Virtual Machine Wizard Assign Memory dialog box, which you can see in Figure 11-4.

The Assign Memory dialog box governs how much memory the virtual machine will have. You should assign the appropriate amount of memory for SQL Server. If you are converting from a physical server to a virtual SQL server system, then you can use the amount of memory in the physical system as a guide. However, bear in mind that you can only assign as much memory as is available in the host server. In Figure 11-3, you can see that this virtual machine will be created with 1GB of RAM. Clicking Next displays the Configure Networking dialog box, which you can see in Figure 11-5.

The New Virtual Machine Wizard Configure Networking dialog box lets you specify that type of network that will be used by the virtual machine; you can choose between not networking, internal networking, or external networking. The options

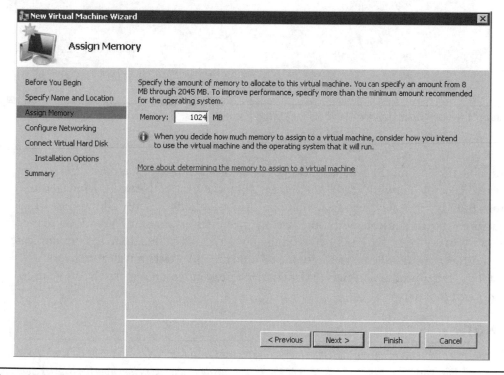

Figure 11-4   *New Virtual Machine Wizard: Assign Memory*

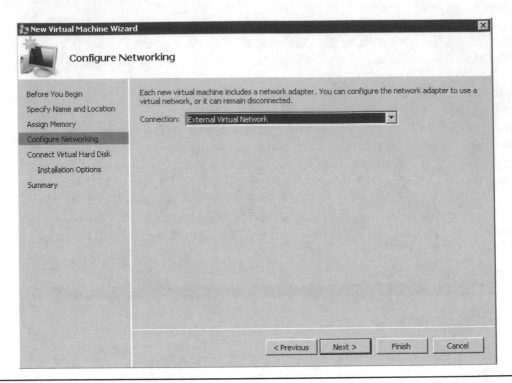

Figure 11-5   *New Virtual Machine Wizard: Configure Networking*

available depend on the type of networking configuration that you have created. You create Hyper-V network configurations by using the Virtual Network Manager link from the Hyper-V Managers's Action pane. Internal network only allows the virtual machine to communicate with other virtual machines on the same Windows Server 2008 Hyper-V host. External networking allows the virtual machine to communicate with other network clients through one of the Hyper-V hosts physical network adapters. For a production Server virtual machine, you would almost always want to select external networking.

NOTE

To use external networking, you must have previously created a virtual network. This can be done when the Hyper-V role is installed, or it can be done using the Virtual Network manager option from the Hyper-V manager. In this example, a virtual network named External Virtual Network has be previously created.

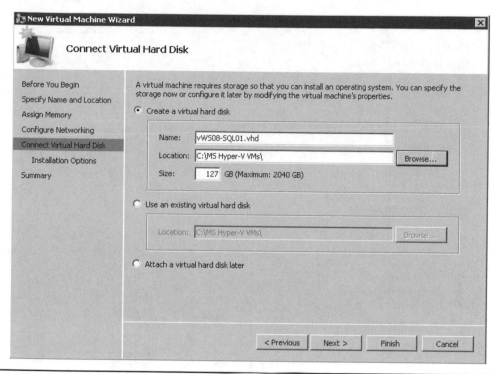

Figure 11-6 *New Virtual Machine Wizard: Connect Virtual Hard Disk*

After selecting the virtual machine network options and clicking Next, you see the Connect Virtual Hard Disk screen, shown in Figure 11-6.

The New Virtual Machine Wizard Connect Virtual Hard Disk dialog box lets you specify the name of the virtual machine's virtual hard disk (VHD) and its location. In Figure 11-6 you can see that the VHD will be named vWS08-SQL01.vhd. As you saw earlier with the virtual machine configuration files, the VHD files must also be located on the CSV mount point. Clicking Browse displays the Select Folder dialog box (see Figure 11-7), which allows you to navigate to the mount point.

In Figure 11-7, you can see that the folder C:\ClusterStorage\Volume1 has been selected. The C:\ClusterStorage\Volume1 folder is created when you enable Cluster Shared Volumes for a failover cluster. By default this folder is created off the root of the

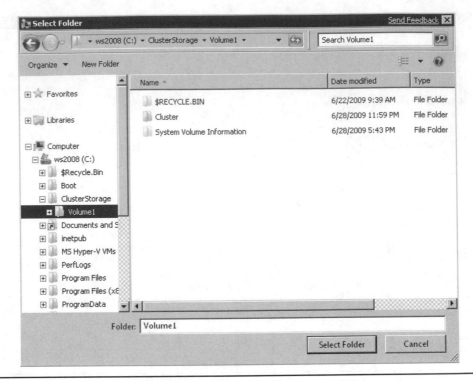

Figure 11-7 *Browsing to the Cluster Shared Volume mount point*

%SystemDrive% drive (typically the C: drive). Click the Volume1 folder to select it and then click Select Folder to return the selected folder to the Connect Virtual Hard Disk dialog box, as you can see in Figure 11-8.

After browsing to the CSV mount point and selecting the Volume1 folder, the new location of C:\ClusterStorage\Volume1 is returned to the Location field in the Connect Virtual Hard Disk dialog box. You can also adjust the size of the VHD. In this example, you can see that it was left at the default value of 127GB. Clicking Next displays the Installation Options Wizard dialog box shown in Figure 11-9.

The Installation Options dialog box allows you to elect to install a guest OS as a part of the virtual machine creation. You have the option of installing the guest OS immediately after the virtual machine is created, or you can install the guest OS at some later time. If you elect to install the guest OS as a part of the virtual machine

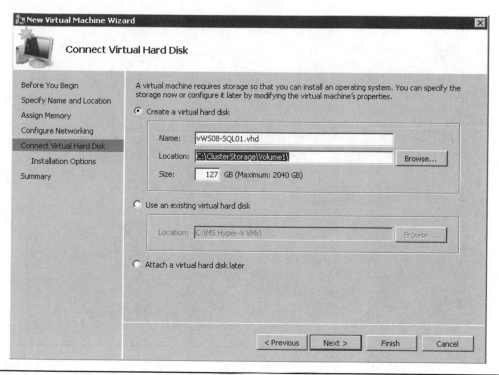

Figure 11-8   *New Virtual Machine Wizard: Connect Virtual Hard Disk*

creation process, you need to specify where Hyper-V can locate the installation media. The installation medium can be a disk or ISO file, a boot floppy, or a network server using PXE. In Figure 11-9, you can see that the guest OS will be installed from the host's DVD drive. Clicking Next completes the virtual machine configuration process and displays the confirmation dialog box that you can see in Figure 11-10.

The Completing the New Virtual Machine Wizard screen shows you the choices that you made on the previous wizard dialog boxes and gives you a chance to change them. If one or more of the values is incorrect, you can click Previous, page back through the wizard dialog boxes, and change correct the configuration choices. If all of the values look good, clicking Finish will create the virtual machine. In this example, clicking Finish will also connect to the virtual machine and start the guest OS installation process.

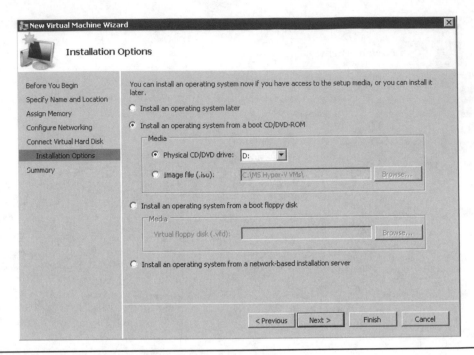

Figure 11-9 *New Virtual Machine Wizard: Installation Options*

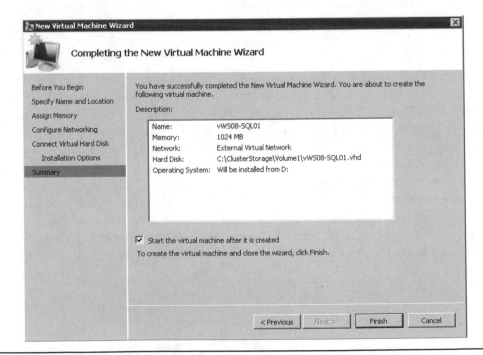

Figure 11-10 *New Virtual Machine Wizard: Completing the New Virtual Machine Wizard*

Installing Windows Server 2008 on the VM

A virtual machine by itself can't really do anything until you install a guest operating systems and applications. The next step in creating a SQL Server virtual machine is to install the guest operating system. In this example, the guest operating system will be Windows Server 2008.

> **NOTE**
>
> *While Live Migration requires Windows Server 2008 R2 on the host, the guest OSes running in the VMs do not need to be the same. They can be other operating systems, including Windows Server 2003 or Windows Server 2008.*

You can see the initial Windows Server 2008 installation screen in Figure 11-11.

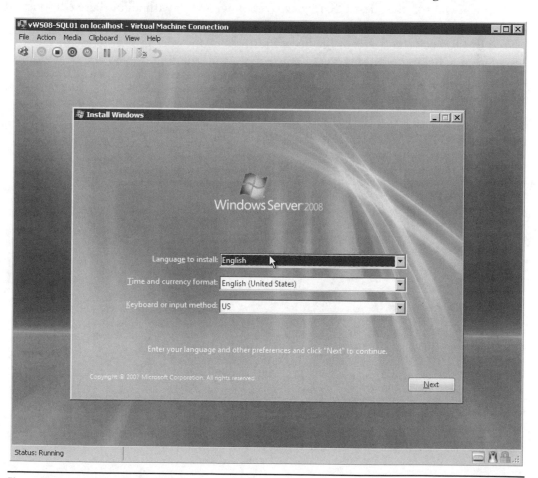

Figure 11-11 *Specifying the virtual machine's guest OS region*

The first Windows Server 2008 dialog box enables you to specify the locale settings for the operating system. In Figure 11-11 you can see that I selected to install the English language and to use the US keyboard layout. Clicking Next displays the Install Now screen illustrated in Figure 11-12.

After you select the locale, this screen starts the Windows Server 2008 installation process. It's important to remember that this installation is being done on the virtual machine, not on a physical system. All of the Windows Server installation files will be written to the virtual machine's VHD. You can see the Virtual Machine Connection around the guest OS installation screen. Clicking "Install now" displays the "Select the operation system you want to install" screen shown in Figure 11-13.

This screen allows you to select the edition of the guest operating system that you want to install. In Figure 11-12 you can see that the Windows Server 2008 Enterprise edition x64 has been selected. The choice of operating systems depends on the feature set that you want in the guest OS. Live Migration will work with all of these editions. Clicking Next displays the End User License Agreement that's shown in Figure 11-14.

You must check the "I accept the license terms" box in order to proceed with the installation. Clicking Next displays "Which type of installation do you want?" window, which you can see in Figure 11-15.

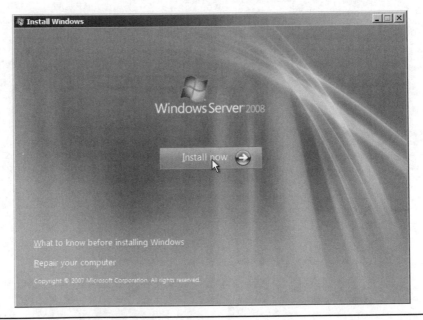

Figure 11-12 *Installing the guest OS on the virtual machine*

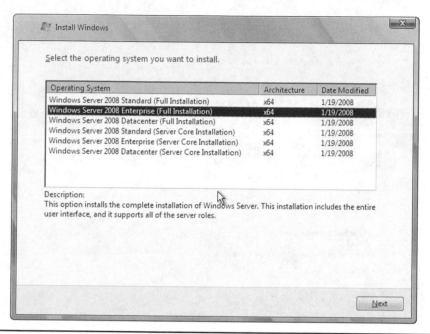

Figure 11-13 *Selecting the guest OS edition*

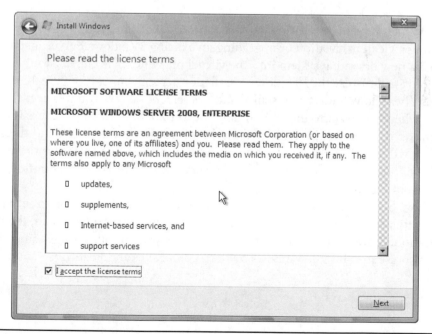

Figure 11-14 *Accepting the guest OS license terms*

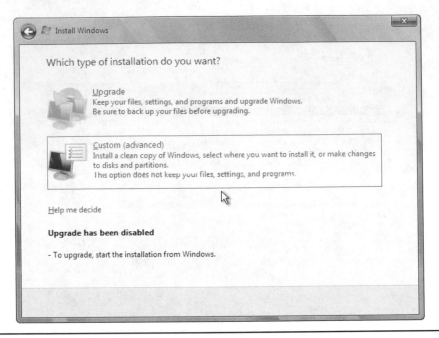

Figure 11-15 *Selecting the new installation option for the guest OS*

The "Which type of installation do you want?" screen allow you to choose between performing a clean installation or upgrading an existing Windows Server installation. To install a new operating system into the virtual machine, click the Custom (advanced) option. This will display the Windows installation screen shown in Figure 11-16.

The "Where do you want to install Windows screen?" allows you to select the disk partition where you want to install Windows Server 2008. In this case, there is only one partition that existing in the virtual machine's VHD. Select Disk 0 and then click Next. This will install the guest operating system, and after a few minutes the virtual machine will reboot and you'll see Windows Server 2008's install configuration dialog box, shown in Figure 11-17.

Windows Server 2008's Configure This Server dialog box allows you to set up the system's initial configuration settings, such as the system name, the domain, the network configuration, firewall, Windows Update, and Windows Firewall settings. In addition, you can also use it to install Windows Server 2008's Roles and Features.

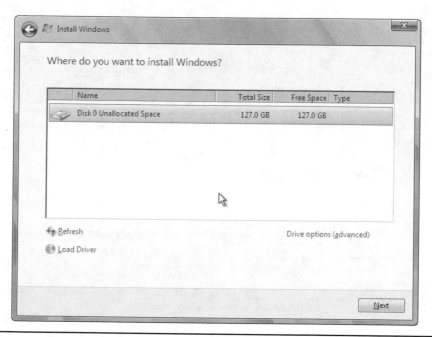

Figure 11-16 *Selecting the Virtual Hard Disk for the guest OS*

Since this is a virtual machine, one of the first things that you should be sure to do is install the Hyper-V Integration Services. Hyper-V Integration Services are installed in the guest operating system of the virtual machine. They provide Hyper-V system drivers for the guest OS as well as time synchronization with the host, a heartbeat service that notifies the host that the VM is active, the ability to shut down the guest OS, and the ability to support Volume Shadow Copy Services in the VM for backup. The simplest way to install Integration Services is by using the Virtual Machine Connection's Action menu. Click the Action menu and then select the Insert Integration Services Setup Disk option. This will install Integration Services and the system will reboot.

After installing the Integration Services, you can go ahead and complete the guest OS configuration. For this example in Figure 11-18 you can see, the guest OS was named vWS08-SQL01. This is the same name as the virtual machine itself, but they

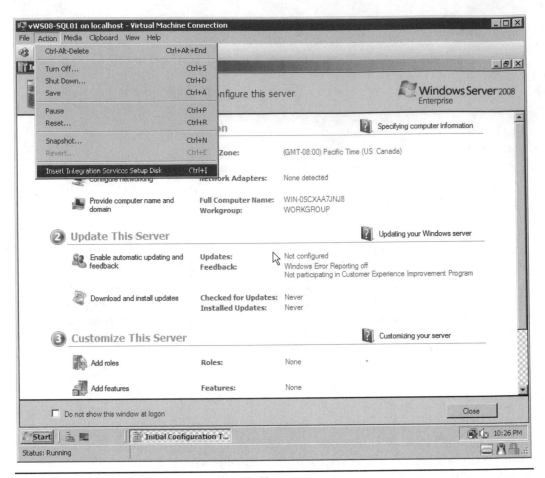

Figure 11-17   *Installing Integration Services on the guest OS*

can be different. The virtual server is also part of the contoso domain and is using a static IP address of 192.168.100.222. It could have also used DHCP for the network configuration. No additional roles or features were installed.

This completes the installation of the virtual machine's guest OS. The next step is to install SQL Server onto the virtual machine. This will create a virtual server that can be protected from planned downtime by Hyper-V R2's Live Migration.

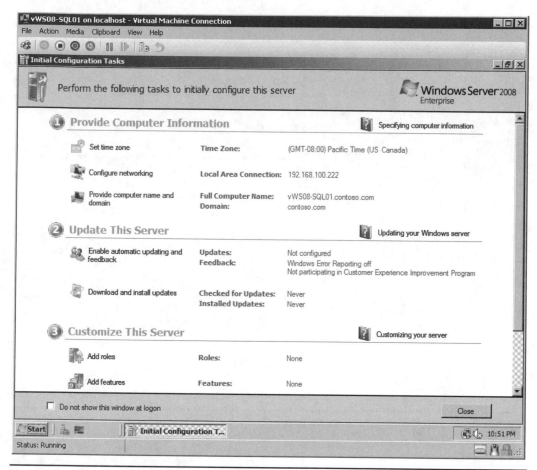

Figure 11-18   *The completed virtual machine guest OS*

Installing SQL Server 2008 on the VM

After the virtual machine has been created and the guest operating system has been loaded, you are ready to install SQL Server. To install SQL Server, insert the installation media into either the host's DVD drive or on a network share that's accessible from the virtual machine. Log in as an administrator on the VM guest and run the SQL Server setup program. This will start the SQL Server Installation Center, which you can see in Figure 11-19.

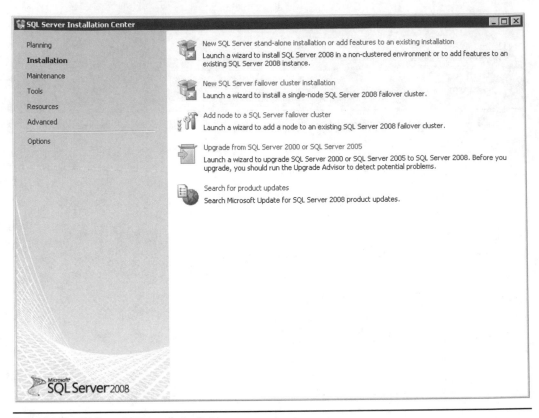

Figure 11-19 *SQL Server 2008 Installation Options*

NOTE

Unlike the failover clustering example that you saw presented in Chapter 4, Live Migration does not require you to install SQL Server on all the different nodes that will participate in Live Migration.

To install a new instance of SQL Server 2008, click the "New SQL Server stand-alone installation or add features to an existing installation" link. This will display the SQL Server 2008 Setup Support Rules dialog box, which you see in Figure 11-20.

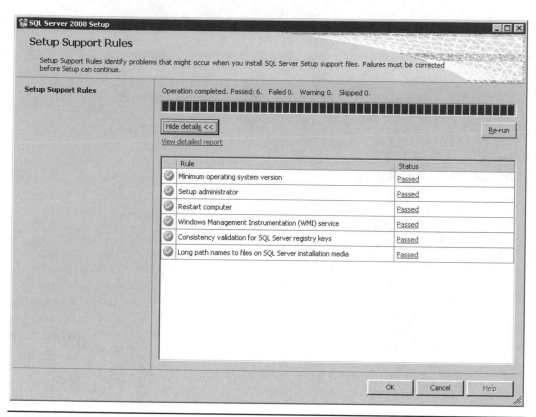

Figure 11-20 *Setup Support Rules*

The Setup Support Rules dialog box automatics checks your system for problems that might prevent the successful installation of SQL Server 2008. In Figure 11-20 you can see that the Setup Support Rules performs tests for six different system requirements. Clicking OK displays the Setup Support Files dialog box, which you can see illustrated in Figure 11-21.

The Setup Support Files dialog box installs the components that are required by the SQL Server 2008 setup program. In this example, since the installation is running on a virtual machine, all of the files will be copied to the virtual machine's VHD. Clicking Install copies the required setup files to the virtual machine and displays the Setup Support Rules screen, which you can see in Figure 11-22.

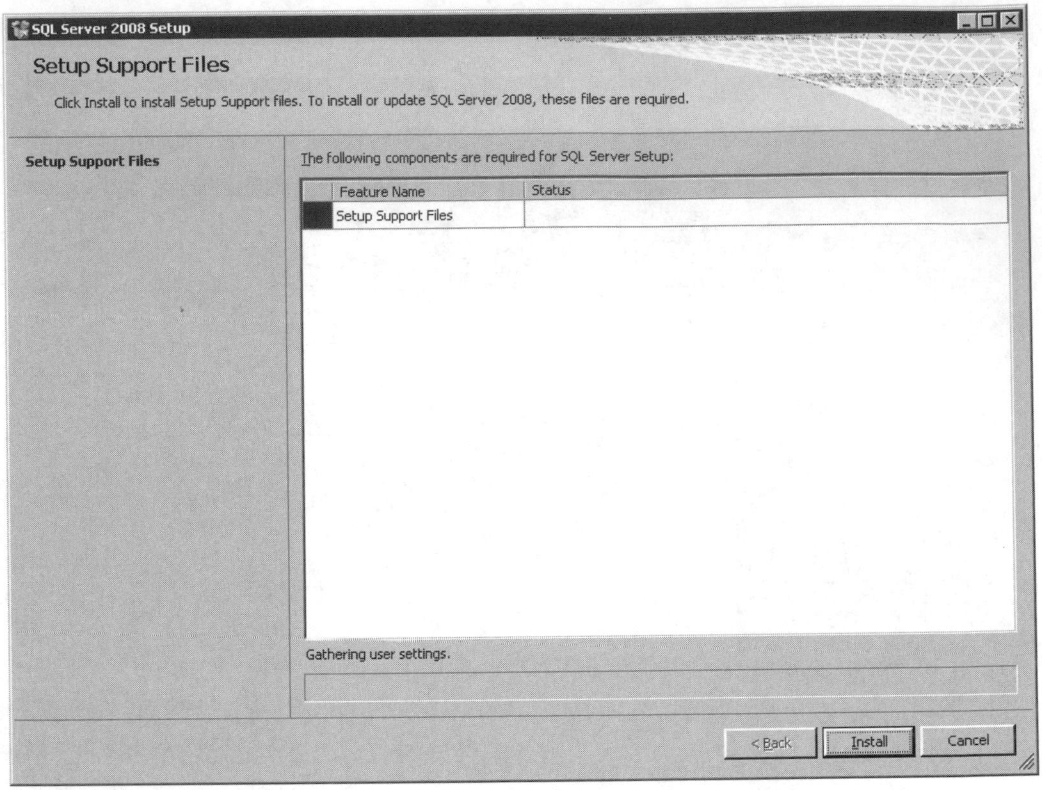

Figure 11-21 *Setup Support Files*

The Setup Support Rules dialog box performs a second set of tests to determine if there will be any problems running the setup program. As on the previous Setup Support Rules screen, a green check indicates the condition is OK and that the installation can proceed. A red *x* indicates that there is a problem that needs to be corrected before the setup can proceed. Clicking the link under the Status column provides more information about any error conditions. If all of the conditions are passed and there are green check marks next to all the items as you can see in Figure 11-22, then you can click Next and proceed with the installation.

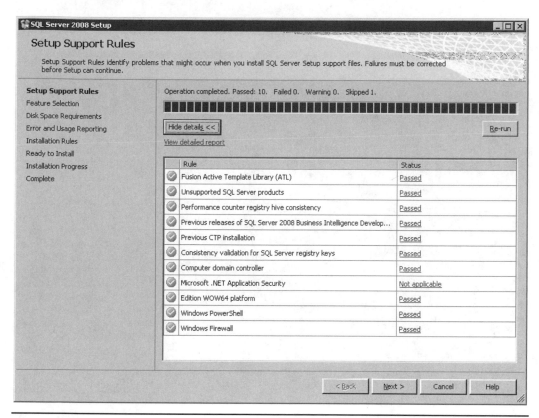

Figure 11-22 *Setup Support Rules*

The next screen in SQL Server 2008 setup process prompts you to enter your product key information (Figure 11-23). If you're installing one of the evaluation versions of SQL Server 2008, select the "Specify a free edition" radio button and click Next. Otherwise, if you are installing a licensed version of SQL Server 2008, select the "Enter the product key" radio button and then type in the product installation key and click Next. This will display the End User License Agreement (EULA) in the License Terms dialog box shown in Figure 11-24.

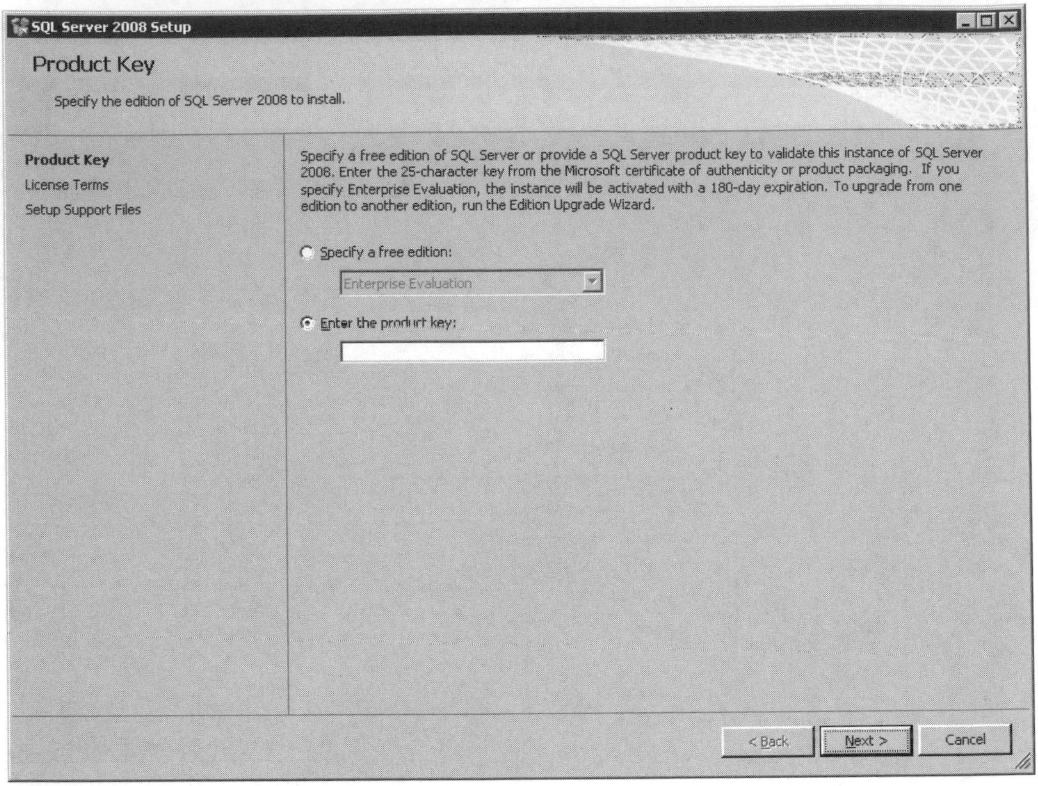

Figure 11-23 *SQL Server 2008 Product Key*

You accept the license agreement by placing a check in the "I accept the license terms" box. Clicking Next will display the SQL Server 2008 Feature Selection dialog box, which you can see in Figure 11-25.

The Feature Selection dialog box enables you to select which SQL Server 2008 components you want to install. After you've selected the database components that you want to install, click Next to display the Instance Configuration dialog box, which you can see in Figure 11-26.

The Instance Configuration dialog box allows you to either select the default instance name or to set up a named instance. Each named instance is essentially an additional copy of SQL Server installed on the same server. Most implementations will

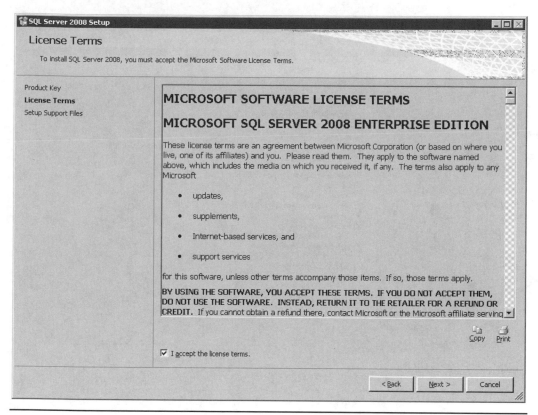

Figure 11-24 *License Terms*

only use the default instance. ISPs and web hosting providers are examples of businesses that most often make use of named instances. If you create a named instance, each name must be 16 characters or fewer. Instance names are not case sensitive, but the first character of the name must be a letter. They cannot have any embedded spaces and must not contain a backslash (\), comma (,), colon (:), single quote('), dash(-), ampersand (&), number sign (#), or at sign (@). Instance names also cannot contain the reserved words "Default" or "MSSQLServer." You can find the complete list of reserved words at http://msdn.microsoft.com/en-us/library/ms143507.aspx. The Enterprise Edition supports up to 50 named instances on a given system. The other SQL Server 2008 editions support up to 16 named instances.

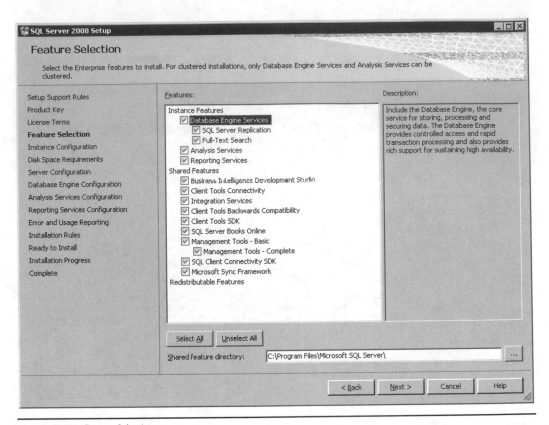

Figure 11-25 *Feature Selection*

NOTE

If you create a named instance, the SQL Server service name will be named as follows: MSSQL$InstanceName (where InstanceName is replaced with the instance name that you create).

You can also specify the directory that you want to use to install the SQL Server instance. The default installation directory is C:\Program Files\Microsoft SQL Server\. In Figure 11-26 you can see that this install will be using the default instance and SQL Server directory locations. Click Next to display the Disk Space Requirements dialog box shown in Figure 11-27.

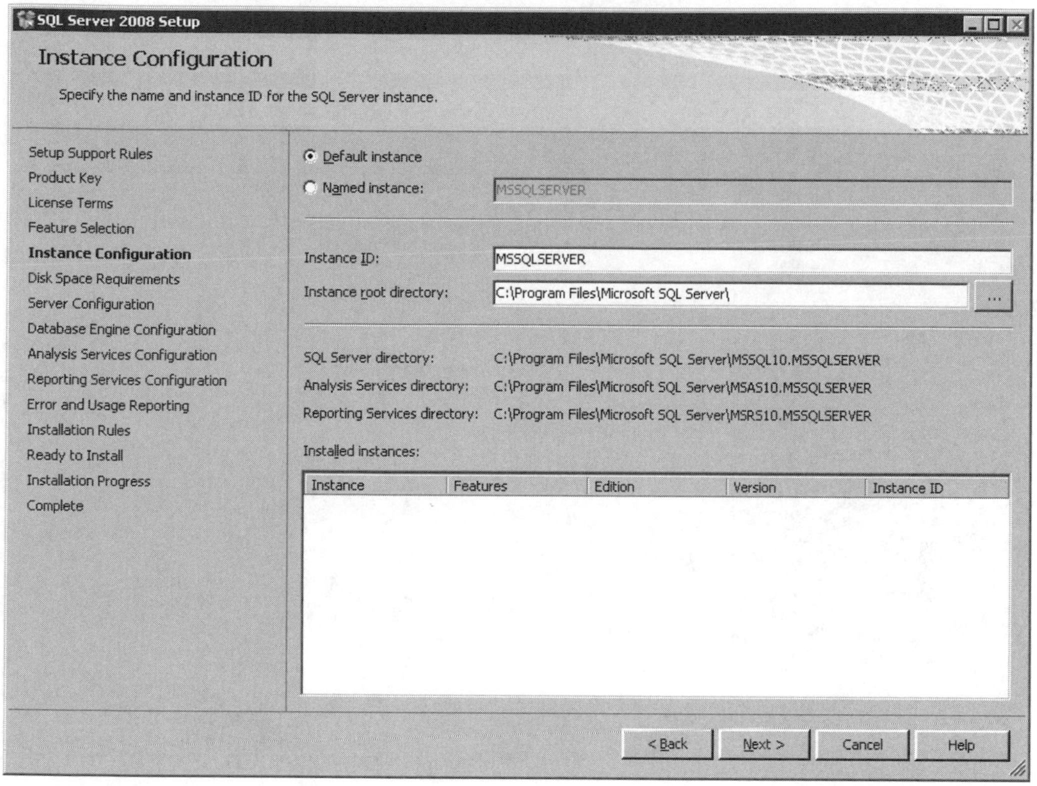

Figure 11-26 *Instance Configuration*

The Disk Space Requirements dialog box displays the installation directories that you previously selected as well as the required and available storage space for each drive. If you need to change the selections, you can use the Back button to page back to the Features Selection and Instance Configuration dialog boxes to change the target directories. If all of the disk requirements are acceptable, click Next to display the Server Configuration dialog box that's illustrated in Figure 11-28.

The Server Configuration dialog box allows you to specify the accounts that each of the different SQL Server services will run under. The values in the Server Configuration dialog box specify the user accounts used by the SQL Server service as well as the SQL

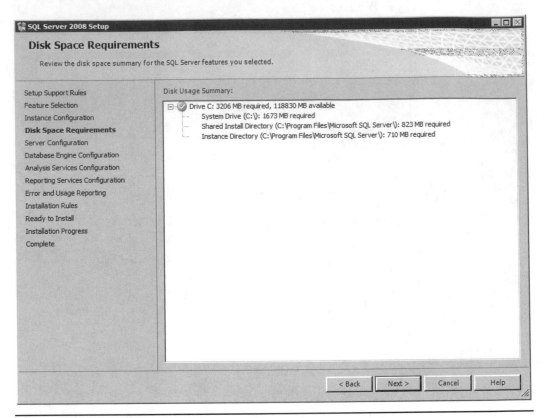

Figure 11-27 *Disk Space Requirements*

Server Agent, Analysis Services, Integration Services, and Reporting Server. This is important because it sets the permissions level that each of these services runs under. Microsoft recommends using a domain account to run each of the services. You can use the administrative account, but because of its high privilege level, that's not recommended. In addition, Microsoft recommends using a separate account for each service. Typically you would want to create a domain user account for each SQL Server service to run under and select these accounts for the corresponding services. This gives you the ability to more granularly control the permissions that the various services possess.

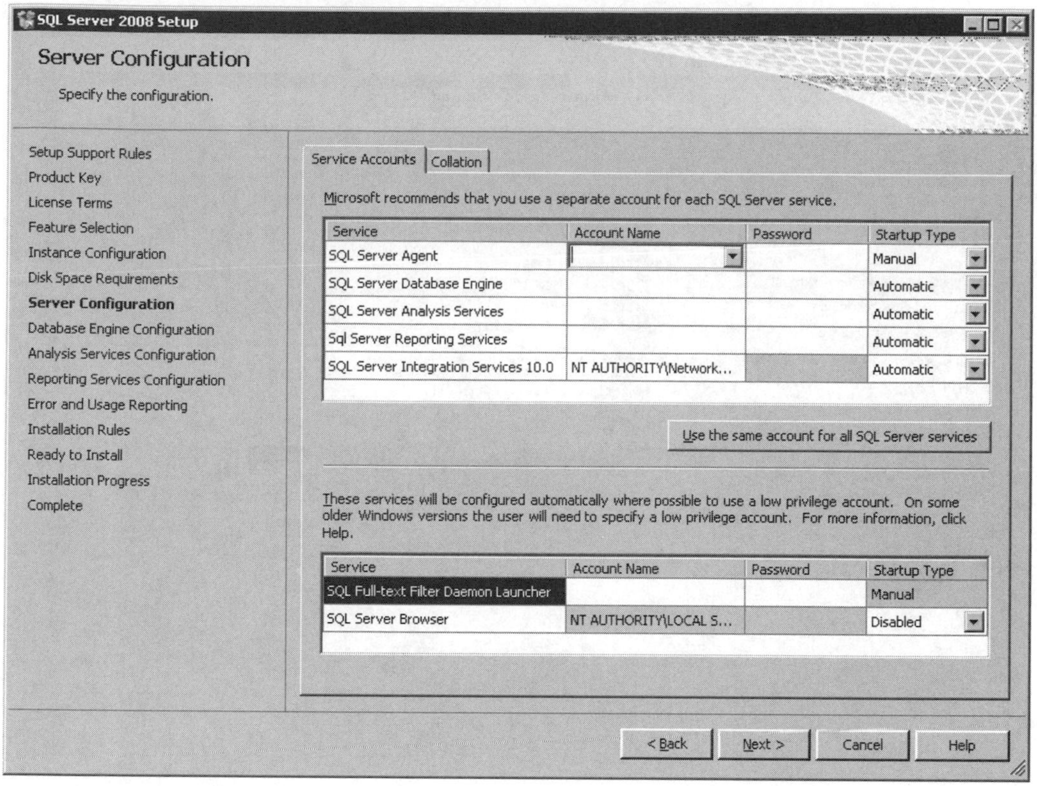

Figure 11-28 *Server Configuration*

In addition to specifying the authentication for the various SQL Server 2008 services, you can also click the Collation tab and change the collation order used by this SQL Server instance. Most organizations will want to use SQL Server's default collation. After supplying the authentication information for the SQL Server services, clicking Next displays the Database Engine Configuration dialog box, which you can see in Figure 11-29.

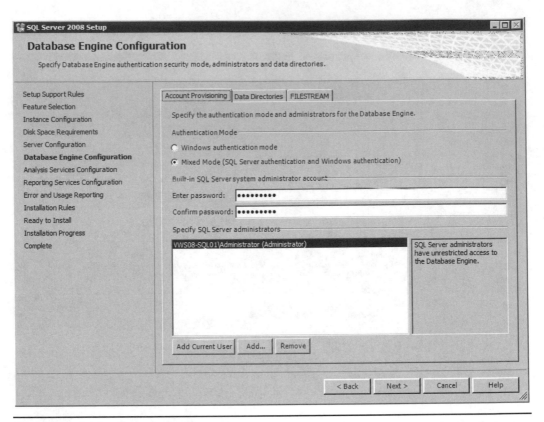

Figure 11-29 *Database Engine Configuration*

The Database Engine Configuration dialog box defines the type of user authentication that SQL Server 2008 will use. The default value is Windows Authentication, meaning that the Windows user accounts will be used to authenticate to SQL Server. Typically this is what you want because it provides easier management in that only one set of login accounts needs to be managed and that set of logins is maintained by the host operating system. It is also more secure because with Windows authentication, the application does not need to pass the user's password across the network. You can also choose Mixed Mode authentication, which means that both Windows logins and SQL Server logins can be accepted. In the case of SQL Server logins, you must manually add these logins to SQL Server, and they are maintained independently from the Windows login. If you're using Windows authentication, you typically would want to click the Add Current User button to add the current user as a SQL Server administrator. If you select Mixed Mode authentication, you then need to select a password for the SQL Server System Administrator (sa) login. For security reasons, you must select a nonblank password. You should strongly consider making this a strong password that's at least eight characters in length, containing characters, numbers, and special characters.

In addition to the SQL Server authentication mode, you can also use the Data Directories and the FILESTREAM tabs to configure SQL Server's data storage options. The Data Directories tab allows you to change the default directories used to store database files, log files, and the temp DB data and log files, as well as where disk backups are stored. By default, user databases and logs are stored in C:\Program Files\ Microsoft SQL Server\MSSQL10.MSSQLSERVER\MSSQL\Data. The default directory for backups is C:\Program Files\Microsoft SQL Server\MSSQL10 .MSSQLSERVER\MSSQL\Backup. The FILESTREAM tab is used to enable FILESTREAM access for the server. In order to enable FILESTREAM access, you need to check the Enable FILESTREAM for Transact-SQL access check box. You also have the option to enable FILESTREAM access for Win32 clients. If you do so, you are prompted to also create a file share. The default name for the file share is MSSQLSERVER. If you don't enable FILESTREAM access during setup, you enable it later using the SQL Server Configuration Manager. For more information on enabling SQL Server's FileStream support, you can refer to http://msdn.microsoft .com/en-us/library/cc645923.aspx.

If you selected to install Analysis Services in the earlier Feature Selection screen, clicking Next displays the Analysis Service Configuration dialog box, which you can see in Figure 11-30.

Like the Database Engine Configuration screen, the Analysis Services Configuration screen allows you to select the administrative account as well as set up the default directories that will be used to store Analysis Services databases. The Account Provisioning tab allows you to select the Analysis Services administrative account. If you want the current user to be the Analysis Services administrator, click Add Current User. Otherwise, click Add and select the windows account that you want to act as Analysis Services Administrator.

To change the default directory that Analysis Services uses, click the Data Directories tab. The Data Directories tab allows you to change the default directories that are used to store Analysis Services data and log files, as well as the Analysis Services temp and backup directories. By default, Analysis Services uses the C:\Program Files\Microsoft SQL Server\MSAS10.MSSQLSERVER\OLAP\Data directory for data files. For log file storage, the default directory is C:\Program Files\Microsoft SQL Server\ MSAS10.MSSQLSERVER\OLAP\Log. The default directory for Analysis Services temp storage is C:\Program Files\Microsoft SQL Server\MSAS10.MSSQLSERVER\ OLAP\Temp. The default directory for Analysis Services backup is C:\Program Files\ Microsoft SQL Server\MSAS10.MSSQLSERVER\OLAP\Backup.

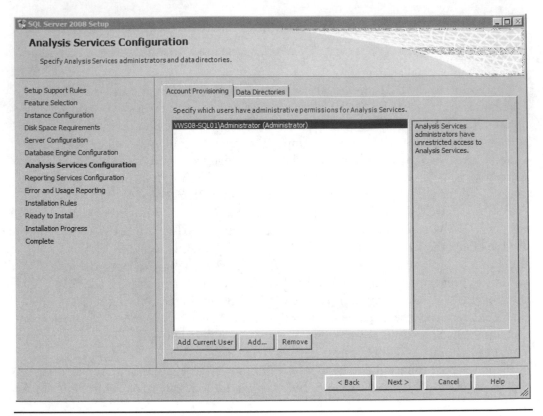

Figure 11-30 *Analysis Services Configuration*

If you selected to install Reporting Services, clicking Next displays the Reporting Services Configuration dialog box, which you can see in Figure 11-31.

The Reporting Services Configuration dialog box enables you to specify the Reporting Services configuration that you want to use. You can choose either to "Install the native mode default configuration," "Install the SharePoint integrated mode default configuration," or "Install, but do not configure the report server." Installing the native mode default configuration will create the Reporting Services database in the current SQL Server instance, and Reporting Service will be usable at the end of the installation. Selecting the SharePoint integrated mode will also create the Reporting Services database. In integrated mode, Reporting Services is managed using SharePoint rather than the built-in Reporting Services Manager. Integrated mode is not active until SharePoint is installed. The final option, "Install, but do not configure the report server," copies the Reporting Services programs to the server but doesn't create the database or

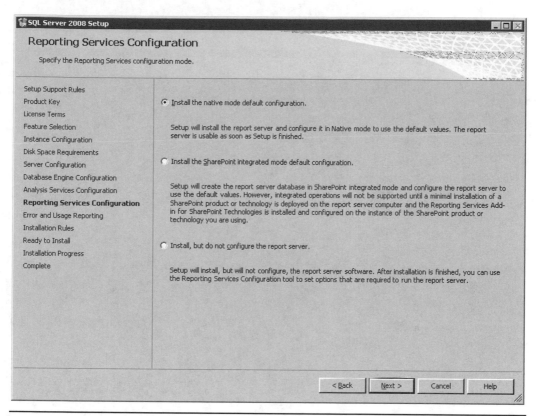

Figure 11-31 *Reporting Services Configuration*

perform any of the other required configuration steps. If you select this option, then you must manually configure Reporting Services after the SQL Server installation.

After selecting the Reporting Services configuration, click Next to view the Error and Usage Reporting screen, which you can see in Figure 11-32.

SQL Server 2008's Error and Usage Reporting screen enables you to optionally report errors in the SQL Server database service to Microsoft. Likewise, the usage reports show Microsoft how you use the product. Microsoft does not collect any personal information from these reports. Microsoft just uses this information to better understand how SQL Server is used as well as to identify and eliminate problems that may occur within SQL Server.

After you address the Error and Usage Reporting dialog box, clicking Next displays the Installation Rules dialog box shown in Figure 11-33.

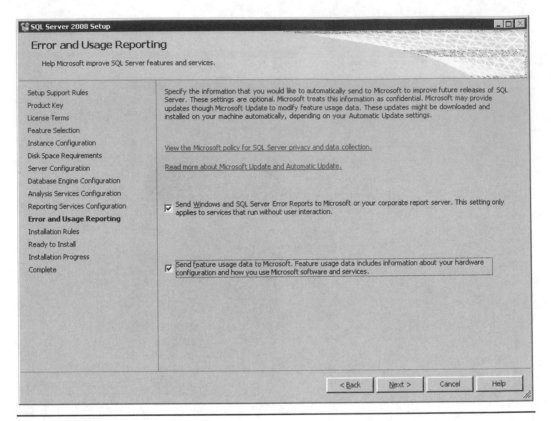

Figure 11-32 *Error and Usage Reporting*

The Installation Rules dialog box performs a final check for any conditions that might block the installation process. If any error condition is found, it will be shown in the Installation Rules dialog box with a red *x*. If all of the items have green check marks as you see in Figure 11-33, then the installation can proceed. Clicking Next displays the Ready to Install dialog box shown in Figure 11-34.

The Ready to Install dialog box enables you to confirm your choices. If you need to change anything, you can use the Back button to page back through the previous installation screens. Clicking the Install button on the Ready to Install dialog box begins the installation process for SQL Server 2008. As the installation program runs, the current status is shown in the Installation Progress window.

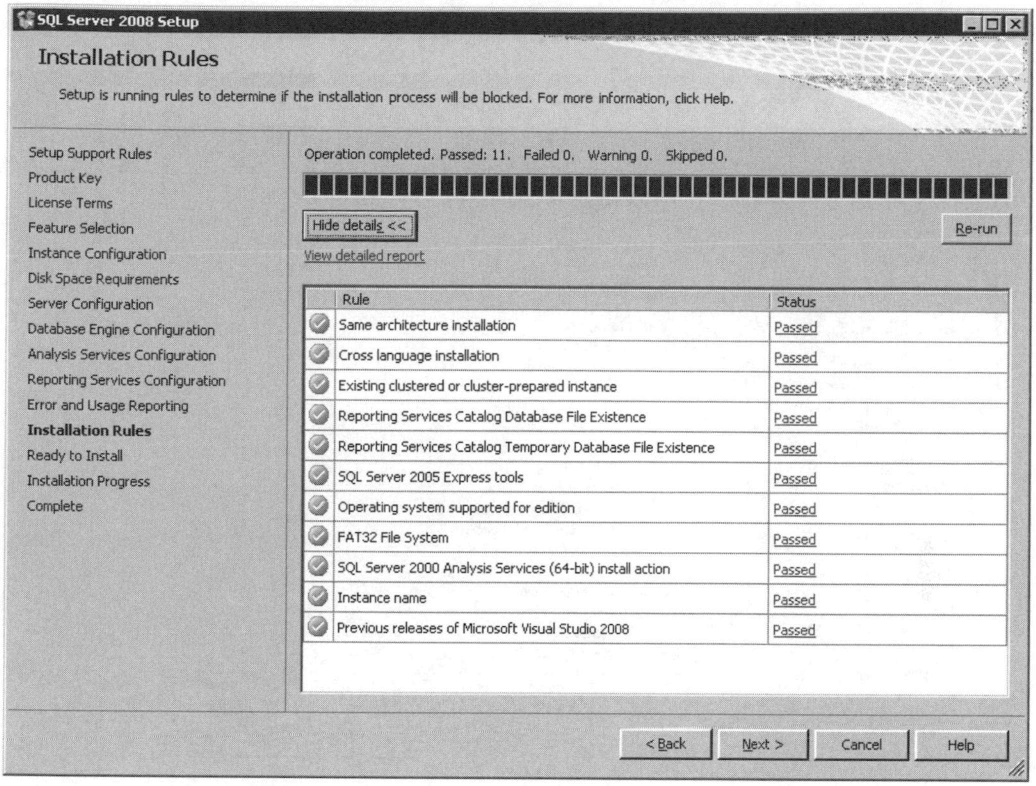

Figure 11-33 *Installation Rules*

When the SQL Server 2008 installation is complete, you'll see the Complete dialog box shown in Figure 11-35.

At this point you have a fully functional virtual SQL Server system. This system is capable of performing all of the same work as a physical SQL Server system. From the network client perspective there is no difference.

A virtual SQL Server system has a couple of advantages over physical SQL Server systems in the areas of disaster recovery and deployment. For disaster recovery the VHD file that stores the virtual SQL Server can be easily backed up and restored to another Hyper-V system. This gives you the ability to have full recovery in the event of server failure in a matter of minutes rather than needing to perform a bare-metal

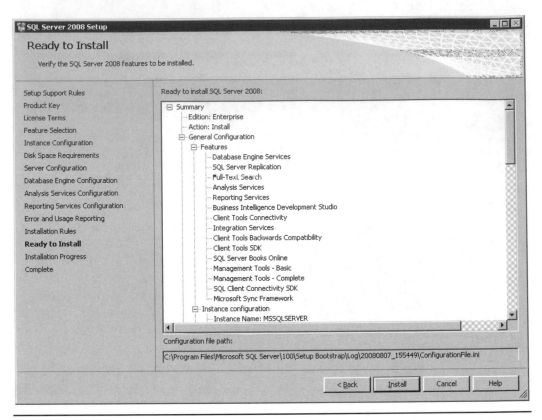

Figure 11-34 *Ready to Install*

install or keep a warm standby server. Combining this ability with the failover clustering solution presented in Chapter 4 can provide very high availability. You can also make copies of the VHD image, allowing you to quickly deploy new SQL Server instances. However, you do need to remember that even though the SQL Server system is running in a virtual machine, product licensing still applies. The primary drawback is in terms of performance. Virtualized SQL Server systems tend to have somewhat lower levels of performance than physical systems. However, they can still meet the service level requirements of the vast majority of businesses.

While the virtualized SQL Server does provide immediate availability benefits, you still need to perform some steps in order to enable Live Migration for the SQL Server virtual machine.

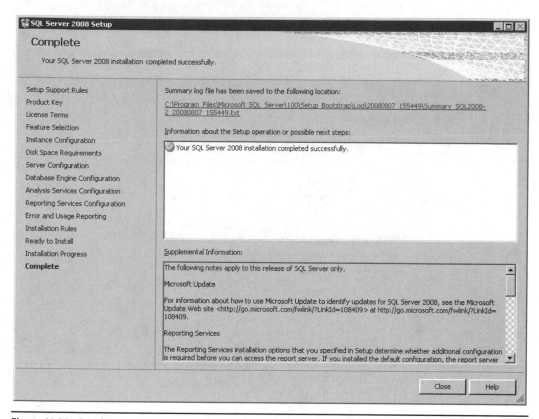

Figure 11-35 *Complete*

Configuring the SQL Server VM for Live Migration

The next step is to configure the SQL Server virtual machine for Live Migration. Begin by opening up the Failover Cluster Manager using the Start | Administrative Tools | Failover Cluster Manager option. You can run this on either of the nodes in your cluster. This will display the Failover Cluster Manager, which you can see in Figure 11-36.

To enable the VWS08-SQL01 virtual machine to use Live Migration, expand the cluster node right-click the Services and Application node and then select Configure a Service or Application from the context menu. This will start the High Availability Wizard, which you can see in Figure 11-37.

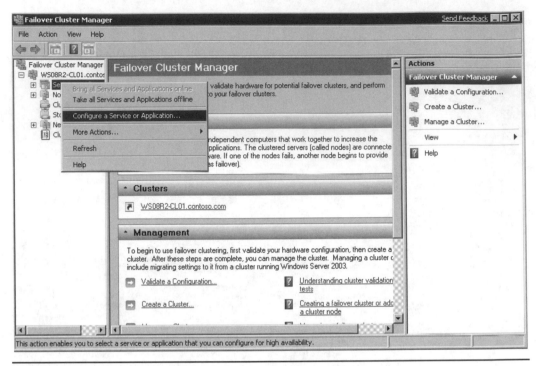

Figure 11-36 *Configuring the Virtual Machine Service*

The High Availability Wizard helps you to enable an application or service to take advantage of the failover cluster services for availability. The Before You Begin dialog box mainly notifies you that you are about to run the wizard. Clicking Next displays the Select Service or Application dialog box, which you can see in Figure 11-38.

To enable a virtual machine for Live Migration, scroll through the list of services and applications in the Select Service or Application pane and select Virtual Machine. Then click Next to display the Select Virtual Machine dialog box as shown in Figure 11-39.

The Select Virtual Machine dialog box lists all the virtual machines that are available on all of the nodes in the cluster. Scroll through the list until you see the virtual machine that you want to enable for Live Migration. In Figure 11-39 you can see the virtual machine named vWS08-SQL01 has been selected by placing a check in the box immediately to the left of the name. Although you can select other virtual machines, unless the virtual machine's artifacts, including the virtual machine configuration file and VHD, are stored in the CSV mount point, they will be unable to take advantage of Live Migration.

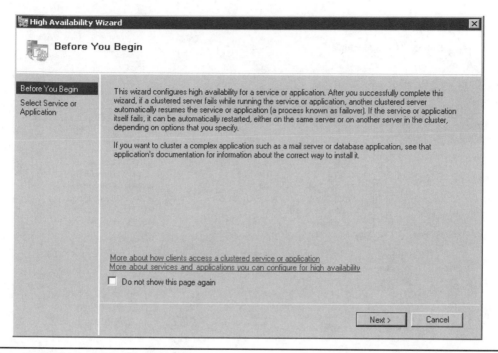

Figure 11-37 *High Availability Wizard: Before You Begin*

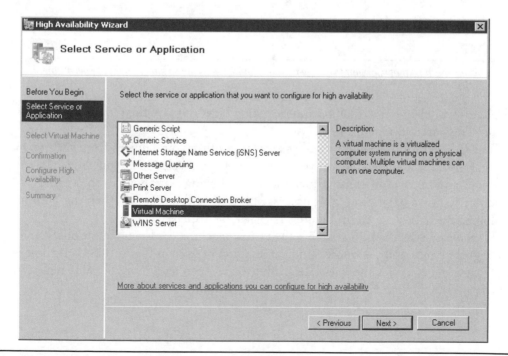

Figure 11-38 *High Availability Wizard: Select Service or Application*

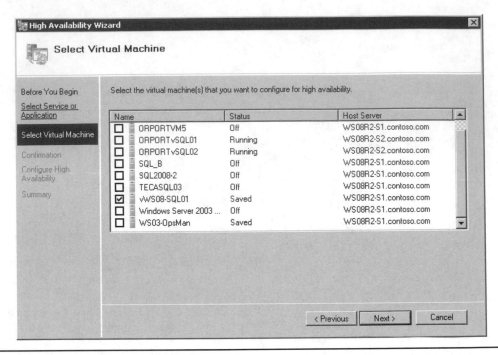

Figure 11-39 *High Availability Wizard: Select Virtual Machine*

NOTE

The virtual machine that you want to enable for Live Migration must be on either an Off or Saved state.

After you select the virtual machine, clicking Next displays the Confirmation dialog box as illustrated in Figure 11-40.

The Configuration dialog box allows you to confirm your choices from the previous Select Virtual Machine screen. If you need to redo your selections, you can click Previous and select a different virtual machine. Clicking Next enables the virtual machine for Live Migration. This process only takes a few seconds; then the Summary dialog box that you can see in Figure 11-41 will be displayed.

If the wizard succeeds in enabling the virtual machine for Live Migrations, you'll see a green check and the Success indicator as you can see in Figure 11-41. If there are warnings, you can click the View Report button to open up a more detailed report in the Browser. Clicking Finish ends the High Availability Wizard.

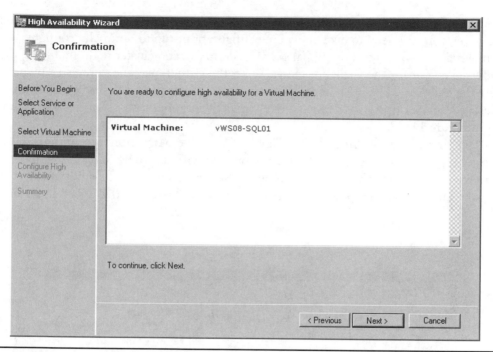

Figure 11-40 *High Availability Wizard: Confirmation*

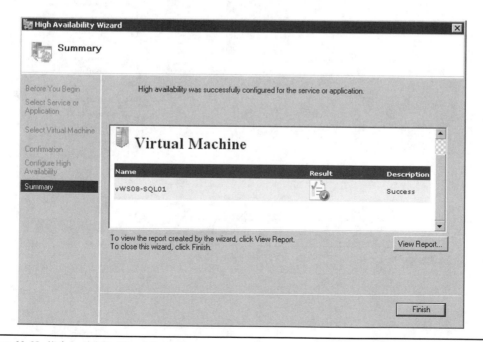

Figure 11-41 *High Availability Wizard: Summary*

When the wizard has completed, the virtual machine is enabled for Live Migration. However, you still need to take one more configuration step to optimally configure the virtual machine. You need to tell Failover Clustering which cluster node should be the preferred owner for the virtual machine. To set the virtual machine's preferred owner, start the Failover Cluster Manager using the Start | Administrative Tools | Failover Cluster Manager option and expand the "Services and applications" node, as you can see in Figure 11-42.

After the virtual machine has been enabled for Live Migration, the Actions pane in the Failover Cluster Manager will be populated with a number of options that enable you to manage the virtual machine. These options include the ability to start and stop the virtual machine as well as to perform Live Migration and Quick Migration.

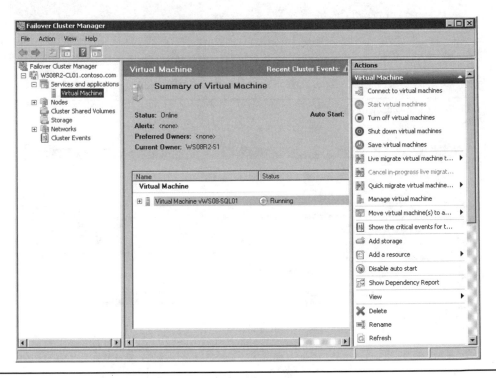

Figure 11-42 *Configuring the Virtual Machines Live Migration Properties*

(More information about managing the virtual machine using the Failover Cluster Manager will be presented in Chapter 12.) To set the preferred owner of the virtual machine, right-click the virtual machine name that's shown in the center pane of the Failover Cluster Manager. This will display the context menu that you can see in Figure 11-43.

To set the virtual machine's preferred owner, select Properties from the context menu. This will display the Virtual Machine Properties window shown in Figure 11-44.

To set the preferred owner for the virtual machine, move the entries in the Preferred owner's list up or down using the buttons on the right side of the screen. The current owner will be indicated with a check mark.

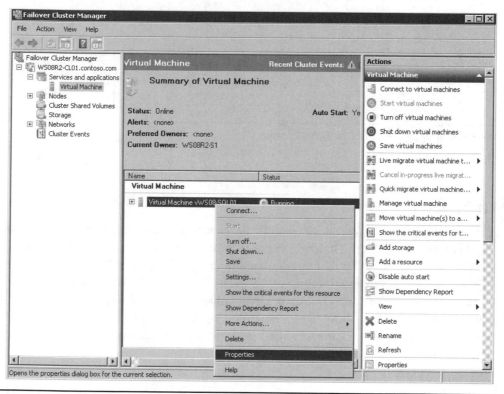

Figure 11-43 *Setting the virtual machine properties*

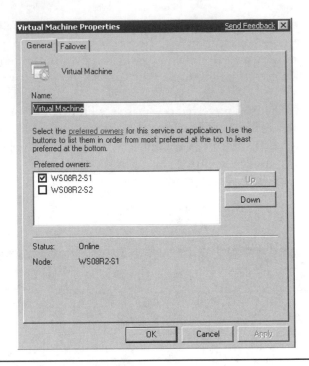

Figure 11-44 *Setting the virtual machine's preferred owner*

Summary

In this chapter, you saw how to create and configure a virtual machine that was on one of the Hyper-V nodes in the failover cluster that was previously created in Chapter 10. Then you saw how to set up that virtual machine by installing Windows Server 2008 as the guest operating system and then SQL Server 2008. In the last part of this chapter, you saw how to prepare the SQL Server virtual machine to use Live Migration. In the next chapter, you'll see how to use the Failover Cluster Manager to perform Live Migration and Quick Migration as well as performing other essential virtual machine management tasks.

Chapter 12

Managing the Virtual SQL Server

In This Chapter

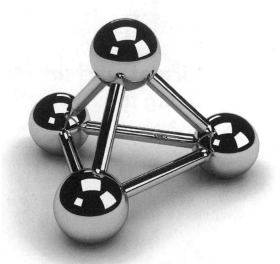

I n Chapters 10 and 11, you saw how to set up a SQL Server virtual machine that is capable of Live Migration. In Chapter 10, you saw how to set up and configure a Windows Server 2008 Failover Cluster that supports the Live Migration feature. In Chapter 11, you saw how to create and configure a SQL Server virtual machine that can be enabled for Live Migration. In this chapter you'll see how to perform the basic SQL Server virtual machine management function as well as how to use both Live Migration and Quick Migration to provide higher levels of availability by reducing planned downtime. You'll also learn about how Microsoft System Center Virtual Machine Manager can provide additional capabilities for enterprise deployments.

Managing the Highly Available Virtual SQL Server

There are two levels of management for virtual machines. There's the level where you manage the virtual machine itself, and there's the level where you manage the guest OS and applications running in the virtual machine. In some ways, managing the virtual machine is quite like managing a physical system. For instance, you can power it on and off. However, the fact that it's a virtual machine also gives it additional management capabilities; for instance, you can save its state, as well as use tools like Live Migration and Quick Migration to move the virtual machine between different physical hosts. Management of the guest OS and the application, in this case SQL Server, is virtually identical to managing a physical server. The primary difference is that you must attach to the virtual server using Remote Desktop or using another remote management method, as there is no physical keyboard, mouse, or monitor. After you've attached with the Remote Desktop, all of the management tools and actions are the same as managing a physical machine.

In the next section, you'll see how perform some of the basic virtual machine management functions as well as how to perform some of the more advanced functions such as Live Migration.

Virtual Machine Management Using the Hyper-V Manager

In Chapter 11, you saw how the Hyper-V Manager was used to create a new virtual machine. The Hyper-V Manager is also the primary management tool for Hyper-V virtual machines. You can see an overview of the Hyper-V Manager in Figure 12-1.

As you can see in Figure 12-1, the Hyper-V Manager is capable of connecting to multiple hosts. For each host, it lists the virtual machines that are running on that host and allows you to manage both the Hyper-V host server and the virtual machines

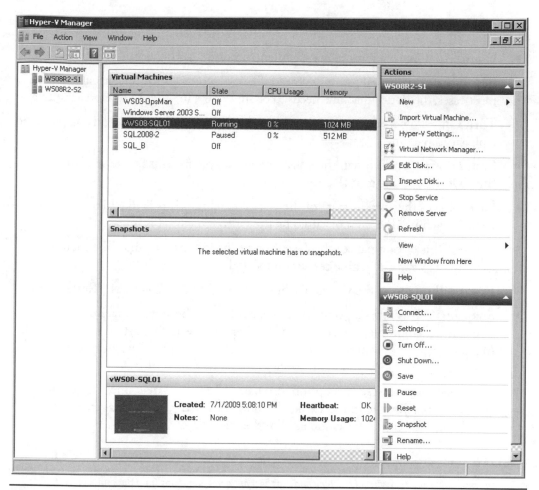

Figure 12-1   *Basic virtual machine management with the Hyper-V Manager*

that are running on the host. Figure 12-1 shows the Hyper-V connected to both the physical hosts WS08R2-S1 and WS08R2-S2. The Virtual Machine pane in the center of the screen shows the virtual machines that are running on WS08R2-S1. The Actions pane shown on the right side of the screen presents the different management options that are available for the virtual machine host and each virtual machine. As you can see in Figure 12-1, the management options for the virtual machine host are shown in the top half of the Actions pane, while the management options for each virtual machine are shown in the lower half of the action pane.

For each virtual machine, the Hyper-V Manager enables you to

- ► **Connect**   Opens a remote management windows to the virtual machine.

- ► **Settings**   Enables you to adjust any configuration settings for the virtual machine. In most cases, the virtual machine needs to be shut down in order to change its settings.

- ► **Turn Off**   Powers down the virtual machine. This is like turning off the power to a physical machine.

- ► **Shut Down**   Shuts down the guest operating system. This is like selecting the Shut Down option from the Start menu.

- ► **Save**   Saves the current state of the virtual machine. This is like hibernating the virtual machine. The memory used by the virtual machine is released.

- ► **Pause**   This option pauses the execution of the virtual machine. The memory used by the virtual machine remains allocated.

- ► **Reset**   This reboots the virtual machine. This is like using the Start | Restart option.

- ► **Snapshot**   This takes a point-in-time snapshot of the virtual machine state. You can take multiple snapshots and use them to revert the virtual machine back to a previous state. Taking and restoring a snapshot can be a useful recovery mechanism to protect you from configuration errors.

- ► **Rename**   You can use this option to rename the virtual machine. This changes the name that you see in the Hyper-V and Failover Cluster Manager, but it does not change the computer name used in the guest OS.

NOTE

You can also right-click each virtual machine and use the management options from the context menu.

The Hyper-V Manager presents the basic virtual machine management options. To use the more advanced high-availability options like Live Migration and Quick Migration, you need to use the Failover Cluster Manager.

Virtual Machine Management Using the Failover Cluster Manager

When you configure a virtual machine for high availability as you saw illustrated in Chapter 11, several virtual machine management options are added to the Failover Cluster Manager. Some of these action items are used to manage the virtual machine cluster resource, while others are used to manage the virtual machines themselves.

You start the Failover Cluster Manager using the Start | Administrative Tools | Failover Cluster Manager option. This will display the Failover Cluster Manager, shown in Figure 12-2.

The Failover Cluster Manager allows you to manage the Virtual Machine Resource as well as the individual virtual machines. You can use the Failover Cluster Manager to start and stop the Virtual Machine Resource by either using the options in the Action pane or right-clicking the Virtual Machines node and then selecting options from the context menu. When the Virtual Machine Resource is started, you can work with the virtual machines themselves.

To manage the virtual machines that have been enabled for high availability, expand the Virtual Machine node and select the virtual machine that you want to manage. This will display the Failover Cluster Manager, as you can see in Figure 12-3.

The virtual machines that have been enabled for high availability will be listed in the Virtual Machine pane that you can see in the middle of the screen. You can manage the

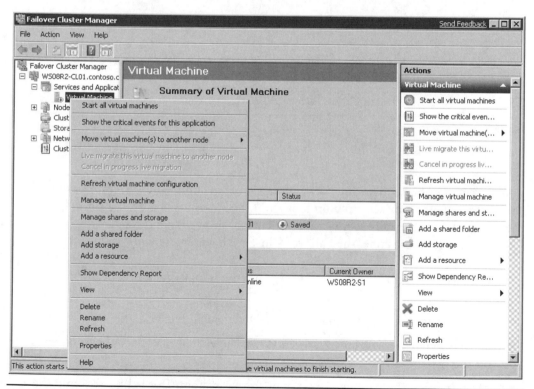

Figure 12-2 *Starting the virtual machine resources*

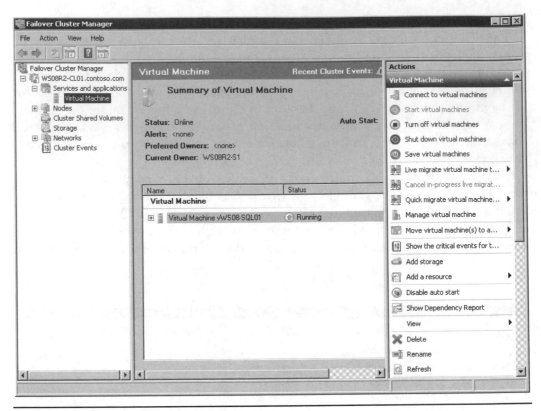

Figure 12-3 *Managing highly available virtual machines*

virtual machines either by right-clicking the virtual machine and selecting options from the context menu or by selecting options from the Actions pane on the right. Some of these options are the same as the management options that are offered.

For each virtual machine, the Failover Cluster Manager lets you

- **Connect to virtual machines**   Opens a remote management window to the virtual machine.

- **Start virtual machines**   Starts the selected virtual machine.

- **Turn off virtual machines**   Powers down the virtual machine. This is like turning off the power to a physical machine.

- **Shut down**   Shuts down the guest operating system. This is like selecting the Shut Down option from the Start menu.

▶ **Save virtual machines**   Save the current state of the virtual machine. This is like hibernating the virtual machine. The memory used by the virtual machine is released.

▶ **Live Migrate virtual machines**   This option moves the virtual machine from one Hyper-V node to another. The operation of the virtual machine is not interrupted.

▶ **Cancel in-progress live migration**   You can select this option to cancel a Live Migration that is currently in progress.

▶ **Quick Migrate virtual machines**   This option moves the virtual machine from one Hyper-V node to another. The operation of the virtual machine is momentarily interrupted as the virtual machine is stopped on the first node and then restarted on the second node.

▶ **Manage virtual machines**   Selecting this option will display the Hyper-V Manager.

▶ **Move virtual machines to another node**   This option can be used to move a virtual machine from one Hyper-V node to another. This is like Quick Migration, but the virtual machine cannot be active.

▶ **Show critical events for the virtual machine**   This option display the events associated with a virtual machine.

Performing a Live Migration

Live Migration enables you to reduce planned downtime by moving the SQL Server virtual machine from one node to another. This can allow you to perform planned maintenance activities like hardware upgrades or operating system updates on the first node without incurring any end-user downtime for your SQL Server applications. Live Migration requires Windows Server 2008 R2 and Hyper-V R2.

NOTE

Live Migration is a solution that reduces planned downtime. Failover Cluster is the solution which address unplanned downtime. For more information on failover clustering, you can refer to Chapters 2, 3, 4, and 5.

Now that you've seen the basic management functions, it's time to jump in and see how to perform a Live Migration. As you'll see, the initial setup is the hard part. Once that's completed, performing the Live Migration is easy. You can manually initiate a Live Migration by using either PowerShell scripts or the Failover Cluster Manager. To perform a Live Migration, use the Start | Administrative Tools | Failover Cluster Manager option to launch the Failover Cluster Manager, which you can see in Figure 12-4.

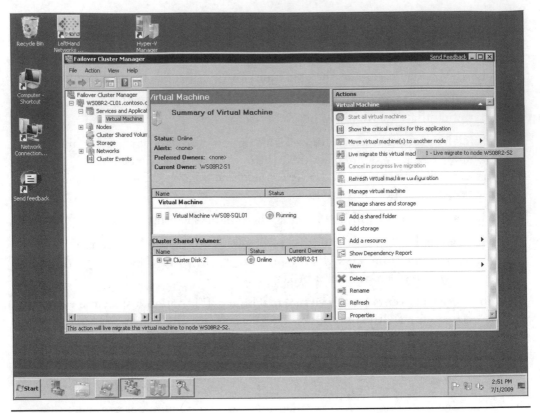

Figure 12-4   *Starting a Live Migration*

Select the Virtual Machine node from the navigation pane on the left side of the window. Then select the virtual machine to be migrated in the Virtual Machine pane shown in the middle of the screen. Next, click the "Live migrate this virtual machine" link shown in the Actions pane at the right. If there are multiple nodes in the cluster, they will all be listed in this dialog and you can choose which node will be the target for the Live Migration. In this case, there is only one other target node, so only the single option of "1 – Live migrate to node WS08R2-S2" will be displayed, as you can see illustrated in Figure 12-4. Clicking the mini-dialog begins the Live Migration, and the progress will be displayed in the Failover Cluster Manager, as you can see demonstrated in Figure 12-5.

The Live Migration process takes about a minute or so. In this example, the virtual machine vWS08-SQL01 is being live-migrated from node WS08R2-S1 to node

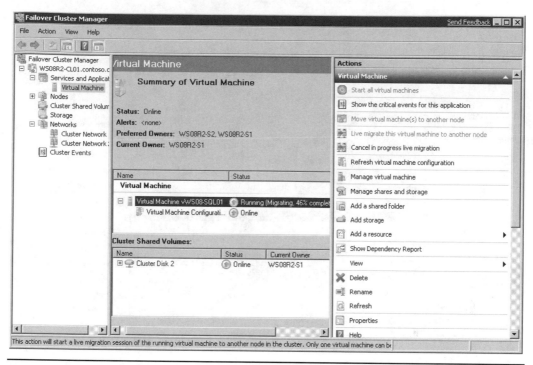

Figure 12-5 *Live Migration in progress*

WS08R2-S2. During that time, the vWS098-SQL01 virtual machine is continuously available and all client connections are maintained. (For more information on the details of how Live Migration works, you can refer back to Chapter 9.) After the Live Migration has completed, the Failover Cluster Manager will be updated with the status of the migrated virtual machine (see Figure 12-6).

In Figure 12-6 you can see the Failover Cluster Manager shows that the new owner of the vWS08-SQL01 virtual is now node WS08R2-S2. This essentially means that the virtual machine is no longer running on the first node, WS08R2-S1, but instead has been moved to the second node, WS08R2-S2.

When all the maintenance work is finished on the first node or when you want to free up resources on the second node, you can perform another Live Migration to move the virtual machine back to node WS08R2-S1. The Failover Cluster Manager keeps track of the current owner and will enable you to perform another Live Migration back to the first node.

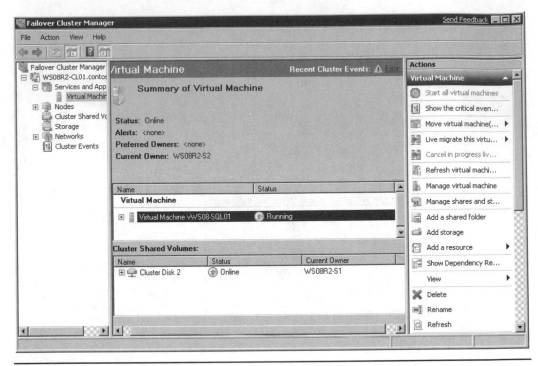

Figure 12-6 *After the successful Live Migration*

Performing a Quick Migration

Like Live Migration, Quick Migration is an option that's intended to reduce planned downtime. Quick Migration was the precursor to Live Migration, and it works on both Windows Server 2008 as well as the newer Windows Server 2008 R2. Unlike Live Migration, Quick Migration will incur some downtime as the virtual machine is moved and restarted on another cluster node.

To perform a Quick Migration, use the Start | Administrative Tools | Failover Cluster Manager option. This will start the Failover Cluster Manager, which you can see shown in Figure 12-7.

After starting the Failover Cluster Manager, select the Virtual Machine node from the navigation pane on the left side of the window. Then select the virtual machine to be moved in the Virtual Machine pane shown in the middle of the screen. Next, click the "Quick migrate this virtual machine" link that you can see in the Actions pane at the right. If there are multiple nodes in the cluster, all of the nodes will be listed in the

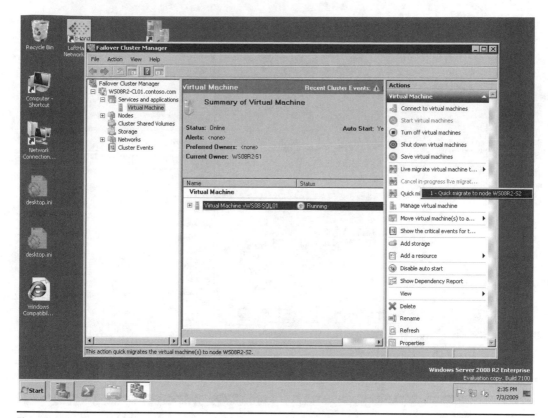

Figure 12-7   *Starting a Quick Migration*

pop-up dialog. In this case, there is only one other target node, so only the single option of "1 – Quick migrate to node WS08R2-S2" will be available, as you can see in Figure 12-7. Clicking "1 – Quick migrate to node WS08R2-S2" starts the Quick Migration. While the Quick Migration process is running, the progress will be displayed in the Failover Cluster Manager, as you can see demonstrated in Figure 12-8.

The Quick Migration process a takes couple of minutes. In Figure 12-8, the virtual machine vWS08-SQL01 is being quick-migrated from node WS08R2-S1 to node WS08R2-S2. During that time, the vWS098-SQL01 virtual machine is not available. (For more information on the details of how Quick Migration works, refer to Chapter 9.) After the Quick Migration has finished, the Failover Cluster Manager will be updated with the status of the migrated virtual machine and the new owner will be WS08R2-S2. You can see the completed migration in Figure 12-9.

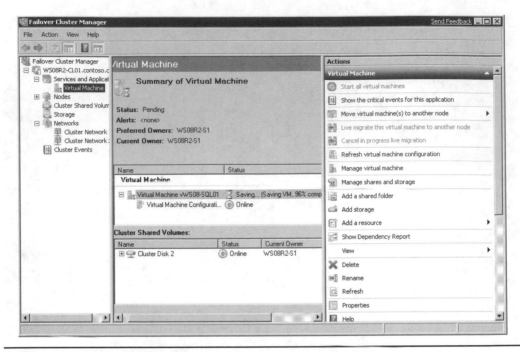

Figure 12-8   *Quick Migration in progress*

Figure 12-9   *After Successful Quick Migration*

System Center Enterprise Suite

In the preceding part of this chapter, you saw how you can perform the basic SQL Server virtual machine management using the tools built in to the Failover Cluster Manager and the Hyper-V Manager. While these tools enable you to perform the basic management functions for the SQL Server virtual machine, Microsoft's System Center Enterprise Suite provides a more full-featured, enterprise-capable virtualization management platform. System Center Enterprise Suite consists of the following components:

► **Configuration Manager 2007 R2**   Configuration Manager is used to deploy both server and client operating systems as well as application software for physical and virtual systems. It can also apply software updates and provide enterprise assets reports.

► **Data Protection Manager 2007**   Data Protection Manager provides the ability to back up and restore the Windows Server operating system as well as key Microsoft server applications like Exchange, SharePoint, and SQL Server running on either physical or virtual servers.

► **Operations Manager 2007**   Operations Manager provides end-to-end monitoring for the health of Windows server operating systems. In addition, management packs extend Operation Manager's monitoring and troubleshooting capabilities to a wide range of enterprise applications such as Hyper-V, SQL Server, Exchange, Oracle, and SAP.

► **Virtual Machine Manager 2008 R2**   Virtual Machine Manager (VMM) provides the ability to manage both Microsoft and VMware virtualization platforms and virtual machines across the enterprise. VMM also enables administrators to create and deploy virtual machines, manage the virtual infrastructure of the data center, troubleshoot and resolve operational issues, and optimize the virtual environment.

System Center Virtual Machine Manager 2008 R2

Virtual Machine Manager 2008 R2 is a feature-rich, enterprise-level virtualization management platform. VMM provides the ability to perform basic management tasks such as creating and deleting VMs, starting and stopping VMs, and saving their state. It also performs more advanced tasks, such as performing Quick Migrations and Live Migrations. VMM is managed using an Administrator Console graphical user interface built on the System Center Operations Manager console. This assures a familiar look and feel for system administrators. You can see the VMM management console in Figure 12-10.

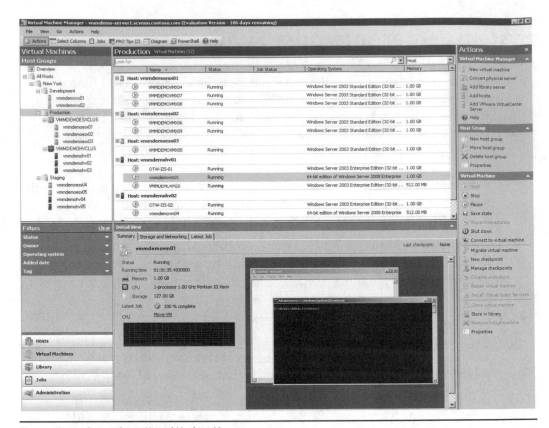

Figure 12-10 *System Center Virtual Machine Manager*

Using the VMM management console, administrators can manage virtual servers and VMs across an entire enterprise. VMM can manage Microsoft Virtual Server 2005, Microsoft Windows Server 2008 Hyper-V, and Microsoft Hyper-V Server 2008, as well as VMware ESX Server and ESXi if VMware's vCenter Server is present. VMM provides the ability to perform these operations:

- ► **VM management**   Using VMM, the administrator can create, delete, start, stop, and save VMs. The administrator can also create VM templates to facilitate the creation of VMs with standard configuration settings. The Live Thumbnail view allows administrators to view and control VMs.

- ► **Centralized library of virtual assets**   VMM provides a library feature that enables you to centrally store and manage virtual server hosts, virtual machines, virtual hard disks, ISO files, Sysprep answer files, and VM templates.

▶ **Intelligent placement**   VMM's Intelligent Placement feature helps administrators to identify the best host servers for new VMs based on a direct analysis of the performance of the virtualization host servers.

▶ **Physical-to-Virtual (P2V) and Virtual-to-Virtual (V2V) conversions**   VMM's Administrative Console enables administrators to perform P2V conversions for existing Windows servers or V2V conversions where you can convert VMware VMs to Microsoft Hyper-V VMs.

▶ **Delegate VM administration**   VMM administrators can delegate administrative functions to other members of the organization for more efficient VM management. This capability is intended to assist management for branch and departmental deployments in allowing local personnel the rights to manage their own environments.

▶ **Self-service provisioning**   VMM's Administrative Console allows specified users to perform self-service provisioning using a web portal. Self-service provisioning enables these users to create and manage their own VMs within the security and storage boundaries set by the VMM administrator.

Summary

In this chapter, you saw how to perform both basic and advanced management functions for highly available Hyper-V virtual machines. First you learned about some of the basic virtual machine management functions that you can perform with the Hyper-V Manager and with the Failover Cluster Manager for highly available virtual machines. The next part of this chapter showed you how to use the Failover Cluster Manager for both Live Migration and Quick Migration. Finally, you learned about how the Microsoft System Center Management Suite Enterprise and the Virtual Machine Manager can be used to streamline virtual machine management in enterprise deployments.

Index

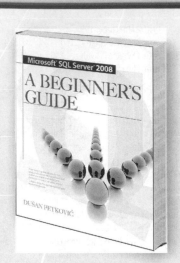
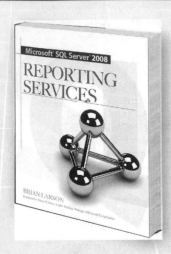